THE COMMON WELFARE

JO GRIMOND

THE COMMON WELFARE

Maurice Temple Smith

First published in Great Britain 1978
by Maurice Temple Smith Ltd
37 Great Russell Street, London WC1

© J Grimond 1978

ISBN 0 85117 159 1

Photoset by Amos Typesetters, Hockley, Essex
in VIP 11/12 Palatino

Printed in Great Britain by
Billing & Sons Ltd
Guildford, Worcester & London

Contents

Acknowledgements	6
Preface	7
1 What sort of Country?	11
2 Politics	34
3 The Economy	43
4 Inflation and Employment	57
5 The Organisation of Industry	72
6 History of the Social Services	87
7 Beveridge and After	101
8 The Urban Programmes	119
9 Previous Experiments in Communal Planning	131
10 Theory and Practice — Greenock	150
11 Practice — Northmavine	170
12 The Big City	194
13 The Community	208
14 The Future	219
Epilogue	239

Acknowledgements

In the course of this book I hope I have made clear how grateful I am to many people for their help in formulating my ideas. In particular I must mention my debt to Professor Peacock from whose views I have benefited much over a long period. I would like to thank Maurice Temple Smith for encouraging the production of this book and his staff for their editorial suggestions. I must also thank Catherine Fisher MBE for her admirable patience and skill in typing and re-typing it.

I am grateful to the following publishers for permission to quote from the works attributed to them: Oxford University Press for R. G. Collingwood, *An Autobiography*, and J. Rawls, *A Theory of Justice*; Macmillan, London and Basingstoke, for G. Watson, *Politics and Literature in Modern Britain*; Allen & Unwin for J. E. Meade, *Planning and the Price Mechanism*, and W. A. Robson, *Welfare State and Welfare Society*; Faber & Faber for E. Howard, *Garden Cities of Tomorrow*; The Times Educational Supplement, Scotland, for articles (published Autumn 1977) on 'The Compulsion Component' by Colin MacLean.

Preface

Human beings are always dissatisfied and always will be. It is part of their nature, 'the troubles of our proud and angry dust are from eternity and shall not fail'. But that does not exonerate each generation from trying to reduce the unjustifiable grievances of their time. Particularly is this true of the present generation which commands more knowledge and better tools than any before it. The people of our time suffer in three ways. Many are still born into deplorable physical conditions of poverty, bad housing and poor surroundings with little chance to make the best of themselves. Secondly, they may become the victims of violence and a fragmented country. Many grow up without faith or standards against which they can test their conduct. They live in a time of disrespect for the individual and some corruption of reason and conduct. They may be caught by the propaganda of competing bureaucracies. They may be the victim of interests, such as those of big business, advertising, broadcasting and the press anxious to stimulate their appetites, regardless of the result. And, thirdly, many are faced with an existence of boredom. I do not hark back to the days of manual labour with nostalgia. A day's stooking in a harvest field can be not only exhausting but very dull. Coal mining, pick and shovel work even above ground, hand-spinning even, must have been worse. But that does not dispose of the tedium of modern big scale production. The corollary and result of much modern work is the alternative of enforced idleness.

Leisure, which many people brought up to demand have little idea how to fill, is considered delectable — individual self-expression which should fill it is not appreciated.

Like all generations our views are coloured by inherited opinions which because they are in some ways unsuitable for our own time, have lost their authority, but like old dead grass smother new growth. Our attitude to work is ambivalent. We still think it virtuous to work hard, we count idleness as a sin yet there may not be enough 'work' in the conventional sense of the word to go round. Some people find individual charity degrading but charity from the taxpayers a 'right'. Christianity teaches that it is blessed to be poor but Christians, like nearly everyone else, would like to see the poor become rich — including themselves.

Also inherited are the categories in which we file our public organisation — work, leisure, housing, transport, social services. It was from contemplating the last that I came to write this book for are not they the instrument by which we are seeking to meet the legitimate grievances of the impoverished? We can hardly be satisfied with their success. Not only do we still have families suffering from economic poverty, but from many other types of impoverishment. May not this be a result of conventional thinking about the human condition and how it can be improved? Does it any longer make sense to think of the social services as simply one branch of central government? Can they be separated from work, leisure and the general framework of life? If these questions are to be answered we must enquire what we want of life.

So I start the book with some discussion of our aim. What should be the objective of our politics?

I pass on to give my view of how a better country, as I would judge it, can be achieved; this entails giving my view of politics and economics. I then give some account of the history of the attempts to increase welfare and improve the lot of the poor and create a way of life which would be more satisfactory for us all. I try to diagnose certain faults in these attempts. We have devoted great resources to welfare services with disappointing results. One of the most pernicious slogans has been 'Public Squalor and Private Affluence' with its conclusion that ever more resources should be swallowed by public expenditure. Yet you only have to look around at housing and clothing, or compare the proliferation of youth officers with the tide of discontent and hooliganism among youth, to see how individuals will make far better use of their money than do public authorities.

I should be quite happy if I only succeeded in adding something to the debate about what is wrong, though I do not by any means believe that everything is wrong. I finish by suggesting some remedies. Much of the diagnosis and much of what I propose as a cure for some of our troubles is tentative, but in a stage of history in which possibilities change and expand so rapidly, surely this is wise. Fundamental aims may remain but we have always had to vary the balance in trying to reach them. Sometimes government has been too strong, sometimes too weak. Sometimes we have to discriminate and offer special help to meet special needs, at others we have to assert general rules and the impartial rule of law against privileged classes. In an age when science opens ever new possibilities, from changing the very process of human procreation and the alteration of human characteristics to the control of the weather and space travel, when there are means of communication only dreamt of by writers of fiction a hundred years ago, it is perhaps all the more necessary to restate fundamental aims and to reconsider how we can come nearer to their achievement in a changing world.

1   What sort of Country?

A development of the sort I have in mind and which is the subject of this book would have to be accompanied by a radically changed attitude to the way we run our affairs. Those who find that no philosophy has been formulated for the welfare state are at once drawn on to comment on the lack of any new political philosophy at all among the established political parties. I would myself avoid the word 'philosophy' because though it no doubt has a precise meaning among philosophers it has a very imprecise meaning outside academic circles. Nor would I pretend that I am capable of devising a 'philosophy' or indeed that a new philosophy in the grandest sense of the word is needed. Several of the most horrible cruelties from which the human race has suffered have been perpetrated in the name of rigid philosophies such as Communism. I am quite in favour of short views — if they are views. 'Social engineering' has been justified so long as there was a general understanding among the politically minded about the nature of a satisfactory country, but that is evaporating. Before carrying out engineering repairs you must know the purpose of the machine you are repairing; the acceptance of 'social engineering', without defining what you want the machine for, has led to the growth of the bureaucratic attitude.

Each bureaucracy becomes an end in itself, as though we made motor cars but put in no seats to carry passengers. Excessive 'social engineering' has resulted, too, in constant tinkering, patching, overlaying, instead of a proper overhaul of our machinery of government. And finally, by degenerating into a barren struggle for perks, office and prestige, it has disgusted some people, forced them to look for a purpose or ideology and convinced them that the only one on offer is Marxism.

Any view about the sort of country we should like, the methods by which it should be run and the services it should offer must be guided by some view of what is good and what is bad. Welfare or communal services deeply affect the nature of our country and its politics and political economy; the way they are administered is certainly part of our general political process. The way we run our industries, conduct our newspapers and broadcasting is ultimately bound up with the wider aspects of community development. Perhaps most important of all is the general moral habit of the country: what is admired and disapproved, what people accept as their responsibility, how far they are prepared to work out their own lives and use their eyes, ears and common sense in so doing. And in all this process, of course, education is a main factor. Whether education should properly be defined as a social service, whether it is a 'right' for all up to an indefinite age, may be discussed but what must be discussed is what should be taught. And it is this which receives far too little attention — at least from politicians. We should be taught to consider what sort of country we want and in this consideration questions about morals and the moral content of politics must arise. What is a 'good' society?

I take as a starting point in discussing the aims of a good society the general conclusions of G. E. Moore:
> By far the most valuable things which we know or can imagine are certain states of consciousness which may be roughly described as the pleasures of human intercourse and the enjoyment of beautiful objects.
>   (*Principia Ethica*, Cambridge, 1959.)

To this I would add the exercise of our own imagination and other faculties.

I am aware that there are objections to Moore's theory but I find it hard to believe that in politics human beings should have any other ends in view than certain states of themselves. Even mystical religions which see the individual being absorbed in some greater spirit mostly believe that on this earth the individual must prepare himself for heaven; in fact he or she is concerned with states of consciousness. I am fortified in my belief by looking at the results of denying it: such denials led to the Inquisition and the Communist system of government. All human beings must be treated as ends, not means; when this principle is not followed we see the threat to human individuality which results from such practices as slavery, the subjugation of women, the exploitation of child labour and doctrines such as communism and nazism which teach that individuals should be ruthlessly murdered if that suits the ruler of the state. Today the greatest threats to the Western world are the bureaucratic attitude and an intellectual nihilism, particularly under communism.

Moore's view also entails the belief that in a sense, the most important sense, all human beings are equal. They are not equal in ability, strength, wealth, success or even in the value they attain, nor should they or could they be, but they are equal in 'God's sight', so to speak. This view also entails accepting the 'golden rule' or 'Do unto others'. The individual cannot reach his or her potential in isolation, we are all members of many communities: the family, the local neighbourhood, our friends, the state, etc. There is no contradiction between believing that moral views are concerned with individual human beings and believing also that community life is essential for their pursuit. If we attempt to promote our own value without taking others into account, in addition to behaving immorally ourselves, the attempt would be self-defeating for others are essential to us. It would also as a practical matter be impossible to run any community in which everyone can get what he wants for himself regardless of others. This can only lead to anarchy, oppression and poverty. It can happen not only when individuals pursue their own ends at the expense of the general good but when groups of individuals do so, whether they are the followers of feudal lords, gangs of brigands, monopolistic companies or trades unions which use their power to exploit their fellows. These are the traits of barbarism, we see all too many of them today: the endless demands for 'more' to be supplied by someone else; the tearing down of our heritage, both literally and in the realm of ideas; the squandering of present resources and the failure to provide for the future.

The great common good is a 'good' community. Two major faults of our society are the neglect of the 'golden rule' or its variants and the belief that while exploitation (by which I mean forcing people against their will to do things which they would not do of their own free will) is quite moral if done by the state, public authorities or organisations approved by general prejudice, yet the market in which people participate to their mutual advantage is immoral. Let me say at once that I am not claiming that all or most state action is exploitation. But too often we experience the use of state power to extort resources, created by the work of the people at large, to carry through a project which those people would never have undertaken voluntarily and which will benefit the prestige and improve the lot of minorities who are already strong and affluent. Again, I am aware that pushed to the extreme there are objections to the doctrine of the 'golden rule' — indeed in certain circumstances it becomes self-contradictory but on the whole the moral reasoning behind Christianity seems to me convincing. Religion is a matter of personal belief which one cannot command but some morality is essential. What I am saying is that whether or not you are a believer in any religion, the running of a satisfactory society requires a view about morals. Even if my particular view of morals is mistaken the need would still be there — politics and morals are intertwined.

A further corollary of my view is that what is valuable can only be achieved by personal voluntary action. It is right and meritorious for me to bring about the circumstances in which you can be, or do, good. It is of no value to either of us for me to order you to do something which you do against your will. It is not necessary to accept Moore's view to agree with one of my main themes, which is that people should be actively concerned in promoting communal welfare so that it is not merely 'handed down'. It seems to me certain that if they are involved we shall be nearer a welfare society and that the services will be more effective. I believe that it is also morally right that they should be involved. In this, too, we seem to have drifted far off the correct course: a social conscience today often means demanding that the state order someone to pay for or do something. I am not saying that this may not sometimes be necessary; what I am saying is that there is nothing moral or conscientious about it and usually it is less effective than giving people the opportunity — or at least persuading them — to do things of their own accord.

Conscription in time of war is an obvious example of the state using its power of compulsion. It can be justified both as essential to the preservation of the community and in the name of fairness. Similar reasoning applies to the provision of resources for some social services so far as they supply public goods. It could be deduced from my view that the rich ought to be willing to provide for community purposes without compulsion through taxation (for a discussion of this point see the chapter on Negative Incomes Taxation by Maynard and Peacock in their essay 'Economic Policies and Social Goals' in *Economic Analysis*, ed. A. J. Culyer, Martin Robertson, 1974.) In general I certainly accept that the government acting on behalf of the people has to make decisions about taxation and such matters which involve coercion. All I am arguing is that to demand that other people be compelled to do or pay for certain things is not in itself meritorious, though it may be necessary. We should remember the saying of Sidney Smith, 'Benevolence is a natural instinct of the human mind. When A sees B in grievous distress his conscience always urges him to entreat C to help him.'

Arising from my views I claim that the social services should aim not merely at the relief of poverty, nor at redistribution, nor at assistance to particular handicapped groups, but at the creation and maintenance of a country in which moral values can flourish. Even if my particular view of morality is not accepted this will, I believe, still be true.

I agree with Collingwood:

Moral philosophy, from the days of Socrates down to our own lifetime, has been regarded as an attempt to think out more clearly the issues involved in conduct, for the sake of acting better. In 1912 Prichard announced that moral philosophy as so understood was based on a mistake, and advocated a new kind of moral philosophy, purely theoretical, in which the workings of the moral consciousness should be scientifically studied as if they were the movement of planets, and no attempt made to interfere with them. And Bertrand Russell at Cambridge proposed in the same spirit, and on grounds whose difference was only superficial, the extrusion of ethics from the body of philosophy.

The 'realist' philosophers who adopted this new programme were all, or nearly all, teachers of young men and young women. Their pupils, with habits and characters yet unformed, stood on the threshold of public life. Half a century earlier, young people in that position had been told that by thinking about what they were doing, or were about to do, they would become likely on the whole to do it better; and that some understanding of the nature of moral or political action, some attempt to formulate ideals and principles, was an indispensable condition of engaging creditably in these activities themselves. And their teachers, when introducing them to the study of moral and political theory would say to them, whether in words or not — the most important things one says are often not said in words — 'Take this subject seriously, because whether you understand it or not, it will make a difference to your whole lives.' The new teachers destroyed (political theory) by denying the conception of a 'common good' the fundamental idea of all social life and insisting that all 'goods' were private.

(*An Autobiography*, R. G. Collingwood, Oxford, 1939.)

Social life, distinct from the state, was and is essential to man. As Hume wrote:

> It is by society alone that he is able to supply his defects and raise himself up to an equality with his fellow creatures and even to acquire a superiority over them. By society all his infirmities are compensated: and though in that situation his wants multiply every moment upon him, yet his abilities are still more augmented and leave him in every respect more satisfied and happy, than it is

possible for him, in his savage and solitary condition, ever to become.

(D. Hume, *A Treatise on Human Nature*.)

If we break the threads which hold society together, if we lose the notion of a common good, we shall indeed be back in the condition of anarchy described by Hobbes:

To this war of every man against every man this is also consequent; that nothing can be unjust. The notions of justice and injustice have there no place. Where there is no common power there is no law, no justice. Force and fraud are the two cardinal virtues. It is consequent also to the same condition, that there is no propriety, no dominion, no mine and thine distinct, but only that to be everyman's that he can get and for so long as he can keep it. (T. Hobbes, *Leviathan*.)

When we read of some modern activities, for example wage bargaining and strikes, we can see that we are not so far from the Hobbesian world as some think.

As Hobbes also pointed out, our respect for the community must spring from our voluntary acceptance of membership, 'For in the act of our submission consisteth both our obligation and our liberty which must therefore be inferred by arguments taken from thence: there being no obligation on any man which ariseth not from some act of his own, for all men are by nature free.'

This notion of common good is fundamental to my argument. The phrase is used in several senses, I myself use it in two senses. First, to describe such undertakings as defence of the realm, for which it is difficult if not impossible to charge individuals. Secondly, to describe the overriding common good which, as the quotations above show, has been an essential of liberal political thinking since the eighteenth century.

What is so serious about modern politics is that the common good which we should enjoy from membership of a good society has become confused with state control, corporatism, collectivism. In fact, these are usually the enemy of the common good. As a result there has grown up, by way of reaction to collectivism, a school of liberal politicians and thinkers who, rightly concerned about our loss of liberty, are inclined to throw out the idea of the common good along with the ideas of state socialism. It is to my mind as essential to reassert the notion of the common good, with all the obligations which go with it, as it is to assert individual liberty and the voluntary character of our acceptance of the common good and the rule of law.

A country which recognises the common good as a political aim and which accepts that even if Moore is wrong the notion of the common good must be linked to some view of what is moral and valuable, should create conditions in which certain states of the human consciousness may flourish.

The beliefs I hold were first formulated in their modern form in the eighteenth century. They stem from the European and American Enlightenment. In many ways they have proved of greater durability in the USA than in Europe. But the tradition, though weakening, is still alive here; how it is put into practice needs constant reappraisal. Tolerance is essential if it is to remain vital: for not only must it allow of individual differences, it is kept alive by dialogue between opposing views which accept its premises.

We are still a tolerant country. Let us be thankful for that. However, in this as in many other things we are living on inherited capital. A tolerant community must be inspired by the kind of liberal ideas which flourished in the age of the Enlightenment, the hundred and fifty years or so which ran from about 1760. The feature of this period was an interest in human beings and their relationships. The decline of dogmatic religion and of subservience to the ruling authorities and to the state encouraged this interest. Human beings were increasingly treated as ends in themselves. At the same time, the governing classes were sufficiently sure of their position to explore new ideas. Economic advance allowed some hope for the general improvement of mankind. The mood was to some extent aristocratic: it revered property, it accepted a hierarchical system of classes, it believed in the victory of the best people, influence was confined to a fairly small segment of the population. But it was also democratic: it saw human beings as all-round individuals, not as confined to particular roles; it believed in open discussion, holding that men were essentially reasonable, and that, out of reasoned dialectic, truth would emerge. Truth would be recognised and ultimately would triumph over special interests. It was devoted, therefore, to individual liberty. It was, however, particularly in the early stages, under no illusions about the nature of mankind. Though truth must be sought by the free exploration of ideas, its victory would not be achieved without effort. Original sin had to be contained: man's aggression and acquisitiveness curbed, morality asserted. Hence the insistence upon the rule of law and upon a constitutional framework for government. Though the state was not to be accorded the prominence which had been claimed for it, the ruling classes looked upon it as a continuing and organic growth for which each generation were to some extent trustees. This view is very apparent in Burke:

> A state without the means of some change is without the means of its conservation. . . . The two principles of conservation and correction operated strongly at the two critical periods of the Restoration and Revolution. The burden of proof lies heavily on those who tear to pieces the whole frame and contexture of their country, that they could find no other way of installing a government fit to obtain its rational ends . . . men have no right to put the well-being of the present generation wholly out of the question. Perhaps the only moral trust with any certainty in our hands is the care of our own time. With regard to posterity we are to treat it like a ward. We are not so to attempt an improvement in his fortune as to put the capital of his estate to any hazard.
>
> (E. Burke, *Observations on a Pamphlet: The Present State of the Nation*.)

The aristocracy planned, built and planted for the future in which, through their heirs, they felt an interest. Minorities were to be respected, especially in the eyes of nineteenth-century liberal writers. It is a great mistake to assume that because Britain has no written constitution it has no constitution at all. On the contrary, nineteenth-century British statesmen felt themselves bound to respect minorities, to ensure that big changes were not forced through against their will and that the different aspects of the nation were taken into account. What affronted Palmerston in so many foreign governments was not that the majority in their countries did not rule but that their sovereigns were unconstitutional: they claimed to exercise arbitrary powers denying the supremacy of the rule of law.

In America, the Founding Fathers in drawing up their written constitution were amply aware of the danger of lust for power. The checks and balances of the British unwritten and the American written constitution were designed to prevent the machinery of state being seized by despots, the individual being subjected to arbitrary curtailment of freedom and the resources of the country being squandered by sectional interests temporarily in power. In Paris (at least up to the Revolution), in London, Edinburgh and the United States, the tolerance which we have inherited was born and developed. It did not spring from apathy. It was far from being an acceptance that everyone could do as they liked. It assumed gradual change but change, nevertheless, which could be brought about by orderly democratic (within the assumptions of various generations) institutions.

The Enlightenment was optimistic. It believed that human reason could discover rules of general validity and by the use of scientific methods increase human well-being. Politics were to be carried on by reasoned argument, which would lead to the discovery of the right solutions; and in these solutions all would acquiesce. Mankind could be weaned from a senseless war of interests which could only lead to mutual destruction. Self-interest under the guidance of economists who understood the workings of a free economy could be harnessed to the general good. If the impediments were removed, human beings would appreciate the benefits of liberalism and by this alone enterprise and imagination would be released. In fact, a cutting-off of burdens, freedom from impediments, tolerance in all its forms would go a long way to improving the human condition — for people would take advantage of it to act rationally and usefully.

To ensure tolerance is difficult enough. To stimulate, or to arrange that a community should stimulate, is even more difficult. Ambition is the commonest stimulation. At various times and places, Athens and Florence being conspicuous examples, men were stimulated in art, adventure, curiosity. Why? We do not exactly know. Did the fall of Constantinople to the Turks by dispersing scholars over Europe accelerate the Renaissance? We can at least be pretty sure that a community is more likely to stimulate if people are given the opportunity to express themselves, if their surroundings are beautiful, if originality is encouraged and choice offered. Movement of both men and ideas is stimulating, so is a mixture of methods and outlook. The great change has been from a society which accepted that very little could be done to improve its material lot, except by conquest, to a society which has seen immense material increases and, by the use of technical inventions, a great expansion in what men can do. This not only improved men's physical condition but also changed their outlook. On the other hand, one source of inspiration has dwindled, the religious source. Faith in the perfectibility of man however strong original sin may be; the drive to make things skilfully and well, in the shape of some platonic ideal, these too have dwindled. If a welfare country is worth working for it is not so that the ambitious can salve their consciences by paying a tithe to keep the unsuccessful out of the mortuary; it is not so as to create a client proletariat dependant upon bureaucrats for their means of life; it is not to stop creation by imposing conformity. It is so as to encourage initiative by insisting on non-conformity — but non-conformity within a framework: non-conformity which arises from the natural relationship which people bear to one another.

Poverty, extremely unpleasant in itself and, therefore, apart from its results, to be eliminated if possible, is not necessarily fatal to tolerance and stimulation. It is certainly not fatal to the leading of a virtuous life — as Christianity shows. Many poor communities have been tolerant. Many poor individuals have risen to great heights of invention. It is poverty without hope which is fatal. And since we should now be able to give everyone hope, not to be a millionaire, nor a senior civil servant, nor a leading lawyer, but to have some opportunity to use their talents, or indeed not to use them, to live in peace if they so desire, this should be an additional aim of our politics.

Professor Rawls near the beginning of *A Theory of Justice* (Oxford University Press, 1972) sets out two principles:

> First, each person to have an equal right to the most extensive basic liberty compatible with a similar liberty for others.
>
> Second, social and economic inequalities are to be arranged so that they are both (a) reasonably to be expected to be to everyone's advantage and (b) attached to positions and offices open to all.

I would accept these principles. The first is a restatement of a view going back at least to the eighteenth century and certainly to J. S. Mill and de Tocqueville. The second, as Rawls admits, is open (as is indeed the first) to various interpretations. But I believe that a society which tolerates individual inequality is for the benefit of all so long as communities give all a reasonably fair start in life and, through the market and the general laws of the country, all have a chance to make their own choice.

But the liberalism of the Enlightenment is waning and this aim is now threatened by a two-sided pincer movement springing from the misuse of power. The lust for power and prestige, for dominance over one's fellows has taken various forms but at present the most obvious are the violent and the bureaucratic. These are the attackers who threaten a liberal society.

The origins of these attacks are not new; indeed, they are as old as original sin. The violent pincer stems from the aggression which stems from hate. At one time aggression may have been useful for the survival of the race, though many animals survive who would never commit the atrocities perpetrated by the Russians or indeed the IRA. But however useful force may once have been in defence of the home, aggression, hate and violence may now, in the age of the hydrogen bomb, exterminate the human race.

Many of those who appeal to violence and practise it by invasion, the forced labour camp, the bomb and kidnapping, justify it by an appeal to Marxism. They never test Marxism by criticising it by the scientific method or by scrutinising its results in the light of experience. Marxists in

What sort of Country?

office everywhere have proved totalitarians, aggressive, cruel and obscurantist. Further, they abuse the tolerance which a free society extends to them by attempting the destruction of that society. Of course in any country there is always much that is wrong, though seldom a fraction of the evil which flourishes in communist states. But because criticism in these communist states leads to death and imprisonment they are excused from the well-publicised attacks which free and open societies (and even South Africa) suffer for their far less heinous misdeeds from communists, fascists, terrorists and anarchists of all kinds.

This pincer formed by destructive and aggressive movements such as the gangs of German terrorists and the IRA is seldom recruited from the ranks of the oppressed. The most active murderers and kidnappers are thwarted and jealous members of the middle class. They are totally different from those, such as the conspirators against Hitler or the wretched poor who have from time to time risen against their oppressors, having no democratic method of raising their grievances and being trussed into a society which denied them freedom or opportunity. There are in the world many idealists shocked by the communist and fascist countries, there are those who dislike some manifestations of the free world and who may feel that the democratic process available to them does not provide them with an adequate means of protest, but their case has been compromised by thugs.

Between the pincer of the left-wing anarchist and the bureaucrat lies the power-hungry intellectual. Some French intellectuals (and some of the British and Americans too) have combined an admiration for regimes committing every type of atrocity with some of the silliest posturing of bourgeois society and pretentious gibberish masquerading as philosophy. Indeed the record of the Western intellectuals should cause us to beware of their successors. Some of them have exploited all the advantages of a liberal society while abetting those who would destroy it.

The attacks are made more dangerous today by the prestige afforded to those engaged in them. A great many people want to dominate, it gives them satisfaction to lay down rules, 'Planning is such fun,' as some planning politician said. If they cannot lord it over someone, they have an itch to destroy. These twin manifestations can be seen most clearly among some of the Left bourgeois intellectuals of the past years. Their record is appalling. In such people you can detect the appetite for dominance accompanied by extraordinary callousness. Take this incident described by a niece of Beatrice Webb and quoted by George Watson in his illuminating book *Politics and Literature in Modern Britain* (Macmillan, 1977):

> I had asked the headmistress of one of our local secondary schools who had been on an extensive tour down the Ukraine to come and meet them [the Webbs]. Over the teacups the headmistress mentioned her horror at finding her party in a station where several cattle trucks of enemies of the State had been pulled up at a siding on their way to Siberia. "Very bad management" said Aunt Bo [Mrs Webb] severely. "Ridiculous to let you see them; the English are always so sentimental." At which the headmistress rather shocked said, "But Mrs Webb they were starving and held out their hands for food — they were in a pitiable condition". "I know," the great one replied, "but you can't make an omelette without breaking eggs."

The other arm of the pincer is the bureaucratic attitude. I must emphasise that the bureaucratic attitude extends far outside the civil service and indeed many civil servants do not suffer from it. Many elected representatives, business managers, professionals and academics do. Whereas the democratic attitude regards human beings in the round, as persons or personalities, endowed with a common divine spark, as choosers, creators, as individuals in a community, entitled to equality of esteem, regardless of their particular classification, the bureaucratic attitude regards people as role-players, as members of this or that trade union, as fathers, criminals, or in the last resort as clients and statistics. While the democrat demands open argument, the bureaucrat demands secrecy. While the democrat demands that he and everyone else should be free to exercise a choice, the bureaucrat insists that decisions should be made by him for his or her clients. While the democrat wants to make his or her way on their own, the bureaucrat expects to be carried up the stairs of a career structure almost regardless of merit. The democrat welcomes eccentricity. The bureaucrat regards it with horror. The bureaucrat is at ease with organisation charts, the democrat is prepared to put up with any number of anomalies. The democrat promotes open discussion, the bureaucrat suspects that it will disturb empires and his place within them.

The democrat is willing to accept defeat, for example at the polls, the bureaucrat can seldom admit that he is wrong. The democrat likes to make his own choice, create his own life, the bureaucrat lives by regulations, perks and payments in kind. The democrat rejoices in a skilful society because he has better things to do than pass memoranda and minutes and read research papers. The democrat is willing to change his job, the bureaucrat will only fight to extend his empire. Indeed he will fight for nothing else. We now know of the appalling treatment of Russians left in our hands after the war. The chief blame for this crime must rest upon the politicians but it is apparent that the bureaucrats of the Foreign Office furthered the policy which led to the death and imprisonment of many thousands. It is argued on their behalf that they acted under orders — the answer, that excuse was not accepted for war crimes. My aim is to promote the democratic society. We must not confuse the bureaucrat with the expert, whose advice is indispensable, nor with the public servant who, if he really is a public servant, is equally indispensable. Bureaucrats are necessary but the dominant element should be democratic. The bureaucratic element should be subordinate in power and small in numbers — the opposite is becoming the case in Britain. Stimulation, widening of individual choice, the promotion of a tolerant community, hospitable to talent to the point of eccentricity and encouraged to run its own affairs, are abhorrent to the bureaucracy because such goals threaten its way of life and its jobs.

Bureaucratic government even at its best gives little satisfaction, it breeds an inert attitude in the receiver and insensitivity in the dispenser. Their failure to find satisfaction or self-respect in their government, or the way we run our services and industries, is a sad feature of our people. The bureaucrats at their worst have replaced the landlords and tyrannical employers as the incubus people feel upon their backs. The new Kremlins, those vast office blocks frowning down on the serfs who support them are indeed the successors to the mediaeval castles and what goes on in them is equally unknown to those outside.

Even when the bureaucrats behave humanely, as indeed they do in many fields of public service and industry, they fail to promote self-respect. And self-respect and respect for others is a very important element in human life. The British eventually governed India better than she had ever been governed before, if you look to the provision of services and the keeping of law and order and indeed economic management. But the Indians felt their self-respect affronted. Any colonial system will collapse because it affronts self-respect. In some ways and in some places Britain itself is becoming a colonial territory. Bureaucratic work is easier and less risky and some ambitious young men therefore choose it because of undefined doubts about their ability to compete. It is easier to sit on committees, write minutes, and to work your way up some ladder which is provided and kept for you. One of the reasons why free enterprise capitalism has been so criticised by academics is perhaps that it does not give enough openings to the man ambitious for power and money but not sure of his ability to stand on his own feet.

Another feature of today's democracies is that the political parties must be forever promising that the state, if entrusted to them, will do something. It is an easy but not wholly true jibe that politicians are always making promises to win votes and then breaking them. The implication being that they mislead an innocent electorate which would respond if they made no promises. In my experience this is untrue. Many politicians in the last thirty years have warned the electorate not to expect too much; on the whole they have got a poor response. However, there is some truth in this old criticism of democracy. But what is more serious is that as the machinery of government is the instrument of politicians, if they want to win power by showing that they will do more for people than their rivals, they are almost bound to extend the range of this machinery. At least they have been up to now. Every party at every election must produce a manifesto which must show that they will make changes in the way our affairs are run. The bureaucracy is strong enough to resist any suggestion that such change should reduce its pay or numbers. The main source of change is the collectivist Left which believes in a bigger public sector and more non-productive offices. So the size of the state machinery grows and inflation increases.

The centralised political machine does its best to snuff out local initiative. However, there are signs of revolt both about the ineffectiveness of the state and the pretensions of those who nevertheless want to extend its interference. There is some movement in favour of local initiatives. It may take many years to off-set the indoctrination of the recent past but unless we are to resign ourselves to a thoroughly unsatisfactory country, it has to be attempted. If some changes of direction are not made, the most likely outcome is the death of the liberal, free, welfare society, a period of rising inflation and unrest exploited by the extreme Left and followed either by a long decline, as in eighteenth — nineteenth-century Spain and Austria, or by communism.

Either would be fatal to a welfare society whether defined as a society capable of supporting the welfare services as now existing or as the type of society I advocate in this book. For either would entail a tyranny incompatible with concern about human relations or the protection of the unfortunate, dissidents or minorities. Neither is inevitable or an immediate threat. But the danger will grow if present tendencies continue.

Our democracy is sometimes criticised for being a dictatorship subject to some assertion of the popular will every few years at a general election. There is some truth in this. Indeed the election itself is a weak demonstration of popular power. The bureaucracies continue. The House of Commons which results from the election is less and less representative of the people's will. Once elected it finds that organised groups prepared to use force have more influence on governments than parliamentary debate. But democratic government is not the whole story of democracy. No system of government will allow of continuous freedom of choice but a market economy can help to do just that — not of course in every aspect of life but in many important aspects. It is a running democracy, going on from day to day and year to year.

It is also often said that we are becoming a corporate state. The word 'corporatism' is used in two senses. It is sometimes the name given to a system by which a government of essentially bureaucratic character, with or without the sanction of an assembly elected from normal constituencies, directs all the main activities of the nation using corporations for this purpose. In some ways this use of the word comes nearest to describing important features of our present condition, for example, government investment through the NEB to Leyland. In the other and older sense 'the corporate state' — the kind of state Mussolini talked about — was a form of socialism in which industry, the professions, the trades unions, elected members to a parliament. Political power rested with those bureaucracies. There are signs of this in Britain today when the trades unions can decide whether, say, an income policy shall or shall not be adopted by a Labour government.

However you view some of the tendencies in Western Europe they are pushing us towards some form of fascism. And, much as some socialists may deplore the idea, fascism is out of the same stable as communism, which is the logical result of socialism. Marx, long before Hitler, spoke of the need to exterminate 'backward' races. Racialism, the superiority of the chosen race, appears in the writings of many socialists and anti-semitism in the writings of the Left intellectuals before they pinned it on the Right. The socialist or communist becomes impatient with all differences, whether of culture, ethnic origin or views which could lead to resistance. The revolution must cut all roots. Once the revolution is achieved and total and permanent destruction of the old ties and distinctions complete there must be a new dictatorial order which will become intensely and permanently conservative. Everyone must submit to the messianic will of the chosen instrument, the Communist Party. The Communist Party elite may indeed rewrite its bible and history from time to time. Those who have won safety, as they thought, by submission may find themselves in the concentration camp but all power still remains with the government which claims total supremacy, its subjects being reduced to a mass trudging on as ordered in the march of history.

This totalitarian hell of Hitlers and Stalins may never, we hope, be achieved. But do not let us be deluded about its nature. Nor let us think that by going half way towards it we shall appease its prophets or find it easy to stop. Do not, above all, let us be blind to the inevitable outcome of revolution. If you tear up the freedom and order of a democratic society — democratic not only in form, through a parliament but in fact, through freedom of expression, information, criticism, work and law, the outcome will not be some return to a happy, liberty-loving, earlier state of human organisation; it will not, except briefly, be to anarchy; it will be to a dictatorship, far worse, because of the means at its disposal, than has hitherto been possible.

The picture, however, is not a simple one of a weak government challenged by powerful interests and with a disorganised and apathetic public opinion as its only ally. For one thing, members of parliament are not as impotent as they themselves sometimes imagine. I would like to see their influence greatly increased, it is much too weak. But by bestirring themselves they can still make themselves felt. If members of parliament believe that weakness would lose them their seats this will stiffen them to press the government for a stronger line. Further, if the public are organised in even the most rudimentary way they have shown that they too can push the authorities to act more in accordance with their wishes. No longer can the enquiry procedure into planning proposals be treated as a routine exercise to keep the children quiet. In parliament the defeat of the guillotine on the Scotland and Wales Bill and other government proposals, whatever you think of the merits of the measures defeated, has shown that the government majority does not always behave as a tame poodle. Debate, pressure, experience, can have an effect, as can the results of economic mismanagement, on the actions of our rulers.

But at present it seems that you must organise and revert very often to force rather than reason if you are to achieve much. This is a very important element in the way we run our affairs. Much as I dislike it, I am nevertheless driven to the conclusion that unless we can rapidly control the disruptive elements already powerfully organised and ready to back each other by striking and picketing in disputes which in no way concern the sympathisers, the consuming public will have to organise its boycotts and direct action. Another turn would be given, therefore, to the screw which is fastening down the instincts upon which welfare communities ought to depend.

The position of the government is also ambivalent. In some respects it is too weak for the good of the country. The trades unions and various bureaucracies exert too much leverage. But potentially a government is exceedingly strong, it has all sorts of weapons at its disposal. I have long thought that one day it would use them — and so it has turned out: it is manipulating grants and contracts to achieve its aims. This could be carried much further. Every sort of service now depends on government money, from university grants to national assistance. If the machinery of government fell into the hands of one interest, one modern feudal baron, or the dictatorship of one party, those in charge would have immense resources under their command. I believe this danger is increased by the hiving-off from parliamentary control of those 'quasi-governmental organisations' such as the Post Office, the BBC and the Manpower Commission. They open up immense fields for patronage. They can easily become irresponsible and oppressive — already the growth in staff is a burden — and in the long run they could become convenient instruments for non-democratic governments.

Our condition should not cause too much surprise. The politics of the Middle Ages were much more like what has been the common state of human society than the politics of the Enlightenment. Barons stalked the land, followed by serfs with a sprinkling of ambitious rivals in the ranks of their armies. Some were strong, some weak. Some were harassed by lesser barons — the little fleas often sucked dry the big. Some had a genuine interest in the well-being

What sort of Country?

of their estates, others could command support only so long as they delivered the booty or had enough tough henchmen to prevent revolt. Against these the Crown was often weak. It had to enforce its interest which was, as near as conditions allowed, the national interest, by manoeuvre. Some of these manoeuvres were very illiberal. It was ruthless when ruthlessness was likely to be successful, it bought off some opposition, it mustered resistance against some feudal practices, it proved itself a better paymaster than some overlords. Unfortunately, we have few, if any, politicians able to practise these skills today. While the mobilisation of public opinion is very important, it is not enough. We have to find a way to make demands for more money unrewarding, and ways to reward those who further the general interests of a free society.

But though we must not be depressed by the onset of violence and the bureaucratic attitude we must reassert democracy. From what I have said it will be apparent, I hope, that by democracy I mean much more than one person one vote. Indeed, I mean much more than democratic government. I mean a democratic society. Just as it is said that the welfare state cannot exist without a welfare society, so I maintain that the democratic state cannot exist without a democratic society. That is to say, a society run for the most part by individual choice and voluntary co-operation, a society of democratic communities. A society which is run by general rules and not the imposition of sectional rule. A society in which the ruled are not reduced to proletarians. A democratic society requires sensitive management and checks upon the seizure of political power at all levels. And a welfare society requires a consideration for others absent from much of today's life. Strikers deliberately choose the occasions on which they can hurt their fellow citizens most. The mentality behind some strikes designed to intimidate the public and the government is the same as that of the kidnapper. And, like the kidnapper, when the striker or his trades union calls off a strike, they almost demand to be thanked. The closed shop too is incompatible with the tolerance and thought for others which should lie behind welfare or communal services. Indeed the whole spirit behind the constant claims by trades unions and other organisations for a constantly increasing share of the national wealth, apart from its results in inflation and the diversion of resources from community development, is as a frame of mind hostile to a welfare society.

Modern British socialism is the enemy of a welfare society though it may run a welfare state. It uses the state and bureaucracies under the state to make the choices which the individual should make. It restricts his opportunities, orders his life and prevents him or her becoming a person in their own right, with opportunities to use their talents to the full.

The intrusive governments of modern times are an interest, or bundle of interests on their own. The new study of the economies of politics and the discussion of 'public choice' by Professor Buchanan and others have done good service in drawing attention to the self-interested motives of governments and their officials. But I believe that they give too little credit to disinterest and public spirit — they commit the error with which Collingwood reproached Prichard. There is magnanimity in government still though we all know that ministers and bureaucrats may be self-seeking.

What I would declare is that there are other political traditions, the traditions of liberalism and of Christian socialism, or guild socialism or syndicalism — the latter has gone by many names. It is these traditions which should be revived and extended. We have to re-assert the virtues of generosity and inspiration and the golden rule and return the economic mechanism to its proper place. We have to affirm that while differing opinions may be held about its nature, and different interests may press their point of view, there can be a general interest. Rawls is right. The advocates of special interests, always claiming more for these interests, must convince us that even if they did not belong to these interest groups, they would still make the same claims for them. And, further, they must be willing to sacrifice the claims of their own interest on occasion. We must free government from the thickets in which it is now entangled, by handing over many of the jobs it attempts to do to individuals or independent institutions. We must save it from enslavement to special interests by strengthening it in its proper sphere of arbiter and protector of the common interest.

Today the old Left, which claimed to stand for the generality of the people against the oligarchies of power and to be the vehicle for popular change has become what Cobbett would have called the Establishment. We are being mesmerized by being told we must submit to technical determinism, which has taken the place of the economic determinism of the nineteenth century. We are constantly told that we ourselves can do nothing, we must surrender to blind forces and characterless organisations. Hence the lapse by some people into frustration and violence. But this fashionable defeatism does not answer those instincts in human beings which demand life, variety, play, enjoyment, innovation — which demand bread not a stone and which I believe should and must be catered for. The new Left — I know Left is an imprecise and misleading word — but what other is there to describe the progressive, populist democratic side of politics? — must assert the democrat against the bureaucrat, must fight for those who start life from too low a level and must battle for the free, welfare society.

2 Politics

A welfare society needs political institutions consonant with its general philosophy. This is not a treatise on government and I do not intend to go into my proposals in detail but some outline must be given because, as I have said, the political methods of the country are very relevant to its social and community arrangements. And if we were to move any considerable degree towards anarchy or bureaucratic dictatorship that would be the end of a decent society in which community development could flourish. For one thing, community development as I see it is about enabling freedom to flourish in a free society.

First then, we must give the people back some of their power. It is apparent that the party system does not correspond with the life and thoughts of the electorate. Few people regard themselves as Labour, Tory or Liberal supporters right across the whole range of their party's policies. The nation is not divided between rich property owners and exploited wage earners. The wealth and power of property owners have been eroded. Some manual workers earn as much as those in positions of responsibility and are in a stronger position than their bosses. A widespread secondary economy has grown up of perks, payments in kind, indexed pensions, free travel, conferences, lunches, expense accounts, free coal for miners (one-fifth of all the coal supplied for domestic purposes goes to the employees of the Coal Board) free telephones, cars provided by the tax payer or the company — the list is endless. Striking does not lead to poverty; hard work can be so heavily taxed that it does not lead to affluence.

I am not saying here whether all this is right or wrong, what I am saying is that it has radically altered the basis of politics. The main disputes today are by no means always between members of the traditional parties. The same elements in the nation find themselves in conflict with governments of different parties. Indeed, the most obvious division is not between the Conservative and Labour parties but between the government and the governed. The government has spread and the public service has become an interest on its own. The emergence of six or more parties in the House of Commons is a reflection of these underlying changes. Possibly the only groups which exhibit the classical characteristics necessary to support a party are immigrants, women, and Scottish, Welsh or Northern Irish nationalists. They form reasonably defined groups, they have recognisable and in some cases genuine grievances and at least some of the remedies they seek can be simply stated. But the two party system — if it ever existed — has gone. Most clearly will this be seen if a Scottish Assembly is set up, three parties will be running neck and neck.

One reform needed is to change the electoral system so that it may reflect the new situation. The electors need a wider choice, a choice within the parties as much as between them. Miss Lakeman founder of the Electoral Reform Society is quite right to reiterate in her long and admirable campaign for electoral reform that proportional representation will allow electors to vote for, say, a left or right wing candidate of the Labour Party without jeopardising the total Labour vote: both can stand and the elector can make them first and second choice. Proportional representation will also ensure a much fairer electoral result; after a general election the parties will return to parliament with a membership representing their vote. Electoral reform should be started by the introduction of some form of proportional representation. The parties may well opt for the list system which will maintain their position. Already, as they lose popular support, they are asking for finance from the exchequer. No more than any other vested interest are they anxious to yield power. Though proportional representation must be introduced somewhere in the system there is still a strong case for preserving the first past the post method because it gives a direct link between the constituency and one member. If we are to have a second chamber, which I favour, it might be elected for a fixed term by proportional reprsentation. If the lower chamber were grossly unrepresentative the second chamber with democratic authority should have power to correct it.

If proportional representation is introduced, and produces a parliament in which the smaller parties have much fairer representation, reform cannot stop there. We shall have to get used to coalitions. No harm in that. The committee system should also be extended so that specialist committees are set up to watch specific subjects and monitor the government's policies and administration.

Scottish, Welsh and Northern Irish parliaments should be established. As far as Scotland is concerned the establishment of a Scottish parliament should be accompanied by the abolition of the regions. As much power as they can reasonably exercise should be left with the districts and with communities smaller than the present districts. When this has been done and a rational view taken of the powers which can and should be exercised by a Scottish parliament, it will be found that very few functions remain to be dealt with at Westminster. Political power should be treated as resting with the people, who surrender some of it upwards to local, national parliaments and to Brussels. It does not flow from Westminster and Whitehall. It is not for these institutions to devolve; it is for the people to allow them to exercise powers over matters which cannot be handled locally. This is of great importance when considering the encouragement of a welfare society and the promotion of community services. The only subjects which I see as being left to London are foreign affairs, defence and over-all economic planning. To discharge its functions as they relate to Scotland the British parliament will require few Scottish members and they should be excluded from English government. The bureaucracy in Whitehall should also be reduced in line with the increased civil service in Edinburgh.

It is vital that the return of power to Scotland (and to Wales, Northern Ireland and the English regions) should not lead to another increase in the size of government. I have an open mind about the necessity for a Bill of Rights; if an effective second chamber is established then it would be unnecessary. But if Scottish, Welsh and Northern Irish parliaments are set up, not merely as another tier of government but with wide ranging authority, I am doubtful whether a second chamber is needed. Proportional representation should then be the method by which the national parliaments were elected. We have at the moment far more government than any Western country and we are not even a federation. The House of Commons is the largest elected assembly in the world, on top of that there are over eight hundred members of the House of Lords and beyond all the European parliament. As we move towards a British federal system, though on a new model, we shall require a constitutional court. It is true that this could administer a Bill of Rights but I would prefer to rely upon the democratic process suitably reformed to protect the citizen.

I remain a strong upholder of one main feature of the British, or rather English, system. The MP was originally sent up to Westminster to curb the executive, he was sent to air the grievances of his constituents. The executive was not elected by the people nor indeed by their representatives. As recently as 1963 Sir Alec Douglas Home, the Prime Minister at that time, was not even elected by his party — he emerged. The backbench member, because of his position and the constituency pressures upon him, was pushed into opposition to the executive. Of course there were other and usually stronger pressures, the pressures of his party, his Whips' Office. Indeed, in recent years, the approval of his party has usually been essential if he is to keep his seat. But the MP is still attached to a constituency and deals not only with its general complaints but with the individual complaints of his constituents. The opposition, of course, opposes: but even government backbenchers are not always wholly subservient to their leaders. This is not the place to go into the position of the MP at great length but in some parliaments the member has become a name on a party list, almost, or indeed entirely, removed from constituency attachment; much government in some countries is carried on through committees. There is, therefore, a danger of losing the distinction between the government, and the member set up not to govern but to stop too much government.

Of course the opposition and all backbenchers have lost much of their power to criticise and thwart. Government has become too big and too secret for them, debate is less important. It is right then that backbenchers should form committees to discharge their critical duties more effectively but these committees must not lead to backbenchers being suborned into sympathy with ministers.

The danger of this happening may be increased by our membership of the Common Market. The 'governmental' committees have much power. Continental politicians are often much better paid and more nearly bureaucrats and specialists than our own. So while I am in favour of more work being done by committees, I do not want the chamber itself abolished nor would I have constituency attachments weakened.

There have been many MPs with no desire to be members of any government; they stood against it — suspicious of the ambitions of power-seeking ministers, mindful that power corrupts and that government throughout history has been seen as a dangerous necessity. Now the scope of government has extended so far and it has so much management to do that this simple traditional role of the MP has had to be modified. I do not object to that. In fact I would like to see an extension of the specialist committee system although it brings the MP into collaboration with the executive. As the two party system is distintegrating and at the same time it is becoming more and more difficult to get important legislation through without a guillotine (which means many clauses of a Bill are not discussed) the House of Commons should set up committees to consider proposed legislation before it is drafted. But we must not lose sight of an essential element in democracy: that is, that representatives who stand for the people and communities of the country must be sent to parliament to probe and criticise the executive — not to excuse it. MPs have to exercise their central functions in new ways; they may indeed have to discharge a dual function of criticism and management but they must not become part of the governing caste, a bureaucracy on their own; nor should they be insulated from the trials and hazards of their constituents. Already with whole-time MPs and a growing army of perks this isolation is happening. Further, a growing proportion of MPs want office and even out of office want to get their oar in on the boat of government. These new developments are one reason why the House of Commons is not discharging its basic role of watchdog with the necessary vigour. Patronage is a most powerful sedative in the hands of the cabinet.

At the same time, more and more public boards have slipped out of parliamentary control. Not only do I believe that bodies such as the Post Office might well be run for motives other than profit, but I believe that to turn them into bogus commercial businesses was a mistake. The government is irresponsible enough as MPs lose their teeth but the position of the public boards is worse.

The nationalised industries, boards such as the Manpower Commission and organisations such as the BBC have ceased to be responsible to the public in any way. Governments have decreed that parliament must not interfere in their conduct. The pretence that they are run commercially is a farce. They are not subject to the market, their ever-increasing staffs are appointed by the patronage of ministers, civil servants or by themselves. This vast patronage is under no scrutiny and those appointed often have no experience or competence. Those irresponsible feudal empires make admirable pastures for retired ministers and civil servants or their City of London favourites. I have little faith in their advisory bodies — too often friendly poodles.

Some little control is exercised by committees of the House of Commons. But at the first questing probe the bureaucrats unite to cover up. The Select Committee had immense difficulty in letting a little light in on British Steel — even when it was losing £10 million a week. The Crown Agents went on their spendthrift way unheeded for years. I wonder if Watergate would ever have been exposed here? By all means let us give the Commons committees more power and staff. They should have permanent staff of their own — far better to equip these committees with permanent accountants and lawyers than to provide ministers and the parties with political aide-de-camps and researchers. These two latter categories could become positively harmful if they proliferate, as they show every sign of doing. They may choke the democratic process.

However, expert staff assigned a definite job by select committees is a different matter and much needed. Indeed I have advocated a counter-civil service. This could be linked to expert bodies such as the Institute of International Affairs and some of the economic institutes so that independent but informed criticism was focused on government policies. But its main job would be to assist the private citizen and his elected representatives. I have not entirely abandoned the idea but I now feel there are three objections to it. First, it is no substitute for reducing the size of government, returning many of the nationalised industries to the market, abolishing many of the boards and bringing others under democratic control. Secondly, it must be accompanied by a drive against corporatism and the bureaucratic attitude: but if this drive were successful, the counter-civil service would be less necessary. Thirdly, at present I hesitate to suggest any reform in Britain because it will unquestionably be bungled. There is a real danger that a counter-civil service might itself swell like the Money Commissions and become a further incubus on the citizen.

It is a pity that we have not used the occasion of the Scotland and Wales Bills to examine the constitutional changes required at Westminster and throughout the system. We have not used the occasion either to make the changes necessary if we are to deal with EEC regulations, or to set up an assembly in Edinburgh which is not a mere copy of Westminster but which would embody some of the changes necessary and some of the features of Scottish democracy.

The rule of law will have to be strengthened. It is weak on two sides. There is no great tradition of constitutional development among British lawyers. We have nothing like the US Supreme Court. Nor indeed could such a court have operated within the traditional English system. But even without a written constitution and a Bill of Rights the court should continue a process which is beginning, for example in the judgements of Lord Denning. They are at least expressing views upon the rights of the citizen and the relevance of what might be called the common law implications of our unwritten constitution. Company law needs to take into account the workers. Trades unions and other workers' organisations should be allowed to enter into legally enforceable contracts. The breaking of individual contracts by sympathetic strikers should be made illegal. The law which needs strengthening is the law against political violence and crimes against the person.

I deal with the organisation of community politics separately. But with general political reform designed to strengthen the democratic as against the bureaucratic elements in our system must go the introduction of democracy into the administration of industry and the public services. In a pluralist country — and pluralism is essential to a welfare society — there should be many ways of running industry. First, we should make the necessary distinction between commercial undertakings and those services which should be run for non-commercial motives — motives of public service. Within the commercial sector the main regulator should be competition within a firm and impartial legal framework. Subject to that, many varieties of organisation should be encouraged: the individual entrepreneur, the joint stock company, the orthodox co-operative and various varieties of workers' co-operatives and industrial partnerships. A country which encourages different geographical communities to flourish in different ways must also encourage different economic communities to run their affairs in different ways.

The least satisfactory way must be the huge state

monopoly. It is irresponsible in that it has neither to make a profit or go out of business, nor is it accountable except in a remote and unsatisfactory way to the public or their elected representatives. Its pricing policies are indeterminate. Its management's motives are much the same as in private enterprise without the sanctions of private enterprise. It is liable to haphazard ministerial interference. It is undemocratic in structure and usually inefficient in operation. It is a main factor in making the economy difficult to manage and a prime cause of inflation.

Services for which the market is inappropriate should be brought under parliamentary control as the Post Office used to be. All other activities should be subject to the market. There should be increased expenditure on community services. The social services should be reduced in number and the present proliferation replaced by a national minimum income. I see no other ways of eradicating three of the evils which damage our country while at the same time maintaining our decency and freedom. The three particular evils I have in mind are the poor condition of some towns, rural areas and, worst of all, those twilight zones of straggling, semi-industrial, characterless and featureless housing; secondly, inflation; thirdly, unemployment. I must stress again that the reason why inflation and unemployment are so disastrous is that they threaten the decent features of a civilised country. They must be tackled not solely for economic reasons nor, in the case of unemployment, because they are necessarily bad in themselves (the rich have never objected to being unemployed) but because they are disastrous for their psychological effects. They are disastrous because they destroy self-respect. They undermine the bonds which pull us together. They deprive men and women of opportunities to use their faculties to the full.

3 The Economy

If we are to tackle inflation and unemployment we must examine how our economy is organised and what is likely to be demanded of it. To take the latter question fiirst, human appetites have proved to be remarkably elastic. New wants are constantly being discovered and boosted by emulation and advertising. In all continents but particularly in Asia, South America and Africa there are masses of people whose way of life is bare subsistence. It is therefore nonsensical and immoral to talk of stopping growth. If the industrialised countries of Europe and America stop growth they will stop any increase in their demands for the products of the less industrialised countries and curtail any rise in the real resources that they are able to contribute to their poorer neighbours. Even at home growth is highly desirable in some directions. The trouble is that growth is a statistical abstraction which leaves out all questions of value. The statistics include the production of alcohol, cigarettes, dangerous drugs and useless, prestige white elephants — all sorts of things for which people would not pay the price if they had a choice. But they do not embrace women's work. Growth, therefore, of itself is neither good nor bad; it depends what grows and some forms of growth are good and necessary.

However, while human beings have shown remarkable ingenuity in finding new wants and while invention and the habit of change in all sorts of consumer goods keep up a high level of demand, there comes a point of decreasing marginal satisfaction when demand slackens. Millionaires usually do not spend all their income, they can eventually be sated even with yachts and dancing girls. Quite a few not so very rich families would rather have more leisure than an increased income from boring or unpleasant work and much work today is boring and in conditions which are unpleasant. The future of demand seems reasonably assured with three provisos. Massive demand will come from the poor of the earth, that being so it will not in the first place be a highly sophisticated demand; home demand should, and probably will, become more discriminating; there is, and will for the immediate future at any rate be, some disposition to forego goods and services for leisure, holidays and civilised employment.

On the supply side, we should certainly be paying more attention to intermediate technology and the sort of goods demanded by the poor; the way to do this is not through state direction but through the market. Concorde is an affront to morality; it is a flaunting by the rich of a prestige project which not even the citizens of Britain want enough to pay for a ticket at the price which would cover its cost. British industry is already over-manned. As technology advances the demand for labour in existing industries will decrease. How far this labour can be absorbed in new industries or services catering for new demands remains to be seen but certainly some of it will be. Nevertheless, until the increased demand from other continents reaches us it seems that for a time unemployment in some form will be endemic in Europe. Technical change is unlikely of itself to make work interesting but may eliminate some unpleasant kinds of labour altogether. It would seem at first sight the supply of service industries will increase. The holiday trade, the trade in sporting events and the demand to have a night out at some entertainment, all point in this direction. But the rising cost of services has led to a growth in 'Do-it-Yourself' activities. The time may be coming when more people will find leisure pursuits in their home. Holiday travel is now little fun and except on package tours or by caravans prohibitively expensive. It looks unlikely, therefore, that we shall get back to a massive demand for the unskilled or semi-unskilled labour such as we saw after

The Economy

the war in the fifties in the big, mass producing basic industries. I would guess that the invasion of Turks, Yugoslavs and Commonwealth immigrants is unlikely to be repeated. The magnet will not be there. The standard of living in Western Europe will remain by comparison very high but markets and governments will continue to resist a further flow which will end up on the unemployment register.

As the world became more and more industrialised it was certain that Britain would have to abate her claim to be its workshop. However hard and efficiently Lancashire worked there was bound to come a day when it could no longer satisfy the British market before breakfast and devote the rest of the day to making goods for the world. And however mobile in theory labour might be, there was certain to be immense friction in the labour market which in any case was declining over the long term. Unemployment, a major source of poverty, is therefore in need of remedies, if remedies could be found, far beyond the social services, improvements in housing and sanitation, the Poor Laws or unemployment insurance.

To the relative decline in the importance of British manufacturing industry must be added the changes in manufacturing methods which all over the world have tended to reduce the demand for labour. I say tended because human appetites being far from sated, the new types of industry which have sprung up have opened up new demands for labour. The discussions which have gone on at least since the eighteenth century about unemployment, it causes and its cure, or the relief of the unemployed have been confused by cross-currents. Unemployment, meaning the failure of those who want paid jobs to get them, has always been admitted to be an evil. Yet shorter hours and more leisure are good. To my mind unemployment is not an absolute evil. It is an evil when it leads to poverty for the unemployed and his or her family. It is an evil when it results in the loss of useful goods for which people of their own free will are prepared to pay a profitable price. It is an evil when it leads to boredom and lack of self-respect. If, therefore, it were possible to stop the trade cycle by which it was held unemployment was caused by impersonal causes which led to slumps in industry which were harmful and unjustified, this would have been a clear gain. But suppose we reach a state where science makes it possible to satisfy most human needs by using machines to the full? Then, if we can distribute fairly the proceeds of, say, a three hour day or a three day week, we should rejoice. Of course, the snag lies in 'distributing fairly' and in regulating 'short time'. But, nevertheless, until we find some way to raise the effective demand of the poorer nations by enabling them to produce goods or materials which the manufacturing nations want and some way to maintain the drive to set up new enterprises and work efficiently, there will always be slack in the economy of the manufacturing nations.

In the immediate future the way to reduce unemployment is to reduce taxation. The money and resources then made available can be used by enterprising people in meeting current demand, for example for repairs to consumer durable goods. Inflexible, large scale industry will not need more labour; smaller industries meeting new and intermediate needs may do but at a higher ratio of output to earnings. So long as it takes five or more men in Britain to do the work of one Japanese or Korean the trades in which they work will not survive except as charities. Nor can we keep up our standards by increasing the number of non-productive workers. Yet the powers that be seem convinced that no economies can be made and everything must proceed as usual. When I suggested that air travel should be made cheaper or the ordinary passenger would be forced out of it, I was seriously told that the only remedy was to close the airports. Another line of argument is that it is very unfair of Koreans to do so much more while claiming so much less. This is a thoroughly immoral argument and makes nonsense of any ambitions to help the poorer countries. If the British cannot compete at present rates of pay they must take less.

If machines can take more of the burden of work the best way to share the benefit would be to give more people a share in the ownership of the machines and in property in general. If nearly everyone owned some property and received some income from it our society would be

The Economy

transformed for the better. Men and women would not be forced to take the first job thrust upon them. They would have a base on which to rest and remove the degradation caused by lack of employment. As Meade says in his chapter on Efficiency, Equality and the Ownership of Property:

> The essential feature of this society would be that work had become rather more a matter of personal choice. The unpleasant work that had to be done would have to be very highly paid to attract to it those whose tastes lead them to wish to supplement considerably their incomes from property. At the other extreme, those who wished to devote themselves to quite uncommercial activities would be able to do so with a reduced standard of living but without starving in a garret.
>
> (J. E. Meade, *Planning and the Price Mechanism*, Allen & Unwin, 1948.)

Meade is being deliberately Utopian but surely he is thinking in the right direction and not only over the wider distribution of property. I am sure we have to get used to new scales of pay — relatively less for those with interesting jobs and more for drudgery.

It is now becoming accepted by an increasing number of people, though not by trades union leaders or bureaucrats, that the retention of workers in unnecessary jobs (the modern Speenhamland system) or the injection of more money into the economy whether by the payment of higher wages, by increasing the amount spent on social services, by government expenditure through local authorities, public boards or the nationalised industries, or indeed by increasing subsidies to private industry, will not cure unemployment. For by increasing inflation it will lead to more undertakings being unable to sell their products with the inevitable result that they lay off staff. Indeed, it is no longer believed that we can spend our way out of a slump, nor reduce unemployment by an increase in the money supply, however calculated. The doctrine of Malthus and Keynes that savings in excess of investment were a cause of recession presupposed that investment would be productive. That is to say that it would be made in the manufacture of goods or provision of services which generated wealth.

They did not envisage either that it would go into expanding the bureaucratic, non-productive top-hamper of the economy, or that savings forced by taxation would be used to bolster inefficient or unwanted industries. They did not in fact foresee the success of the trades unions and other bodies in directing savings to unproductive investment. They also, it seems to me, supposed that prices and costs were not rising at anything like the present rate. In fact, they assumed a stable or deflationary state of the economy. Inflation, therefore, is now seen as not only an evil in that it destroys many of the pillars on which a decent free society rests, but as itself a cause of unemployment. Inflation is therefore the root evil.

As we have destroyed the free regulator and the possibility of reducing prices, salary and wage rates, at least in monetary terms, we have killed one way in which the labour market could be extended. Let us be honest about this: if we really feel that unemployment is a disaster, there is a simple way of reducing it — by reducing wage rates. Indeed we have now deterred management from taking on extra labour for which it may have an opening because the Protection of Employment Act saddles it with such responsibilities and makes it so difficult to dismiss anyone. Such, therefore, are the difficulties within constantly changing human demands and inventions, and in the face of international trade cycles and all the friction which retards the movement of labour, that cures for unemployment are often methods of alleviating the distresses caused by it. Even public works programmes and job creation schemes are often palliatives. Even when public work programmes seem eminently sensible, for example the building of roads during recessions, they have to be used with caution. Nowadays many of the traditional areas of public work do not use much labour. And it is difficult to tailor them to the length of the recession. Particularly today when organised labour demands that jobs should continue long after their justification has disappeared. It is also noticeable that job creation schemes which have a lot to be said for them if they prevent boys and girls going straight from school on to the dole do not pay very much in wages and are kept to the fringe of the economy. So although at

The Economy

the time of writing we are bedevilled by what is optimistically considered a temporary lack of work we may have to resign ourselves to a higher level of unemployment than was once thought necessary. Certainly the Keynsian remedies of low interest rates and deficit budgeting have been found unusable in the face of restrictive practices and trades unions rigidity without rates of inflation which in turn will destroy our society and certainly make even semi-full employment in a free society impossible.

The public debate then usually turns back to the question not of curing or abolishing or conquering unemployment but of providing the unemployed in their leisure with a reasonable standard of living. But I must emphasise that to provide a reasonable standard of living for the unemployed we must both accept the presuppositions of a liberal society and also provide the wealth to do it. The economists who immediately after the war advocated a 'liberal socialist' economy assumed that the common good and the general will should prevail and the laws of political economy be respected. These assumptions are no longer valid. Beveridge thought that poverty could be abolished, without even touching the rich, by a redistribution of income within the working classes — though he did not recommend this, believing that some redistribution between classes was essential. It is to providing better incomes for the unemployed and for the disabled, the old and the sick, that his plan was directed. It is to this rather than reforming the economy that our efforts have been directed since 1945.

Indeed changes in the economy through government intervention and nationalisation of industries have been introduced not to make it more possible for more people to be employed usefully in trades which produce goods or services which can be profitably sold but in maintaining occupations which produce goods or services for which consumers in a free market will not pay a price which covers investment and allows for the rate of wages which the unions consider essential. This in the long run, if carried to excess, (as it is being carried) can only produce a lower than possible standard of living and unemployment, open or concealed.

It is not difficult to see how inflation is being generated. Unless in a free society there is a free market and there are more goods and services for which people are willing to pay a profitable price, any increase in money or credit must lead to a rise in prices (leaving aside the velocity of circulation). The supply of goods can be increased by imports but Britain cannot increase her imports unless exports increase very greatly. It is salutary to look at these matters in real terms: if there are ten apples in a shop, even if each customer has one thousand pounds to spend on apples they cannot get more than ten out of the shop. The classical corollary to this is that if the demand for apples increases then more people will grow apples. But in our present circumstances there are obstacles to this, even in the long run.

In the short run, the argument about how to keep down the cost of apples is between those who want to prevent people getting more money to spend — that is, between the advocates of a wages and prices policy and the monetarists (of which there are several species) who demand that there should be less money; and the advocates of a wages policy who claim that it isn't, or isn't mainly, the availability of money which drives up the cost of apples. The supply of money in their eyes is only increased because of rising demand and does not cause that demand. The monetarists reply that if the money was not available the demand would not arise. At least the monetarists can claim that the availability of money is a condition of rising prices — a *causa sine qua non*. To suggest a not very exact analogy, it may be that it is the will to violence which matters and which would exist even if there were no weapons. But the absence of weapons would nevertheless make violence much more difficult and less damaging. The monetarists have won considerable support over the last few years. Although the hopes of the Labour government have been pinned on a prices and incomes policy, they have accompanied this by control of the money supply and the public spending borrowing requirement. They have announced cash limits to the grants available to local authorities. If these measures have been taken at the orders of their creditors, nevertheless there would appear to have been a genuine conversion by some Labour ministers to monetarist policies.

But the monetarists used to put less emphasis upon the effect of the money supply on prices. As Hicks points out in his essay on 'Monetary Experience and the Theory of Money' (Sir John Hicks, *Economic Perspectives*, Clarendon Press, 1977): 'The initial effect of an increase in the supply of money, Hume was aware, was to stimulate industry. It must first stimulate the diligence of every individual before it increases the price of labour.' Unfortunately, the restrictions on home industry being so strong and taxation so heavy, an increase in the supply of money in Britain no longer has the results expected.

Inflation is a political problem. It is not to be solved by economic sleight of hand but by political decisions. Once the government determines to stop inflation it will be stopped. What makes the task of the government difficult is not ignorance as to how to do it but uncertainty about the political consequences of taking the necessary measures. Either strict monetary control or a strict incomes policy allowing virtually no increases until production rises will stop inflation. But can any government ride out the storm which will be raised by selfish bureaucratic interests? The problem is made more difficult by the existence of such a large public sector. Today over sixty per cent of the national income passes through the public sector. This sector is immune from the operations of the market. If it were subjected to the discipline of the market large portions of it would go out of business. So long as the public sector was small compared to the rest of the economy it was possible to manage it. A central and local government service which was only a fraction of the free market sector could have its payments fixed by reference to that sector with allowances for security, pensions and the satisfaction of public service jobs. Taking these characteristics into account the rates should be lower than in private business. Now, however, the public service is becoming the pacemaker. Its size and the position it has won with indexed pensions and annual increments puts it in the lead over productive private employment. In the nationalised industries a similar development has taken place. Here, however, there is the additional complication that they are supposed to be run commercially. If they were, they would have to be greatly reduced in size, the wages paid to their employees would have to be reduced and the number of employees cut. Such measures would of course be unthinkable to the unions involved. Ten years or so after nationalisation the chairman of British Steel himself says it is bankrupt. Bankrupt businesses cannot legally trade.

It is the size and nature of the public sector which makes the economy so difficult, politically, to manage. It makes it difficult whether you believe in an incomes policy or a monetary policy, whether you believe that the cause of inflation is the uncovered borrowing liability of the government or whether you think that a return to laissez-faire will put everything right. For the public sector will resist any cure. The commanding heights of the economy were to be scaled and conquered by socialists so that the general interest should prevail. What has happened is that sufficient areas of the economy have been taken over by nationalisation to guarantee, not that the general interest will prevail, but that the sectional interests in these areas can get their own way.

This is of profound importance to the welfare state or the welfare services. First, it is a prime cause of inflation and inflation is now a more serious threat to our standard of living and a decent society than is unemployment. Further, the aggression with which each trades union and profession fights for higher monetary rewards is incompatible with a welfare society. As Professor Robson has pointed out:

> The leaders of the Trades Unions insist with all the emphasis at their command that unfettered collective bargaining between the parties to a dispute with no holds barred is the only proper and acceptable method of determining wages and conditions of employment. Such arrangements are appropriate to a laissez faire state, they are certainly not compatible with a welfare society, for in such a society welfare is not only something created by the state through the action of public authorities but is also generated by the actions and attitudes of individuals, groups and institutions.

(W. A. Robson, *Welfare State and Welfare Society*, Allen & Unwin, 1976.)

'Free collective bargaining' is a misuse of words as used by the trades union leaders. It is in the same class as 'The German Democratic Republic'; that phrase is designed to mislead, to use the language of freedom and democracy to conceal something quite different. They do not intend that as a result of free collective bargaining the steel industry might, for instance, reduce wages and lay off numbers of its workmen. Circumstances may force a reduction in staff as is happening at British Steel but such reductions are not the aim of the unions when they call for free collective bargaining. Yet for an industry making a loss as big as that of British Steel reductions on a much bigger scale than contemplated should be the result of any such process. Free collective bargaining would certainly not be free, for the unions retain their right of coercion by strikes — and strikes not only in the industry concerned but in other industries as well. It would not be bargaining for a bargain presupposes that both sides would take responsibility for the result and would abide by it. As Adam Smith said, 'Whoever proposes to another a bargain of any kind proposes to do this. Give me that which I want and you shall have this which you want, is the meaning of every such offer.' But what the trades union officials mean by bargaining is that they should, in the public sector, be able to extort payments from the tax payer in return for services which he or she does not want. And similar demands are now being made by trades union officials in the private sector as well.

The union leaders look beyond the managers of industry to the tax payer and expect him to pay up. Nor have they any intention of allowing themselves to be subjected to the ordinary law of contract. If they wish to break a bargain in Britain they can do so and are not liable for the consequences. Nor is it even collective, except within the industry concerned and doubtfully there. We have seen many groups of workers break agreements entered into by their unions. And there is no nationwide bargain. The TUC have constantly and correctly said that they could not deliver their side of such a bargain. The threat to a welfare society in the sense the term is generally used arises today not from millionaires, great concentrations of capital, nor international companies but from powerful unions and closely organised groups of workers, often led by men who want to destroy a free society and what socialists describe as welfare state, and from professional bodies and bureaucrats using their strength at the expense of the weaker or less organised elements in the country. The methods of using this strength, the strike and the sympathetic strike, are now no longer aimed at the wicked employers but at the general public. This again, as Professor Robson has pointed out, strikes at the root of a welfare society:

> When an industrialised nation becomes a welfare state the need for a strong sense of individual, group and institutional responsibility and the need for social discipline become far greater because irresponsibility and indiscipline cause disruption, fear and suffering of many different kinds. Air line pilots or ground staff on strike can destroy beyond repair the holiday plans of thousands of families.

The Grunwick affair was not only a terrifying example of how fragile now is the rule of law but a demonstration of how little some sections of our people care for their neighbours. Ordinary life, business and employment in an area of London were put in jeopardy by some Post Office workers though the sufferers had nothing to do with the Grunwick dispute. The immorality of the kidnappers who hope to coerce the public and their representatives into accepting their demands by threatening to kill innocent victims stems in a more savage form from the reasoning which prompts the sympathetic strike. Firemen demanding higher pay from the government hope to win more for themselves by allowing the public's property to burn and its lives to be endangered. They even demand that fire equipment, which belongs to the public authorities not to them, shall stand idle. It is, or was, true that take-over bids can deprive workers of their jobs. But at present this is much the lesser danger. No take-over can now take place without considerable reaction from the workers and it may well provoke interference from the Monopolies or other

The Economy

Commissions. It is intimidation by pressure groups and the mentality of those who demand ransom money that threaten us.

So the existence of such a large public sector and the power of the organisations to defend and extend it are a major reason for our difficulty in dealing with inflation and are in several ways incompatible with a welfare society. With production stagnant and the country heavily in debt there can be no justification for any over-all wage increases. If a trades union or professional body gets a rise somebody else will get less. Prices will increase and weaker members of the community will suffer. The other illusion is that if the price of imported goods goes up, for example oil, then wages must go up to meet it. The only way to meet it is to use less or cut down on something else or work harder to pay for it. The mobilisation of public opinion has proved less effective of late in general political controversies. There is probably a large majority now antagonistic to many trades union demands. But whether this opposition can be effective, even if it is reflected in a big Parliamentary majority is doubtful. The majority do not necessarily win the day — large measures of nationalisation have been carried through by a government which only commanded thirty-eight per cent of the votes. The nationalisation measures themselves were probably supported by less than half even of those who voted Labour. And the majority in parliament is not governed by reason. What decides Government action is usually an amalgam of what was in the Manifesto, what their advisers both in the civil service and the new backroom research units want, the pet theories of a few ministers and the buffetings of unforeseen events. What is in the Manifesto is often largely irrelevant to the situation the government have to meet on taking office.

But clause four still remains in the constitution of the Labour Party. If the advance towards total nationalisation has been haphazard it has been remorseless — and always by way of state monopoly. Municipal enterprise, as fostered by Joseph Chamberlain, has not been encouraged of late: indeed the local authority gas and electricity undertakings have been swallowed by national monopolies.

Until recently the Labour Party set its face against workers' participation and even now when it talks of workers being associated in management it means the trades union bureaucrats. Socialists would like to kill all competition in education. They have done their best to eliminate the private landlord and would prefer all housing to be publicly owned. That prominent Socialists send their children to private schools and live in expensive private houses is merely part of the general hypocrisy which pervades much of their conduct — particularly in regard to equality.

Conservatives and Liberals have been tainted with the same prejudices. Collectivism has been in the air. More and more people have seen the extension of centralised bureaucracy as the means to achieving their aims or ambitions. It has been assumed that because you cannot put the clock back you must accept the current wisdom, ignoring the fact that collectivism is putting the clock back to mercantilism and Marx. Surely we should consider the possibility of putting the clock forward.

4 Inflation and Employment

There must be freedom to choose, create and criticise. You cannot have freedom without economic freedom. A welfare society and effective welfare services even of the existing variety depend upon an economy in which by far the largest sector including both manufacturing and servicing is run by free enterprise subject to the market. Socialism in Britain means state or bureaucratic socialism. So far from this being necessary for a welfare society, I believe it is the very opposite: that the lack of satisfaction, of self-respect, of skilful management and efficient use of our resources are caused by the present brand of socialism. Inflation is the result of the divisive and greedy activities of various bureaucracies. The failure to change the use of our resources, which is also caused by the tenacity with which socialist bureaucrats cling to their vested interests is a major cause of unemployment with its consequent poverty. The reinstallation, therefore, of the market within a firm framework of law and leaving aside for the moment the question of the organisation and ownership of industry and services is a first essential.

The working of the market economy has been fully examined from Adam Smith to Marshall, Pigou, Keynes, Hayek, Friedman, Peacock and other present day economists. But, nevertheless, there seems widespread ignorance about how it operates. In essence the market allows those with something to offer and those who want something to come together and effect an exchange to their mutual advantage. Adam Smith found in human nature 'the propensity to truck, barter and exchange one thing for another.' He claimed that this was a characteristic common to all men which was to be found in no other race of animals. 'Nobody ever saw a dog make a fair and deliberate exchange of one bone for another.' Bargaining can cover every economic activity which results in the main benefit accruing to the individuals concerned. It is usually held to be inappropriate where either many who have not taken part in the bargain and have paid no part of the price yet benefit from the result (public goods) or where services are considered essential but a charge for them would not pay the cost of collection. I shall return to this subject later.

Bargaining through a price mechanism in a market allows for continual variation in production and demand. It encourages the distribution of labour and capital so that entrepreneurs and workers produce what they can produce most efficiently. It will regulate the provision and allocation of savings for investment as well as the exchange of consumable goods. It has proved by far and away the best means of raising the standard of life. But it also provides freedom of choice — laissez-faire, freedom to choose what you produce, laissez-aller, freedom to move around and freedom to lay out your money as you want. These freedoms cannot be afforded to the citizen of a planned economy, if by a planned economy is meant an economy in which the greater part of production, distribution and exchange is controlled by the government and not the market. If the government decrees that, come what may, however reluctant people may be to buy British cars at a price which car workers will accept and however stubborn these workers are in refusing to take any cut in wages, yet the factory producing these cars must be kept in operation, then somehow or other the public must be forced to pay for the cars and other workers must be forced to take less. The first stage of the planned economy is usually planned consumption (a variety of demand management). The government subsidises out of taxation the sale of some line of goods below its market price and so stimulates consumption. The eventual stage of planning dominating more and more of the economy must be the direction of labour.

The free market economy provides the means by which a country can improve the various communities which compose it. As Adam Smith wrote in his introduction to *The Wealth of Nations*: 'Political economy considered as a branch of the science of a statesman or legislator proposes two distinct objects: first, to provide a plentiful revenue or subsistence for the people or, more properly, to enable them to provide such a revenue or subsistence for themselves.' This is vital to a good community. Even if planning carried beyond a certain point were not hopelessly inefficient, thereby preventing people from providing a rising subsistence for themselves, it removes from people an essential ingredient of a good society in my sense of the word, or of any society in which the current welfare services are backed by an attitude consistent with them. Adam Smith goes on, 'and secondly to supply the state or commonwealth with a revenue sufficient for the public services.' As creeping bureaucracies strangle the market, production of real resources falls and the wealth to support communal or social services is not to be found. This can be illustrated from our own experience. Whether you think that some services, for example items provided by the health services such as medicine and spectacles, should be charged to taxes and not to the recipient, there is no doubt that governments have wanted to charge them to the tax payer but have found that the taxable wealth to pay for them was lacking.

A feature of the free market is the emergence of surplus value. This surplus value, it has been alleged, is, under the market system, annexed by a small part of the nation. This criticism is tied up with the labour theory of value which holds that it is labour (in conjunction with some other elements such as land which are not the product of human activity) which creates value. Because the labourer does not receive the full price of the product, he or she is held to be exploited by the employer. It should be noted that even if this theory was correct, exploitation still arises under socialism as can be seen very clearly in the Marxist countries. The surplus value may be taken by the state but it is not returned to the worker.

The value of any commodity is what someone else will pay for it. As Adam Smith wrote: What everything is really worth to the man who has acquired it and who wants to dispose of it, or exchange it for something else, is the toil and trouble which it can save to himself and which it can impose upon other people.' However hard I toil away producing something, unless someone else is willing to give me something that I want more than what I have produced, then my production is of no economic value (though it may have great artistic value or have provided me with useful exercise). The taking of risk, the postponement of consumption so that savings may be accumulated and investment undertaken, the organisation of the market and the provision of credit, all have to be paid for. If they are not, the economy will be stagnant as Adam Smith also pointed out, 'It is not the actual greatness of national wealth, but its continued increase which occasions a rise in the wages of labour.'

A most welcome feature of the market economy is that it breaks down decision-making into a multitude of individual bargains. This has several advantages. If some decisions are wrong they will only affect part of the economy; they will not be so disastrous as a mistake in a national plan. The cost of wrong decisions is borne by those who make them and not by the public at large. The autonomous and multifarious process of decision-making ensures flexibility. And the process also removes a source of friction, for the market is an impartial organisation — it cannot be bullied. Once the government starts to interfere then the way to improve your place in the economy is to exert influence on the government, or seize power. The strong win; the unsuccessful have a grievance and become disaffected.

The market is democratic. It allows everyone to decide what they want to do with their earnings. In a free market everyone should have some opportunity to offer his wares, use his skills, show his enterprise. The free market is far more egalitarian than planning by a department of state. It has as its end the satisfaction of all human wants. What is

Inflation and Employment

the end, the purpose to which planning by a department is directed? In certain circumstances this may be a clear and simple need which justifies the concentration of resources upon it. In war it is the need to win the war and to make the munitions that will help do so but in peace there is no such simple end. The choice of end is therefore arbitrary, it is what those in charge decide it shall be. Very often abstractions are involved because the desires of flesh and blood, the aims of people, are multitudinous.

The market also encourages innovation which is all too often anathema to the bureaucratic planner. The waste of the non-market economy should be emphasised. If resources are switched to uses which yield no profit, that is to say, for which no one of their own free will is willing to pay an adequate price, then they are switched from something else which people want.

The free market system *is* a system. To describe it as 'the law of the jungle' is the reverse of the truth. The law of the jungle puts all power into the hands of the strong; this is what happens in the planned economy — it is what the market prevents. It is not a random, haphazard way of conducting affairs. To accuse it of that is like saying a thermostat is haphazard because it does away with hand operation. The automatic changes of prices, responsive to supply and demand, are a much more scientific regulator than haphazard interference by ministers at the request of this or that pressure group. Because it is a system it must be set up and sustained. Human beings may have a propensity to bargain but their bargaining will not be satisfactory without a framework of law and institutions within which it can operate. The enforcement of contracts, the defence of person and property and the maintenance of a stable currency are some of these prerequisites.

Markets can be modified, some economic activities (if economic is the right word) can be taken out of the market but the free enterprise system hangs together and if its working is too seriously dislocated it will not function at all. If the nationalised industries do not have to raise their capital in the free market, even though they sell their products competitively, they are not subject to a true market. Further, if too much of the economy is taken out of the market no one has yet found a way (at least in a free society and probably this is true even of a complete dictatorship) of allocating resources or rewards. One obvious example of this is fixing the rates of pay in the public service. This is difficult enough at the best of times. Buf if there is a large private market sector the pay of public servants and those who work in nationalised industries can be fixed by reference to comparable jobs in that private sector with some allowance for pensions, security of tenure, absence of risk, etc. But without such a sector what is the criterion? Again, without a rate of interest — the price people are prepared to pay for lending their money — how do we judge which investment should be undertaken?

I have mentioned a stable currency as essential to a market. Money is both a means of exchange and a store of value. If violent inflation or deflation takes place, as well as hindering the production of wealth (as Keynes explained) it destroys everyone's ability to save and invest and plan their future. Our present inflation, therefore, threatens the free society, and certainly, if pushed too far, threatens the sort of society which I have outlined as being desirable. The provision and regulation of money has usually been considered the prerogative of the state. But all governments have a penchant for debasing the currency. It is very doubtful, therefore, whether it is in the long term interests of a free society to leave it in their hands.

The market economy has severe drawbacks and limitations. However, unless its nature is understood, the genuine limitations and drawbacks cannot be defined. First, let us be clear that since a market is an artificial creation, protected by the laws of the state, the state is entitled to regulate it. Were it not, for instance, for the law giving limited liability to joint stock companies the great expansion of industry which has taken place would never have come about.

Secondly, there are many, many human activities which should not be subject to the market. There are the public goods already noticed. There are services — for instance, in my view, a basic health service and a postal service — which although they can be made subject to a market, should not be. There is the use of resources, such as the supply of land which cannot be increased to meet increased demand. For a discussion of what should or should not be subject to a market see Arthur Seldon's book *Charge* (Temple Smith, 1977). It is not my intention to go into this in detail.

Thirdly, and very relevant to any discussion about what activities should be withdrawn from the market, there is the perennial inequality of those who have to operate the market. The weak position of consumers faced by a monopoly can sometimes be rectified by anti-monopoly legislation though this should usually aim at creating a market and not at setting up ministries, commissions or consumer councils to curb monopolies while allowing them to continue. There can be the weakness of labour in the face of employers, though today this is not the danger it once was. But most important of all, there is the basic difficulty facing market economies — that some of those operating in it have, through no fault of their own, far less chance of benefiting from it than do others. The advantage of inherited wealth, for instance, is very great. Far too many people still suffer from the disadvantage of being born poor in a poor community.

As justification for interference in the market economy it is sometimes said that it cannot raise the huge sums needed for capital investment. This is extremely doubtful. Private savings and investment, certainly by individuals and small companies and to a lesser extent by big companies, have been discouraged by taxation, dividend limitation and nationalisation. In spite of this, the savings available in investment which the public expects to be profitable (such as the oil industry) are immense. If private saving and investment were actively encouraged their volume would be very large. Our main trouble today is not so much lack of investment but the justifiable reluctance of savers, faced with restriction and taxation and the general climate of a collectivist country, to put their money in risk enterprises. It is of course true that industry in a market economy will not deliberately invest in capital projects which will not yield a profit. Therefore, if you want Concorde, the tax payers have to pay for it. But over the greatest part of the economy this refusal of industry to back prestige white elephants (or flying pyramids) with shareholders' money seems to me very much to its credit. Let it be noted too that many of the undertakings of which some of those on the Left at the moment most disapprove, for example nuclear development and the pushing of arms sales, are in the hands of governments or public authorities.

Just as I would argue that there are services which should be provided outside the market, so there are investments of a non-commercial kind which public authorities should undertake with forced savings raised through taxation, though these are far fewer than is generally supposed. As it is we waste a high proportion of savings. It is an enlightening commentary on the confidence which trades unions and nationalised corporations have in our corporate state that they invest their pensions funds in pictures and foreign property. They know full well how inefficient much of British industry has become.

How far is there scope for co-operation between government and private entrepreneurs? Two common forms of this are the support of agriculture and assistance to firms in difficulties, believed to be temporary. British agricultural policy has been a success. Britain produces more food than Canada or Australia, her farming is technically efficient and prices, at least until inflation mounted, seem to have given reasonable satisfaction to the farmer and the consumer. The cost to the tax payer has been high but at least he or she has got something for it. The technical services provided by the state have been fairly widely used. It is impossible to guess what would have happened had food and fodder been left to the market but in an imperfect world British agriculture must be rated a success; the policies which have guided it must therefore be rated successful too, though the chief credit must go to the farmers and the farm servants themselves.

One of the features of British agricultural policy seems to have been the use of co-operative effort. The state has not gone into farming itself on any scale. When it has done so its work has not been very productive. The Scottish Office has been losing of the order of £1½ million annually on trading from the land it owns. The farmer has kept his personal interest and his personal incentive. The market, though much modified by guaranteed prices, capital grants, subsidies etc., has functioned to some extent. A balance has been struck between change and security of tenure. Probably any strict economic balance sheet would show that some of the capital sunk in British farms and largely supplied by the state has not earned as much as it should. But if we add to the production of food, the relief to the balance of payments and the preservation of rural life, British agricultural policy is an example which should be studied. We should at the same time consider whether even better results might not have been obtained by providing money for farming through agricultural banks and other non-government channels.

Assistance to ailing businesses is a different matter. I do not believe that a very small increase in general economic results justifies hardship to small minorities. And hardship can result when firms go out of business, especially in towns where they account for a large proportion of the jobs. But it has proved impossible to know whether difficulties are temporary or permanent. The tendency has been to ignore symptoms indicating a permanent decline. The bolstering up of firms of every size from Leyland's downwards by injections of tax payers' money has contributed to the inefficiency of British industry. In the long run too it has harmed many communities. For it has directed attention from their real needs. But I do not rule out the supply of capital by public bodies to firms essential in their neighbourhoods. I would rather, however, such capital was raised locally where this can be done.

What is incompatible with a free society and therefore with a society in which communal and social services can perform their proper tasks is a further extension of corporatism, whether through centralised government direction or further nationalisation. However the march is disguised and however slow progress may be, this can only end up in all-pervading state socialism. The consequences of state socialism have now been known for sixty years. There is no excuse for anyone being unaware of what they entail. Nor is there any room for doubting that the consequences flow, and must flow, from the nature of communism. Yet communists and their sympathisers frequently appear amazed when, for instance, Russia invades Hungary or when liberty is further restricted. They pretend that these are deviations from some humane and liberal communist norm.

All the appalling consequences of extreme socialism as evinced in every communist state are shrugged off as aberrations yet communism clearly is appalling in practice. Russia is a monumental tragedy. Its record of massacre, imperialism, terror, suppression of all new thought and art, religious and social persecution and cruelty is unparalleled in history; and this has happened not in a primitive people but in a nation with vast resources in the twentieth century. It is grossly inefficient. It was in a fairly advanced state of industrialisation in 1917, it has agricultural, mineral and energy resources unequalled in the world, yet it has to import food and skills from the West and remains far behind Western Europe, America or Japan. I read in a report by efficiency experts on the University of Warwick that we must choose between democracy and efficiency. This just shows how dotty efficiency experts are. Democracy under the rule of law and a system of free enterprise has proved incomparably efficient. If planning and control of resources and population were the foundation of wealth Russia would be the richest and Switzerland the poorest country in Europe. For a description of how inefficient planned economies can be even in war read Speers' book *Inside the Third Reich* (translated by R. & C. Winston, Weidenfeld & Nicolson, 1970).

Nor does Russia make any contribution to the poorer countries. On the contrary, she herself depends upon resources provided by the West. If the underdeveloped countries were wise, they would examine how America and Japan pulled themselves up without foreign aid to become the richest countries in the world. 'Ah,' I shall be told, 'Russia has indeed taken a wrong turning but she is not really an example of communism.' What is? The appalling massacres of the Khmer Rouge, the bayonetting of children, the terror imposed by communists in

Inflation and Employment

South-East Asia? Czechoslovakia? The darkness which has descended on perhaps the world's oldest civilisation — China? It is an error to believe that oppression and cruelty are aberrations from communism. Communism believes that the individual must be sacrificed to the state, that he or she is unimportant. Some time, of course, when everyone has been reduced to nonentity in a proletariat the state can relax. But no one can seriously believe even this. The size of the communist state apparatus and its power grow ever greater. If communism were to relax it would be instantly overthrown. Communism is like the extreme form of fifteenth and sixteenth-century Catholicism which maintained itself by the Inquisition and the Index. Indeed it is much, much worse. To expect it to embrace liberty or the welfare of individuals and the community is more absurd than to expect the most bigotted Catholics of the late middle ages to tolerate atheism.

I shall then be told 'socialism is not communism' yet the current difference in much of Western Europe is only in the methods of achieving the communist state. The British Socialist party is committed to an indefinite programme of nationalisation. And, of course, communism or socialism suits the bureaucracy. No doubt very few Russian bureaucrats take Marx seriously but communism is a marvellous vehicle for satisfying the ambitions and extending the empires of bureaucrats; so to a lesser extent is socialism. What is to my mind a valid argument for communal action is that a country run entirely for all purposes and without restraint by the motives of self-interest will be an unsatisfactory country. The mainspring of capitalist free enterprise can be represented as the quality — greed — which all religions and moralities have rejected. The answer to this is threefold. First, to get on, to produce, to improve your own and your family's condition by market activities helps others as well. Secondly, however, this process must be kept under control by a general morality and a legal framework, by being excluded from certain operations and by concern for the weak. Thirdly, by expelling the free market you do not snuff out greed or personal ambition, you transfer it to far more dangerous activities in the bureaucracies. At the back of communism or socialism there is the very appealing notion of a country run by altruism — we all long sometimes to talk with some old communist ghost who lived before any communist party was born — but bureaucratic state communism or socialism is not altruistic. Indeed its rise has at least coincided with, and certainly contributed to, the decay of altruism in our society. That is a major reason why we must think again and see if altruism can be reinstated.

What part have altruism or ethical considerations to play in the running of the economy?

Most decisions have ethical implications or belong to a chain of decision-making which has such implications, apart, that is, from purely technical decisions (should I use this size of screwdriver or that?). And ethical decisions must be made by individuals. They often entail resolving different claims because two or more of the possibilities open may increase or reduce the chances of promoting the values which to my mind are the test of right or wrong action. Thus no system, planned, market or otherwise can relieve individuals of their responsibility. We may have to reconcile complicated competing claims. For instance, should I invest in South Africa if the market tells me that such an investment is profitable in a freely working economy? I have to consider the claims of the black workers. Will these be furthered or hindered by such investment? Is the market in fact free? And many other claims as well. The market will not tell me what is morally right. It will tell me what people want and for me at any rate this is an important consideration. It also enables each buyer or seller to make moral decisions and provides an important piece of information before he or she does so. Thus so far from being immoral or amoral, the market imposes an obligation to decide between right or wrong.

Enthusiasts for the market often maintain that it can regulate all economic life except those activities which are public goods. They maintain therefore that the test of whether something should be paid for compulsorily by all out of taxation, or by charging, is whether or not the benefits accrue to all or can be particularised. For instance, defence

Inflation and Employment

must be paid for by taxes because if the country is defended all will gain (or perhaps lose). There is force in this argument. But I do not think it entirely adequately defines the limits of the market. For one thing, it may be possible to pay for public goods by charging; it is possible to provide them by free enterprise, as has often been done even in war by hiring *condottiere* or mercenaries.

Secondly, there are some commodities of which the sale, if unfettered, is clearly against the public interest, that is instead of promoting a society in which freedom can flourish will hinder it. This is a tricky area. I remember Winston Churchill giving Gwillym Lloyd George, the Home Secretary, a severe dressing down for forbidding the sale of some drug. It is one of the many areas of decision where competing claims have to be weighed. But most important when considering the concept of the common good, there are services and activities for which the profit motive, the free market, the process of bargaining is inappropriate. To take an extreme instance, somebody of course has to pay for the work of the clergy. In fact, the congregations do but the thought of bargaining outside each church door before each service is surely unattractive. The same is true of all services in which there should be a strong personal and ethical bond between the persons concerned. In fact, services in which the motive is altruistic are not suitable for regulation by the market alone. It is not only the fact that the army is a public good which makes bargaining for its upkeep difficult. It is that soldiers (leaving aside mercenaries) are altruistic. Our country does not offer sufficient opportunities to the altruistic. It must be the only conceivably justifiable reason for the nationalised industries that they should be run for different motives from private enterprise. But they are not.

Socialism as practised in this country has not increased the scope for altruism. It has served to obscure the division between those operations which should be subject to the market and those which should not. It has made the overseeing of the economy and the regulation of the price mechanism, a legitimate task for government, more difficult.

It is sometimes assumed that the social services are an

extension of socialism and that they receive most support from Labour governments. It is strange that this should be so. Action by the government to alleviate poverty goes back a long way, before socialism was thought of. Important steps in health and housing were taken by Tory governments in the nineteenth century and, of course, Lord Shaftesbury was a Tory. Pensions, unemployment and sickness insurance were Liberal measures. The Chamberlains were never socialists. Beveridge was a Liberal member of parliament. Of recent years Tories and Liberals in parliament have shown at least as much concern for the social services as socialists. If it is argued that laissez-faire economics created some of the conditions which these services sought to better it is certain that it also created the wealth to support these services. Nineteenth-century governments never produced laissez-faire; they introduced constant legislation to control it. Nor is it true that similar conditions are not created under various types of socialism. A glance round the world will show that.

What is true is that collectivism has been the dominant strain in British (and indeed in Western) thinking for the last forty years or so. This has affected the social services as it has all sides of politics. State or bureaucratic socialism has won the day over rival varieties of Christian or democratic socialism such as syndicalism. Control by officials on behalf of the public has been largely accepted.

Though logically socialists should welcome profits, in fact they have treated them as evidence of exploitation. It often seems that in their eyes it is a positive asset that nationalised industries should declare a loss. It is important to understand the implications of this. It could be taken to show a pleasure in failure as against success. Or perhaps it means that no margin over current expenditure is necessary for future investment? Or is it that those who postpone consumption and take risks are immoral? Whatever be the springs from which condemnation of profit arises they are poisoned springs, destined to reduce all human progress. They diminish the wealth available for social or community services. They hinder the will and ability of people to improve their own and their community's welfare.

So for many reasons I see a market economy as being essential to a good society and its services. But I see too a large segment of human activity in which the market is inappropriate. I believe we have both damaged the working of the market and allowed market values to invade fields where they have no place. We should distinguish much more sharply between what activities are appropriate to the market disciplines and those which are not.

But within the proper sphere of the market could we not eliminate some at least of its imperfections — the inequality to which it can lead and the domination of some individuals or organisations over their employees? Laissez-faire has led in practice to huge inequalities of wealth and power which have led to stresses within Western civilisation and driven the majority of workers away from a free market system.

5 The Organisation of Industry

While pondering on the means whereby our industrial system might give more satisfaction while retaining its essential freedom I was introduced by Robert Oakeshott to the Mondragon workers' co-operatives. Mondragon is a town in the province of Biscaya in the Basque part of Spain. It is the headquarters of a group of co-operatives which have spread through the province. Robert has clung to the central idea, which I share, that a free society must be a libertarian society, that a libertarian society must incorporate a free market and voluntary co-operation and that efforts to supplement or improve the capitalist system had taken a wrong turning.

Partnership or co-ownership between owners, managers and workers has in one form or another long been a part of the Liberal Party programme and a part in which I personally was much interested. It was obviously sensible if you wanted to run a free economic system to interest as many people as possible in its success. That means giving them a say in how it is run and a share in the profits. Industrial partnership also means an extension of democracy into a field important to everyone — the field of work. If workers who produced successfully were rewarded through profits this would not be inflationary and would be an incentive to effort.

But though they should be praised for their efforts, the firms which have practised partnership, co-operation, co-ownership or profit sharing have not been outstand-

The Organisation of Industry

ingly more successful than those which have not. Mondragon co-operatives, on the other hand, seem to have been a conspicuous success. Why is this?

The features of the Mondragon type of co-operative are first that it is a regional, or perhaps I should say national, development (if you count the Basques as a nation). The inspiration is Basque. The movement was closely bound up with Basque aspirations and the retention of Basque culture and language. It harnessed Basque patriotism to industry. What an excellent thing it would be if Scottish and Welsh nationalism or the patriotism of the regions of England could be harnessed to such purposes. I have remarked upon the effects of over-centralisation and I shall have something to say about Iain Noble's experiment in Skye to both of which the Mondragon co-operatives are very relevant.

Mondragon indeed was not only intensely Basque, it was anti-Madrid. It is rather creditable to Franco's regime that in spite of this, Mondragon was able to claim the initial concessions given to co-operatives in Spain. And incidentally Fascist Spain was in fiscal policy much more favourable to workers' co-operatives than were Labour or Tory governments in Britain. I believe this antipathy between the co-operatives and the central government was a positive boon. The Basque workers had not been taught to rely on government. They had not been brought up to believe that the state or any public authority would look after them. Their reaction to difficulties was not that 'They' must 'do something' about them and they did not unconsciously or consciously feel that the government would always bail them out, however they behaved, which seems to be the attitude of too many British firms.

The salient features which struck me after a visit to Mondragon with Robert and others are as follows.

The great success of the co-operatives, which have now been operating for twenty years, has been achieved during a time when the Spanish economy was growing; nevertheless, it is remarkable. There are over sixty co-operatives engaged in all sorts of pursuits from agriculture to foundries but with emphasis on production rather than services. Some fifteen thousand people are involved generating sales in excess of £200 million a year and a considerable export trade. But the success is not only in the goods made and the wealth generated. I have constantly reiterated that an effort to improve the opportunities which a community gives to its members must aim high. The co-operatives aim very high, for example in the quality of their research. Indeed, I was somewhat dismayed by the conspicuous grandeur of the headquarters with fountains outside, marble halls within, a cinema and all the trappings of big business public relations. But the psychology behind this may well be right. Workers have no need to be humble; they can outstrip the biggest capitalist or state companies.

The founder of the Mondragon co-operative was Arismende, a priest. He was horrified by the poverty and depression of the Basques. He started first to improve their education, particularly their technical education. The school came first. He was himself a Basque nationalist in revolt against the neglect, indeed the oppression, of Madrid. He set out to give the Basques an opportunity to foster their own language and civilisation and show what they could do. Madrid provided some help — but not too much — and this was an advantage: the local people looked to themselves, they had to make their own way. This was, and is, the keystone of the whole enterprise. It is a demonstration of what communities, imbued with a spirit of their own, can achieve. Had the Mondragon experiment been able to rely on large external help, it would neither have taken the productive and efficient course which it has followed, nor would it have given the satisfaction which I believe it does.

How, with only the initial grant all co-operatives get from the public authorities in Spain, did Arismende's experiment grow to the organisation it has become? It has mobilized not only the patriotism of the Basque communities but their money. If the psychological keystone has been self-reliance, the economic keystone has been the bank, the Caja Laboral Popular. Into the branches of this bank the Basques deposit their savings. These savings go into co-operatives, that is, into productive industry in their own provinces. Compare this with the

The Organisation of Industry

position in Britain where the Savings Banks, the Building Societies and indeed to some extent the Joint Stock Banks, carry savings away from the home communities and place them in government loans or in housing or largescale industry, usually in the big cities. Caja Laboral Popular is itself a co-operative; it is one of the chain of co-operatives and it exists with and for them. It is not an alien institution disinterested in its investments except as a source of profit. It has an expert management department. Proposals for new co-operatives, which are presently being founded at the rate of four a year, are stringently vetted by this department. It is available to monitor and help existing co-operatives. To some bankers it may be alarming that it should invest in long-term projects. But it claims so far to have suffered hardly any serious bad debts: only one co-operative has failed. Everyone who wishes to join a co-operative has to put down about £1,000. Surprising as it may seem to the British, this does not appear to be a serious obstacle to would-be co-operative workers. There is a waiting list. If anyone cannot find £1,000 the Bank will lend it, against repayment of course.

In the group are a secondary school and a technical college. The secondary school has about half its pupils boarding. It draws them from all over the Spanish Basque provinces. Like everything else it is run co-operatively by the teachers. Although it deliberately gives preference to children from poor families every family pays something. There are also primary schools associated with Mondragon and co-operatively run, though not part of the group. In one at least of these the families of the children pay sixty per cent of the running costs, the balance being raised by the school — no public funds. If it seems incredible to us that working class families should pay for education, it seems incredible to some Basques that they should pay for cars, television sets, drink, but not education. As a result of charging, the schools are far more economically run, the teaching is of a high standard and truancy at a minimum. When the pupils at the secondary school have passed their first technical examinations they can join a co-operative of their own — Aleco-op — which itself manufactures at a profit. From their wages and shares in this co-operative they pay for their own further education. Also at Mondragon there is a research and development centre which those who have experience of such places in other parts of Europe, and in America, tell me is of a high order.

Finally, since the co-operators were excluded from the social services of the Spanish state, they have their own sickness, unemployment benefit, pension scheme, etc. At present co-operative retiring after twenty years' service can expect a pension and a lump sum payment of around £15,000. The antagonism of the state and the need to arrange their own social services appear to have been a blessing. They now offer better services than the state.

The co-operatives claim to have dissolved the tension between capital and labour. All the workers are capitalists. Not everyone is so sure that they have completely broken down the distrust of worker for management. But in twenty years they have only had one strike (though there have been demonstrations in sympathy with other workers). The top salaries are limited to four and a half times the lowest wage. On a brief visit one certainly gets the impression of much more solidarity between the shop floor and the top offices than is common in British business. Canteens are shared. The managers (mostly in their early thirties) seem close to the workers. Some workers belong to trades unions, but with the elimination of the boss, whether private or state, the loyalty of all is to the co-operative, the institution, and not to something outside. It is a 'vertical' not a 'horizontal' loyalty. The whole operation, of course, is a lesson in how to reduce class distinctions and bureaucratic top-hamper. It is socialism without the state.

The co-operatives function as one element in a competitive system. Wages, for instance, are fixed by reference to comparable wages in the private sector. They are free, therefore, from the danger of state socialism: that it becomes a system of compulsion. They do not want to expand too far or at the expense of other enterprises. They have only taken over one or two firms and then only to prevent them going out of business. Nor do they want to build up too big units. The Fragor factory, making washing machines and cookers, which already employs some eleven hundred workers, is big enough. In education they offer one of several alternatives, there are other 'private' schools (that is, those run by the Church) as well as the state system. They do not own housing. So they are free from the temptation to run their members' lives. The schools are not merely technical; there is a strong emphasis on Basque traditions and the Basque language. Though there are no political tests, there is some indoctrination into the advantages of co-operation on the Mondragon model. Nevertheless, they seem at least to have come near answering the usual criticism of syndicalism — that it exploits the consumer. They appear to have employed freedom and individual choice without subjecting workers to the harsher disciplines of private enterprise. Workers redundant in one operation are offered, wherever possible, jobs in another co-operative. Experiments have been made in breaking down the assembly line into small groups as at Volvo.

It may be too that Mondragon is contributing to a possible solution of the difficulties thrown up by technical advance. The technology at the disposal of the co-operatives is sophisticated. But new co-operatives are set up to cater for the needs not at present met. Thus they respond to real demand. They are not the result of a bureaucratic urge to behave according to Parkinson's Law so that only existing organisations can expand. If this can be maintained it would seem a way to meet an underlying problem of industrial capitalism (whether state or private). That is the problem of finding new jobs which are a contribution to welfare for those workers threatened with unemployment from technical change. Mondragon also shows how the profits of improved efficiency can benefit a whole community.

Mondragon cannot claim to solve all problems — what system dealing with human beings could possibly do that? It may well be unsuitable for certain operations. It must be emphasised that it does not, and should not, claim to supersede all other varieties of industrial (or agricultural) organisation. But it surely has very valuable lessons to teach. The existence of a whole range of co-operatives and the crucial pivot of the bank seem to have overcome some of the snags on which other attempts at co-operatives have foundered. The absence both of workers who are not owners and of shareholders who are not workers seems to be an advantage. I must confess, however, that I do not see why a co-operative should not employ labour outside its ranks on contract. Those with money to save can deposit it in the Casa Laboral Popular which supports the co-operatives. Such depositors do not share in the profits but are paid a fixed rate of interest. But this system could be amended. The important point is that savings stay in their homeland and are put to productive use.

For the Mondragon system to be translated to Britain we should have radically to change our attitudes. One only has to think of the vested interests it threatens. Employers' federations, trades unions and whole departments of the bureaucratic state would lose much of their significance. Once the divisions between capital and labour, teacher and pupil, bureaucrat and client, governor and governed are blurred the very framework of modern society is altered. Many of the non-productive organisations which cause such a drain on our resources, which divert talent up dead-ends and prolong the struggle which perpetuated inefficiency, dissatisfaction and inflation no longer serve a purpose. And as one such organisation withers so its mirror image, or partner across the net, also becomes unnecessary. If the state does not wither away (which it certainly will not do) Mondragon holds out a much more realistic solution for a reduction in its power than does orthodox socialism. Nor is Mondragon unique. The same features can be traced, for instance, in some of the co-operatives in the West of Ireland.

So we come round again to the possibility of general community development as a development of the welfare society and we meet pointers to the way in which a wider background can be established for a satisfactory way of life.

How boring many modern industrial processes may be is not easy to calculate. Most work is unpleasant in one way or another, at least after a time. Hobbies such as gardening or carpentry, which if done for wages would be considered work, are enjoyable only so long as undertaken voluntarily

The Organisation of Industry

and at times chosen by the practitioner. But there seems to me little doubt that the division of labour and the conveyor belt processes have taken the interest out of much work where the worker sometimes does not know what the final product is, can feel little interest in it and certainly is not consulted about it. The endless repetition of a single process for eight hours a day does not give a human being satisfaction, no matter whether he himself takes part in it or watches a machine do it. I found myself driven to distraction after watching a printing machine for half an hour. I longed for any interruption, tea, breakdown or strike. I am, therefore, very sympathetic to the experiments made in their motor industries in Sweden and elsewhere in the introduction of group working.

It may well be that mass production of the conventional sort is not the most efficient form of production. The motor industry seems to show that this is so. A chronically disgruntled labour force and constant strikes lower efficiency. And, let me remark once again, that the state of men's minds is as much a fact to be taken into account as is the state of the machinery. The woollen industry seems to have a much better record which may be due to its organisation.

But suppose that, in some occupations at least, huge units using assembly lines prove to be able to make better products at less cost, even allowing for labour unrest. Must we then accept them so long as we have a market economy? Our answer must lie in putting a price upon good conditions of work. Workers may have to accept less for less soul-destroying work. As far as I am concerned, to take an extreme case, I would need at least treble the pay I now get as a member of parliament before I would work eight hours on an endless belt. I am sure we must expect to get less for interesting jobs than for exceedingly dull jobs. I recognise that this will upset the entire wage structure but I believe it must come. Nor am I too much impressed by the claims of skilled workers or responsible managers for very big differentials. Mondragon so far has shown that it is possible to get good management at a salary which is never more than four and a half times the wage of the lowest paid worker.

However, if a change in our attitudes to differentials is not the whole answer should we not consider bringing in the community? Some well-intentioned employers have always been prepared to shoulder responsibility for providing services usually set up by public authorities — Rowntree housing for instance. Of late some employers seem to have gone to the other extreme and looked to the state to relieve them of burdens which might well be considered a cost they should bear. Not only do they expect direct subsidies but when they have finished, even temporarily, with workers they return them to the unemployed pool. And in spite of severance pay and the employer's contribution the tax payer must foot a large proportion of the bill for maintaining them. This to my mind should give the tax payer some right to a say in how business is organised. A community may gain, may obtain a common good, if its members are reasonably happy at their work.

Let me repeat: if you want a society in which every community gives as much satisfaction to its members as its circumstances will allow, a society in which there is the maximum opportunity in every community for its members to use their talents and lead an interesting life, a community in which all activities can reach a high standard — you cannot ignore the organisation of work. Most people spend up to half their waking day at work and the same outlook will cover their work and other activities including social and community development.

A community should be able to say to a potential employer — whether individual, co-operative, or public — if you want to set up a factory or farm or service among us and, above all, if you want help whether by direct subsidy or from the community bank, you must accept some conditions about the organisation of your business. So long as the community does not attempt to run the business this should be as acceptable to employers in general as are the conditions imposed on farmers who want grants. I am not talking about nationwide regulations but conditions which would make the employment a better contribution to the particular circumstances of a particular community. If such

The Organisation of Industry

a partnership is established, then the community will require funds to play its part.

There is a growing and welcome tendency for industry to devolve management as far as possible — another sign that the days of bigger meaning better are ended. Mergers and take-overs still continue and a smaller proportion of Britain's output is in the hands of small companies than in any other Western European country. The grip of central ownership remains and there are certain advantages in big scale operations, for example in buying and in diversity of operation with some financial control. But many conglomerates have proved inefficient. There is much to be said for a firm concentrating on business it knows. And some of the amalgamations between industrial processes no longer have much justification. Industry, like life, is a changing affair and must remain so if it is to be efficient in the use of resources, responsive to consumer demand and sensitive to its workers who must be treated as human beings, not machines. It is no wonder and no loss then that the future changes in industry should be difficult to predict. As I say, we should welcome many types of organisation, old and new. What we should try to ensure is that changes are brought about for the right reasons. If they are the response to more efficient technology, new needs, new enterprises, then they should be willingly accepted; but not if they are the result of restrictive practices, prestige seeking, empire building, monopoly or seizure of quick fortunes.

In some industries many processes are combined. In the production of newspapers, for instance, there is the editorial department, news gathering, printing and distribution. News gathering is to some extent already done by separate agencies. Distribution of, say, evening papers which circulate largely in one city is done by the paper's own vans. National distribution of a morning paper concerning the whole country involves rail and air. Newspapers do not own fleets of long distance vans. Printing might well be hived off. The most efficient use of presses involves printing two or three newspapers. The printers and their work are quite different from the editorial staff and their work. To some extent newspaper management is already engaged in bargaining with the printing unions. It might encourage efficiency and provide a greater incentive to sensible bargaining if the editorial management openly contracted with printers who owned the presses. At present the printing industry is one of the worst in the country for restrictive practices.

The same charge might be made in the docks. The restrictive practices of dockers are gravely damaging British trade and the well-being of the dockers themselves. Parts of London docks are now a desert. It takes two men to unload a piece of machinery at the works in central Scotland but at Grangemouth docks the unions insist upon twenty to do a similar job. Dockers even at the smaller ports enforce the most absurd practices, receive huge payments and exercise a nepotism far worse than that of the old school tie brigade. They should not be allowed to enforce a closed shop at the docks. It might well be that those who want their services should contract with one group of dockers or another. There are signs that industry is moving in this direction. The expense of acquiring sophisticated modern equipment is such that it should not be left standing idle, there has therefore been an increase in the hiring of machinery. Small firms offering specialised services have sprung up here and there. But at the same time some firms are doing jobs which previously they contracted out because contractors are sometimes so late or unsatisfactory. On the whole it would seem that industry would benefit from contracting out more operations, many to workers' co-operatives, and the workmen would also benefit by being able to work in smaller units with a more immediate interest in their work. Mr. Norman Macrae described such proposals in the *Economist* of January, 1977. 'The lump' has raised the ire of the trades union bureaucrats because it is a threat to their empire. It has its drawbacks but in some ways it is a welcome advance.

If it was essential to absorb us all into very big units then it would indeed be difficult to allow us each to take that personal responsibility which is the prerequisite of any morality and of the sort of life which I believe should be offered to everyone. Big units, whether of government, services or industry, do not necessarily preclude a diffusion

The Organisation of Industry

of moral responsibility. It is quite possible to run, say, a division in the army and allow a field of decision-making to every NCO and indeed private soldier while maintaining general rules. It is not only possible: it is indeed essential. However, in practice big units tend to become bureaucratically run. They tend to treat human beings as hands, not whole persons, their directors are often tempted to accumulate more and more power at the centre. The casting of the block vote at the TUC Congress, for instance, is a distortion of what is intended as a democratic process. We have not been very successful in handling those organisations in which there is justification for large units — nor have we shown great skill in extending or contracting units. We could, I am sure, have learnt more in this regard (and in other regards also, for instance, education) from the army. At the Coal Board too Lord Robens did a good job in humanely running down the number of coal mines. But there seem to me very few human activities which really demand large-scale organisation.

From the standpoint of economic efficiency, as a means of increasing the opportunities of the less well-off, and certainly as a cure for inflation and unemployment, corporatism as it has been increasingly practised in the last forty years is a failure. Indeed, it could not be otherwise for it is a prime cause of our economic troubles.

People's attitude to work may also be influenced by who they work for — even the most boring work is made more tolerable if I work for myself. Apart then from the structure of industrial units there is the question of their ownership. Many people work most willingly for employers — and long may this continue — but I am convinced by the example of Mondragon, and to a lesser extent Yugoslavia, that workers' co-operatives have a major part to play. They offer many of the advantages of socialism without the state. They are not open to the usual criticism of syndicalism — that it can hold the consumer to ransom — for they operate in a free market which offers various alternatives. They seem to have gone some way to dissolving the antagonism between capital and labour while retaining a free society. I believe it is an advantage that they have no outside shareholders. But I favour a state of affairs in which all sorts of organisations flourish. The presence of shareholders in the company who are not workers does not nullify the advantages of partnership.

Though having some say in the end product or the organisation of the working day may not either alter the actual process of manufacture nor therefore its tedium, it must make life more interesting. This must be so even leaving aside the obvious satisfaction to be got from sharing in the profits of a successful firm. The association, therefore, of the workers with the control of the firm and the decisions of management is to my mind essential to improving the condition of industrial life.

If the workers in a firm look to the success of that firm for the major contribution to their well-being and not to the bargaining strength of their trades union, they will have a direct interest in increasing productivity, checking over-manning and restraining the demands which make inflation inevitable. Wage bargaining can then be genuinely free. If profits are earned and distributed they will not add to costs for profits are not a cost. Thus one of the chief difficulties in stopping the demands which lead to inflation — the failure to reward restraint and efficiency — will be diminished if not abolished. Of late we have heard less of productivity in relation to wage rates. The difficulty has been that the work of many essential workers cannot under present methods be directly related to increasing productivity. This is so for various reasons but it largely arises because wage rates, if not always earnings, are fixed by various trades unions across the industry. If everyone working in an individual firm has a substantial share in the profits of that firm and is a part owner of the firm the position is transformed.

It is sometimes objected that many workers do not want to be owners and certainly do not want to be responsible for management. This is so. It is a valid argument against imposing any universal and rigid framework on industry. But there is no reason why because some workers do not want to participate those who do should be frustrated. In Yugoslavia there are at least enough workers willing, indeed eager, to take responsibility. In this country among those who do not are some who do not want a free economy, and therefore a free society, to continue. Just as it would lead to better maintenance of our houses if more people owned their own homes, so it would make more sense to give the mines to the miners rather than continue the present bureaucratic system with its manifest failings. Competition must of course be retained and must operate not only between existing businesses but also by allowing new firms to enter the market. For this purpose there must be an improved capital market. But the ease with which large amounts of capital are raised on the open market, for example by British Petroleum, shows that there is no lack of risk capital, if only it can see a profit.

In bringing about these changes I see the community as an essential element. It certainly is in Mondragon. Not only should its savings be available for local investment (either in the form of loans at fixed interest or equity) but again it should itself be able to borrow funds or obtain grants from the central government for such investment where local resources are inadequate. But, as I say, it should not attempt itself to run competitive business and such borrowing should be phased out as the community becomes richer. In fact, I am advocating a return to the attitudes, if not the methods, of Joseph Chamberlain. A start would be made by handing over such services as gas and electricity to local co-operatives with community involvement. The need for a nationwide grid does not preclude this. It merely requires some collaboration between authorities.

But how are we to handle the possibility of a permanent decrease in the number of jobs available — however we change the structure or ownership of industry? Co-operation in itself will help over this. The £15,000 received (in addition to a pension) by the Mondragon worker as a lump sum on retirement obviously makes retirement more acceptable. Earlier retirement may be one step to be taken.

But to change the structure and ownership of industry will take time. Nor, I must say again, do I look for a change in all industry. What I am looking for is a much wider spread of ownership by individuals and by individuals acting in groups. Availability of credit, so that individuals can start their own firm, or take a share in local firms, is one essential. And useful lessons can be learnt, not only from Spain, but from Germany where small businesses can obtain credit cheaply and locally. Some general guarantee of local loans (as is available in Germany) would be necessary. Training is important. The Business Schools seem to have been used chiefly by big business to recruit management, rather than by would-be entrepreneurs. Changes in company law and in taxation could also encourage a wider spread of ownership. The cleverest pupils today are too often persuaded to try for academic or bureaucratic jobs; indeed education as a whole could pay more attention to training children's minds and hands to creative work on their own.

We must also accept the likelihood that the type of work to be done will change. Many communities are aware of jobs needing to be done in their area — despite the existence of a large national pool of unemployed. They may also contain entrepreneurs willing to undertake them. One of the curious factors of the last two or three years has been the difficulty of getting repairs and improvements done to houses, despite the slump in the building trade.

Training could be made available locally for this increase in 'Do-it-Yourself' operations. (The technical colleges are too elaborate and expensive). Nor should the acquiring of a paper qualification be the end of such training.

On the international level there is the need to encourage and finance trade. There is the huge task of improving the economies of Africa, Asia and South America. A discussion of this topic lies outside the scope of this book but community development must be constantly aware of its place in a wider, indeed world-wide, community and of the need to look outward.

6 History of the Social Services

Having sketched in the features of a country which I would think agreeable, and having dealt briefly with the political and economic background which I would advocate, and also with the dangers, I turn to the welfare or community services which we should now devise. First, let us look at the history of the present welfare services.

Governments from time immemorial have intervened to deal with the poor citizens of their country. But usually neither welfare nor social service would appropriately describe the methods of such governments. The poor were often treated in the same way as vagabonds. Such truly welfare services as existed in earlier ages were largely the responsibility of the church. The main tasks of government throughout history have been the defence of the country and the keeping of order. The poor were of interest primarily as a source of disorder. It was not believed that much could be done about poverty and if it could it was not a primary function of the state.

In 1834 when rising to call the attention of the Commons to the existing laws for the relief of the poor in England, Lord Althorp said that the operation of the Poor Laws had been injurious to every class connected with the land, 'the landed proprietors, the farmers and the poor themselves.' This general mischief he traced to a statute of George III which suggested that relief to paupers ought to be given in such a manner as to place them in a situation of comfort. This he held was the business of private charity. The magistrates had ordered relief to the poor to be given in their own dwellings. 'All the feelings of independence on the part of labourers had been almost entirely extinguished in many parts of the country.' 'Some parishes had been abandoned owing to pressure on the rates.' He suggested that there should be a board of control commissioners who would oversee the whole system and prevent extravagance by orders (approved by a minute). The Commissioners would also form parishes and make general rules. The Poor Law would be administered locally by Boards of Guardians.

In committee (6 June 1834) Mr Cobbett challenged the reason behind the Poor Law Bill and the need for it. He denied that the existing position was 'frightful' as Lord Althorp had suggested, disputed the damage to agriculture and suggested that if the evils of pauperism could not be shown to have increased they should not legislate at all. 'The House in fact treated the subject as if the poor had been guilty of some crime . . . it was afraid to investigate the causes of the present condition of the poor.' And a good Cobbett passage: 'In the parish of Breed, in Sussex, fifty years ago, there was but one cottage that did not belong to the labourers that occupied them; now there were but two cottages the property of the labourers, 182 of whom were upon the rates. In another place the labourers formerly brewed their own beer, now they neither brewed beer nor drank it.'

The debates of 1834 show up clearly the general attitudes to the very poor and their relief. Of course a large proportion of the nation was poor; these debates were not concerned with them, nor was the Poor Law. It was only concerned with the destitute. The acceptance of inevitability, the anxiety that begging should not be encouraged, concern about local finances and the effect on the labour market, all these considerations were much in people's minds. Only a few wanted to examine the causes of poverty.

The nineteenth-century system largely dated from an Act of 1834. It was based on the harsh and indeed illogical belief that poverty was both inevitable and blameworthy. As well, therefore, as providing some minimal relief to poverty, the Poor Laws were designed to frighten off the poor from public funds. They were naturally loathed. The Act of 1871 continued this tradition.

Stricter standards for sanitation were recommended by a Commission which reported in 1871. In 1875 Disraeli's government introduced measures to strengthen the powers of local authorities over sanitation and also to condemn, demolish and rebuild slums. Thus the principle of public interference in the private lives of citizens was now well established. Disraeli's government also passed the Artisans' Dwellings Act and the Sale of Food and Drugs Act of 1875 which until 1937, according to Ensor, remained the backbone of our sanitary laws.

But these laws were aimed at specific evils. They were designed to help the poorer members of the community who suffered from bad pay, bad conditions of employment, bad housing, bad sanitation and health.

So while the Poor Laws continued important steps were taken to improve what may be generally called welfare; these had a very considerable effect on the lives of the poorer people. I refer to such things as the factory and sanitation Acts and the notion that planning of various sorts was necessary. Legislation on the factories goes back well into the nineteenth century influenced by various reports and owing a particular debt to Lord Shaftesbury and the representations of various voluntary bodies. (It is wholly untrue to suggest that nineteenth-century politicians were not interested in the conditions of the poor. Laissez-faire economics did not stop the state from interfering in housing, industry, health or commerce. In fact, laissez-faire has never been the policy of Britain — nor in its extreme form the doctrine of liberal economists such as Adam Smith.)

Mr Cross, in asking leave to introduce the Artisan Dwelling Bill of 1874 mentioned memorials sent by the Charity Organisation Society and the Royal College of Physicians. He also drew attention to the practical work done by, for instance, the Peabody Trustees. But the total was small — accommodation for some thirty thousand.

Mr Cross went on to say:

I take it as a starting point that it is not the duty of the government to provide any class of citizens with any of the necessaries of life. . . .It would not be possible to teach a worse lesson than this — that if you do not take care of yourselves the State will take care of you, nor is it wise to encourage large bodies to provide the working classes with habitations at greatly lower rents than the market value paid elsewhere. . . .But no one will doubt the propriety of the state to interfere in matters relating to the sanitary laws.

He went on to point out the waste caused by bad housing and physical conditions — in asylums and gaols etc. 'In one district of London having a population of 2,000 to 2,100 there have been more people sick in five years than the whole population and in one district of Manchester the death rate was sixty-seven per 1,000'.

Mr Cross's speech sets out the approach of later nineteenth-century governments to improvement in the living conditions of the poor. It does not accord with modern fashions. However, many modern fashions are equally absurd as I shall suggest in due course. In fact nineteenth-century governments of both parties did rather more in fits and starts to improve these conditions than they have been given credit for.

After Disraeli's government in the '70s, Irish Home Rule, South Africa and other such issues dominated politics. Mr Joseph Chamberlain, the apostle of civic activity, became absorbed in the Irish issue. Apart from the Workmen's Compensation Act of 1887 he achieved little.

However, while the causes of poverty in general were considered outside the scope of governments, unemployment was more and more recognised as unwanted misfortune. It was no longer assumed to be due to idleness and could no longer be shrugged off as 'inevitable'. It was a growing source of unrest and the same was true of poverty and low wages in general.

As for tackling the causes of poverty, there was still little academic or political activity. It was assumed, as I have said, that the poor were either to blame or were the victims of fate. Any attempt, for instance, to raise wages or undertake public works were by the majority of economists and statesmen considered to be self-defeating. One economist of note, Malthus, and as far as I know only he, looked at demand as a factor in stimulating unemployment. Keynes appropriately congratulated him for to some extent he forestalled the Keynesian analysis. It was Malthus who said, 'When profits are low and uncertain and when capitalists are quite at a loss where they can certainly employ their capitals is it not contrary to the general principles of political economy . . . to recommend saving?' Or again, 'Adam Smith has stated that capitals are increased by parsimony, that every frugal man is a public benefactor and that the increase in wealth depends upon the balance of production above consumption. That these propositions are true to a great extent is perfectly unquestionable. . . . But it is quite obvious that they are not true to an indefinite extent and that the principles of saving, pushed to excess will destroy the motive to production.' Public works were suggested by Joseph Chamberlain but even in his time there was no enthusiasm for them.

In 1905 a Conservative minister had set up a Royal Commission under Lord George Hamilton which presented two famous reports, the Majority and Minority Reports on the Poor Laws.

There is much of importance in both these reports. The particular points which, in the context of this book, should be stressed are the disagreement between the reports as to whether the different classes of poor (children, the old, the insane, etc.) should come under one or different authorities and the concern of the Commission over the causes of poverty. For almost the first time, too, an official body suggested that local authorities should help the poor and that in turn the central government should help the local authorities. The slow change from disapproval to acceptance of obligation was accelerated.

These controversies aroused little political interest. (It is strange how little political interest the social services have aroused. They do not figure much in the history books and, considering their importance, they have played a comparatively minor part in political controversy or the reputation of politicians.) The Liberal government did little to resolve them. This is often blamed on John Burns, head of the local government board; there is some justice in this, but he was not alone in his lack of interest in any philosophy of welfare.

The Report of the Majority of the Royal Commission on the Poor Laws remarked on the absence of any general interest in the Poor Law work or election to the Boards of Guardians. They attributed this 'to the fact that Poor Law work stands in no organic relation to the rest of local government'. They concluded, 'We do not recommend any alteration of the law which would extend the qualification for relief to individuals not now entitled to it'. They did, however, recommend more central control which indeed has been the theme of commissions and governments since the 1830s. 'The central authority should assume a more direct position of guidance and initiative in regard to local authorities.' They also recommended unemployment insurances, labour exchanges, voluntary aid committees which would focus contributions from voluntary funds and public assistance to necessitous workmen. Supplements paid out of public funds to augment wages had a long history in agriculture. They were constantly criticised but they continued.

The Minority Report came out strongly against workhouses in which all sorts of people suffering from different troubles — lunatics, tramps, the old and sick, children and the feckless — were lumped together. This again was an old complaint, but it was still going on in the late 1920s. They noted the large sums expended in outdoor relief to the 'non-able-bodied' which was then costing four million pounds a year and they returned to that theme which had entered constantly into discussions about poor relief — the unemployed. They suggested, 'that the duty of so organising the national labour market as to prevent or minimise unemployment should be placed upon a Minister responsible to Parliament who should be called the Minister of Labour'. They also recommended unemployment insurance and training. 'Decasualisation and suppression of under-employment must be accompanied by action to ensure the immediate absorption of such labour or else to provide the full and honourable maintenance at public expense of the surplus of labourers.'

The Liberal government of 1905 decided to introduce Old

Age Pensions. Mr Asquith, who was originally in charge of the pension proposals, speaking in the debate on the address in 1907 said, 'The figure of a man or woman who through no fault or default is compelled to beg bread or lodging is an eyesore in our social system.' He assured the House that there was no object which his colleagues and himself more ardently desired than old age pensions.

In one way old age pensions continued the tradition of the old Poor Laws in that they were aimed in a pragmatic way at the relief of poverty, they were not concerned with the cause of it. The government were acutely worried by the expense of paying for them. But in other ways they broke important new ground. They were much wider in their scope. Though aimed at the relief of those 'compelled to beg bread or lodging' everyone in need could claim them. There was no contribution. They were the responsibility of the central government not the local authorities. There was no suggestion that those who were poor were to blame for their condition; the idea of guilt was scotched but not killed.

The next social services to be introduced were the Employment Exchanges in 1909. These too were brought in by Mr Asquith's government, the minister responsible being Mr Winston Churchill at the Board of Trade. Again they were introduced for pragmatic reasons. Unemployment had been troubling the consciences of MPs and others for some time.

The reports of the Poor Law commissioners had recommended their introduction. A few exchanges run by local authorities or private individuals already existed but nothing like a national network. But, above all, in Mr Churchill's words, 'The old method, the demoralising method of personal application, hawking labour about . . . and treating a job as if it were a favour was thought by the government to be inhuman.' And as Mr Gooch pointed out in the second reading debate, employers, though they could usually get as much unskilled labour as they wanted, would gain in their search for skilled labour — 'a great convenience to the employer to be able to lay his hands on the particular kind of specialised labour he requires.' It was also remarked that the labour exchange would provide valuable statistics.

But little if any notice was taken of a feature which labour exchanges introduced. They were a social service which was a service. The state undertook, not to pay money to the individual, but to assist him. The Poor Laws had provided workhouses etc. but these were as much a deterrent as a service.

The National Insurance Act of 1911 was also a new departure. Again there was little attention to theory in the speeches introducing it. Mr Sydney Buxton, moving the second reading of the Bill, said, 'The principle on which these two schemes are based is that the burden of insurance against sickness and unemployment should be shared by the workmen, employers and the state'. He referred to two schemes because the Bill dealt with unemployment and sickness separately. The Bill was entitled, 'To provide insurance against loss of health and for the prevention and cure of sickness and for insurance against unemployment and for the purposes incidental thereto'. Rather odd, as apart from giving some money for sanatoria etc. it did little or nothing to prevent or cure sickness. It was an insurance bill in both parts.

Mr Lloyd George, asking leave to introduce the Bill, described it as aimed at 'an evil to be remedied'. He told the Commons that thirty per cent of pauperism was due to sickness and 'a considerable percentage would probably have to be added for unemployment.' As far as unemployment was concerned the Bill was designed only to cover the 'precarious' trades and would affect a sixth of the working population.

As for insurance against sickness Mr Lloyd George gave some interesting figures about the existing situation. 42,000,000 industrial policies against death were already issued by the friendly societies, insurance companies etc., 6,000,000 policies against sickness and only 1,400,000 against unemployment. About 250,000 policies lapsed every year. Few workers could afford to insure against all three and of the three possible disasters death had priority. The sickness part of the scheme was in two parts. One part was compulsory and applied to weekly wage earners and those in employment under the income tax limits. There was then a voluntary part of the scheme which could be joined by the self-employed etc. Mr Lloyd George described the interest which each of the three parties had in the scheme to which they jointly contributed. The employer had an interest in the efficiency of his workmen and the state in a happy, contented and prosperous people.

The decision not to work insurance through the insurance companies and societies was based largely on the inability of the insurers to pay the premiums. But these organisations were still to be encouraged and indeed to some extent involved in the purposes of the scheme. There appears to have been little argument about applying what passed as insurance methods to sickness and unemployment. It was apparently largely accepted that it was a true insurance. For practical reasons of ability to pay, the principle applied in the case of pensions — no premiums — was abandoned. Thus 'insurance' came to be accepted in the social services (see Ensor, *England 1870-1914*, p.445).

Asquith, Lloyd George and Churchill all quoted the experience already gained in Germany where social services had been operating for some years. The welfare services have many parents but among the most important is a streak of paternalism. However, that did not restrain the Tories from making violent attacks on the National Insurance Act with their famous denouncement of the licking of stamps. As Mr Ensor has noted, 'The Conservatives slid a stage further down the perilous slope of "direct action".' In other ways besides the social services do we find the origins of modern methods in this period.

Rowntree had calculated that the incomes of nearly twenty-eight per cent of the population or forty-three per cent of the working class were below that sufficient to satisfy bare physical needs. Winston Churchill as President of the Board of Trade introduced the Trades Boards Bill in 1909. William Beveridge, who was already active in this field, wrote a book entitled *Unemployment* and, as I have said, the Royal Commission on the Poor Laws drew attention not only to the need for help to the unemployed but for measures to increase employment.

So Britain entered the 1914-18 war and emerged from it

with the activities of the central government greatly extended. After the war, unemployment insurance was extended to cover most trades, instead of being confined to four. At the same time under Lloyd George's government housing became a national responsibility. Indeed it was at this period that the building of houses to be let at a loss started. Housing has never been considered a social service but in so far as the state provided housing at the tax payers' expense, ostensibly at least for the poorer sections of the nation, it bore many of the characteristics of a social service. At the same time the Poor Laws still continued under local Boards of Guardians while the central government extended its operations. The war itself had led to a huge increase of government interference and to a new frame of mind which accepted such increase as natural. The surprising thing, however, is that given the circumstances there was not a bigger increase in interference by the central government, nor among politicians was any theory of social service developed.

When the Conservatives took office, however, in 1924 they brought with them Neville Chamberlain, a more than worthy son of his father and among the politicians of the twenties the one most interested in social administration. Neville Chamberlain had clear ideas about making the administration of the social services efficient. He disciplined those Boards of Guardians which had been paying more in relief than was approved by the government and to that extent he brought the social services further under the control of the central government. At last the pre-war controversy was resolved and the Minority Report of the Royal Commission on the Poor Laws won the day. In 1928 the Boards of Guardians were abolished. The local authorities took over a great range of services.

In moving the second reading of the Local Government Bill 1928 Chamberlain described the condition of the machinery which he found:

> Sitting here at the centre of things I can see the cracks and flaws in the machinery; I can hear its creaks and groans. I can note how in one place the load has been growing and growing until it has become far greater than

the shaft that was originally designed can hoist. In another place I can see remnants of old gears designed long ago which now only serve to weaken and hamper the workings of the more modern plant.

He listed the defects under five main heads: the existence of the Guardians who overlapped with the local authorities, the heavy charges on the country districts for roads, the lack of elasticity in adjusting boundaries of local authorities, the inequitable system of rates and the chaos between national and local expenditure. He drew attention to the different weight of the burden borne by various parts of the country. In Bradford the Poor Law was responsible for fivepence in the pound, in Gateshead for ten shillings and fivepence.

He also drew attention to the drawbacks entailed by treating many types of infirmity in one institution, 'The whole trend of practice in modern medicine and surgery is towards the treatment of many cases in institutions where there can be accumulated the special equipment and specialized skill.' Yet one institution in a rural area contained seven acutely sick persons, fifty-five infirm and seventy-six epileptics, eight certified lunatics, nine uncertified mental deficients, one able-bodied man and three healthy infants.

How had the insurance principle been faring in the meantime? Chamberlain like his predecessors, and indeed most of his successors, never questioned it for sickness or unemployment. The analogy with commercial insurance was too strong, though the two seem to me quite different. Commercial insurance is, so to speak, like a bet: the company bets that I will not get ill, I bet that I will. Or like a contract: for the sake of laying their hands on some of my money now the company contracts to pay out at a later date. But the state is not a company, it is engaged in neither betting nor contracting for profit. What it says is that the elderly deserve support and it will arrange for them to have some of current production. That will affect the government's management of the economy. One way or another somebody has to go without to make room for the pensioners' demand but whether he has or has not paid contributions, whether there is or is not a fund is irrelevant.

The insurance payments may provide the state with resources for the payment of current claims; they cannot do so for the claims of those who pay. Obviously each insurer does not set aside some food, fuel, etc. for his or her old age. All the insurer can claim is that having contributed out of current production in his time to the welfare of the old, the next generation ought to contribute to his, but the circumstances may be entirely different.

There is an illuminating paragraph on insurance in the Beveridge Report of 1942. The report claims to have given effect to two views, 'The first view is that benefit in return for contributions rather than free allowances from the state is what the people of Britain desire'. Note the phrase 'free allowances from the state'. The state, of course, has no money to spend on allowances. What is meant is allowances provided by taxation or paid for at the expense of other people or by printing or borrowing money. The second view is that, 'Whatever money is required for the provision of insurance benefits, so long as they are needed, should come from a fund to which the recipients have contributed'. Benefits without contributions are wrong in principle according to these views. The insured person should not feel that income for idleness, however caused, can come from a bottomless purse. What matters, however, is not what has been put into the purse but what resources are available when benefit comes to be paid. These passages make it clear that the argument for insurance is an ethical or psychological argument. It is either morally right that people should contribute or it makes them feel good and independent. Though why it should be morally superior to pay through insurance rather than through taxation is not clear. It is not an economic argument. The Beveridge Report goes on to accept a departure from normal insurance methods: in commercial insurance the premiums are usually adjusted to the risk (the bad risks are asked to pay more) but it is not considered that the state need do this. The decision cuts both ways. No doubt it relieves the bad risks but flat rate contributions were not always fair to the good risks who had little money.

Further, it should have been apparent by the end of the twenties that unemployment, though cyclical in degree, was a permanent feature of the economy. Some trades, particularly those such as dock work, which by their nature employed casual labour, were obviously more subject to it than others, but all trades suffered. Yet suggestions for its cure were greeted with suspicion by governments. It was left to opposition members such as the Liberal Party with their Yellow Book to suggest large schemes of public works. Some economists, Keynes, Henderson and so forth, revived thoughts not entertained since Malthus but it was not until well into the thirties that Keynesian ideas became orthodox.

Though the social services themselves in so far as they existed up to the thirties probably were not a major factor in Britain's economy, the fears of the nineteenth-century ministers and economists have been too readily written off. They have been denounced as cruel, reactionary and class conscious but the case for some of the nineteenth-century hesitations has been pushed under the carpet. The kind of effect which nineteenth-century politicians of all parties feared came more from general attitudes, the growth of reliance upon government, creeping bureaucracy and the general doctrines of state socialism than from particular social services. Of course it is difficult to disentangle the social services from the general increase in government, and the effect of the services was certainly not uniform, but the state of Britain should have made those who saw salvation in ever-increasing state responsibility pause in their tracks. However, a disease of the British is to ignore the lessons to be learnt by applying common sense to the life around us. Even in the thirties British industry was hampered by a lack of mobility and the dead hand of centralisation. A contributory cause of trouble was the disbursement of rather small sums of money to areas of unemployment and declining industry which were just sufficient to keep the poorer wage earners and unemployed alive but in poverty in their home areas, and without any serious effort being made to retain capital for investment in those areas.

Another disease of the British which has done great damage and is getting steadily worse was very evident in this field. Instead of diagnosing faults and eradicating their causes the habit has grown up of laying over them poultice upon poultice. A very obvious reason why certain areas in the North of England and Scotland and Wales were running down was the exhaustion of raw materials, the change in the world economy and the concentration of all prestige and decision-making in London. As mergers (much approved by the bureaucratic Left) grew, head offices moved to the South-East where power lay. The pull of the centre ensured new industries were sited in the South-East. Instead of dispersing power, encouraging the head offices of industry to move from London, discouraging mergers and encouraging such counter-pulls as there were (for example in Cardiff and particularly in Edinburgh, where lingering Scottish and Welsh traditions had put up some resistance to London centralisation) and looking to the creation of new, rather than bolstering up old, industries, governments shelled out subsidies and doles of one sort or another to off-set the results of the very policies they were pursuing. Nor was there any effective criticism of this strange policy. The state socialists were bent upon creating more centralisation, bigger bureaucracies and monopoly. They dominated Labour thinking. If the Left has anything to do with increasing the freedom and responsibility of ordinary people and distributing power, then what has passed for the Left in this country for eighty years has little claim to the name.

Up to the war the social services had been pragmatic. They had grown somewhat haphazardly. Increasingly, though locally administered, their direction and much of their finance has been centralised. Had Neville Chamberlain remained a dominating figure in home affairs they would have been reduced to some system and attention paid to their successes and failings. As it was, by the end of the thirties academic theorizing which had gone on for some time was beginning to penetrate all parties but particularly the Labour Party. And vested interests among bureaucrats and others in perpetuating the system were already taking root.

7 Beveridge and After

Then came the Beveridge Report. It was a grand affair in the eyes of the government (or at least a large segment of the government), the newspapers and broadcasting. It got immense publicity. Beveridge himself, who had followed a long and honourable career in public service, became rather carried away by dreams of grandeur. He was convinced that under his name and proposals the Liberal Party, for which he stood in the 1945 election, would sweep the country. Unfortunately, this proved a delusion. He himself was defeated and the Liberals returned twelve members. How far the Report assisted the Labour Party I cannot say. It certainly did to some extent. Though the Tory Party was committed to it and the Liberals could claim to be the fathers of the welfare services and to possess the author of the Report, Labour looked to be the most likely vehicle for carrying it into effect. The British seldom vote for any definite policy — contenting themselves by voting against something and less often giving their hearts rather than their heads to some cause or figure. There were many other factors in the Labour victory of 1945 besides the Beveridge Report.

Beveridge in his autobiography has mentioned the fame which came to him — how people greeted him in the street as the equal of Churchill and made sketches of him in trains. It has been said that the Beveridge proposals became part of our war aims. This may be true as far as politicians, civil servants and academics were concerned. But despite

Beveridge's personal experiences I must enter a mild note of disagreement. I do not remember that in the army Beveridge was part of the aim for which soldiers fought. He and his Plan became a hope for many who were in poverty and hoped to gain by it. It is not nearly so obvious that the public wanted to pay for it or understood the redistribution of wealth and demand which, if carried out, it was intended to procure.

It is strange that Keynes should have so readily accepted the economic implications of the Report. Possibly Keynes like Beveridge did not pay much regard to the psychology of the individuals who would have to pay. But even aside from that the more astringent criticisms of Hubert Henderson on the economic aspects proved much nearer the mark, 'Want could have been abolished before the present war by a redistribution of income within the earning classes without touching any of the wealthier classes.' This is a breath-taking passage in the Report. As a matter of common sense, history or observation it must surely have been apparent to the Beveridge Committee that though particular groups have from time to time lived together with some equality of means (Jesuit settlements in South America, I believe, and Kibbutzim certainly) an economically egalitarian society has never been sustained for long. It is sometimes argued that it could be done by dictatorship. But one only has to look East of the Iron Curtain to Russia or to her conquered territories to see slavery and gross inequality. So to suggest that if half the nation has £2 per week and half £4 you can divide the difference and pay everyone £3 is naive, to say the least of it. The Beveridge Committee, though Beveridge was a Liberal, seems to have been bemused by the dogma constantly repeated both by active Socialists and academics, for example Tawney, that socialism is about equality — not equality of opportunity but equality of means and reward. But, of course, in practice it isn't. British socialist leaders have been as keen to acquire large salaries, perks, farms, houses, as anyone else. They have not nobly thrust aside the money to be made from their memoirs. 'The rate for the job' is much more the cry — a pretty

Beveridge and After

meaningless phrase implying the highest rate anyone can get.

The right wing of the Labour Party, the so-called social democrats, have been particularly forward in having no truck with equality in practice. Children are educated privately. They take their medical treatment at Manor House. Hugh Gaitskell, for whom I had a great admiration, seemed a little surprised when after announcing that socialism was indeed about equality there was some carping about his investment in the 'Invest in Success' unit trust. And now the most highly rewarded British citizen in the world (probably) after tax is a leading social democrat. Good luck to them but let us drop equality as the hallmark of modern socialism in practice.

Nor are the academic socialists any different. The most vociferous clamour for more grants and perks comes from left wing lecturers and students. Even some of the professors most critical of the capitalist system do not hesitate to engage in profitable private enterprises.

As for the Labour supporters the trades unions laugh at the idea of equality. They will join, of course, in trying to extract more money from the tax payers for the old age pensions but as for abating their claims for higher pay which are one of the chief causes of the difficulty of the old, oh, dear me, what a ridiculous suggestion. Men earning £150-£250 a week for unskilled work vote Labour and demand more. Nor do the already rich socialist managers feel there is anything peculiar in collaring all the free cars, expensive offices, trips to conferences and higher salaries that they can find. Equality for social democrats is strictly for other people.

There are of course those in the Labour Party who are genuinely egalitarian and revolt against the official ethic but within the Labour movement they are regarded as mavericks, if not lunatics. No, in so far as equality has ever caught on with sections of the human race we have to look at some aspects of the Christian tradition — and indeed other religious traditions and classical restraint. (Some Bishops have actually refused a rise in salary and in my experience the Churches are the only institutions which do not constantly bleat that the tax payers must provide, and provide more, for them.) I would suggest that more non-socialist councillors and officials have foregone their attendance allowances and travel on deputations etc. than have their socialist colleagues.

Just as peculiar is the apparent implication of the Beveridge Report that if a vast amount of purchasing power was transferred to the less well-off members of the community it would have no effect on the economy. I have already suggested that the nineteenth-century Scrooges had a little more reason on their side than has been allowed. What surely cannot be denied is that if you set up a society in which it is just as meritorious to receive assistance as to work, in which you will be looked after from the cradle to the grave and in which the general ethic is against enterprise and production and in favour of bureaucracy, research and the expenditure of public money and (partly as a result) there grow powerful vested interests for these purposes, you will have considerable effect on the economy. Whether that effect is good or bad is a matter for argument. I shall in fact argue in connection with a national minimum income that a free society should be able to generate the wealth and harness the ability to pay such an income — but only if it reforms its whole attitude and political economy. To pretend that the creation of a welfare state will not affect the drive and output of the economy, the will to work, efficiency and demand, is nonsense. Yet the Beveridge Report and most of the discussion since its publication seem to have ignored this.

The assumptions since Beveridge too often have been (a) that the free enterprise system is wicked; (b) that, in spite of being denigrated, clobbered, regulated and whenever possible put out of business, it will yet continue to produce the wealth which the nationalised industries manifestly do not but which is essential to the well-being of bureaucrats, academics and the social services; (c) that it is more meritorious to spend other people's earnings than either to save or spend your own. Lately I read of a woman who had given up working in Marks & Spencers for a more 'worthwhile' job in social service. Apart from the fact that a job in social services carries complete security and a pension linked to prices and beyond the dreams of most producers, I would suspect that Marks & Spencers have done more to improve the living standards of the worse-off than do most social workers. But the climate of the time deludes people into thinking that civil service jobs are more meritorious than production or distribution.

The third peculiarity of the Beveridge Report is to assume that if by a miracle equality were to be accepted and a huge redistribution of producing power took place without any effect on the economy, all would be well. This peculiarity springs from a strong streak of materialism. While denouncing the capitalist system as promoting greed, vice and the wrong values, all too many instructors of the public at the same time believe that its vices should be more widely spread. But poverty is not merely inability to purchase: it is being deprived of opportunity, it is to be condemned to boredom and it is frustration, loss of self-respect or self-fulfillment. There is much more sense in equality of opportunity than in equality of purchasing power. The blight and curse of inequality is not being poorer than some other people — it is being brought up in depressing third-rate surroundings, it is having little prospect of employment, or having unsatisfactory employment. The Beveridge Report largely ignored this. In many ways it was a continuation of nineteenth-century attitudes. It was not concerned with the causes of general poverty. Nor was it much concerned with people as individuals. It was concerned with extending the help given to people in trouble once they were in trouble by the creation of a large bureaucratic system of social insurance. Curiously the Report was in some ways a large extension of pragmatism but it overlaid this with mistaken theory. At this time too the subject became seriously choked by jargon such as 'social deprivation' — as though people were born with specified rights of which someone was depriving them. A curious return to the social contract or the state of nature. Nothing is more certain than that in the state of nature no one had any rights, and force, aggression and acquisitiveness reigned.

A further result of the atmosphere surrounding Beveridge was to spread a view among the influential coteries of politicians and academics that poverty or inability to cope with life was never the fault of the sufferer. The Poor Laws lent too far one way but the pendulum of the dominating fashion now swung to the other extreme. It is one thing to recognise that much poverty is due to accidents such as birth or unemployment, quite another to say that the individual has not a responsibility to do the best he or she can and should be encouraged to rely entirely on public charity. Further, this new fashion was far out of touch with the public. It is often right to govern ahead of public opinion but it is important that you are going in the right direction. Beveridge to his credit undertook a vast programme of speeches and articles designed to explain the proposals of his commission but he was unable to create an atmosphere of informed attention and discussion.

'Beveridge' was, as heralded by academics, publicists and politicians, a war aim (though, as I say, this was rather a sophisticated opinion) — a land fit for heroes and that was that, even if the heroes had no clear idea of what it meant. It didn't mean that no one would be impoverished, feckless, badly housed, mad or bad. It did, according to popular interpretation (for which the Report must take responsibility) mean that all such people could be raised to a standard of life well above that suggested by Rowntree and maintained there by the employed population. As for unemployment, that was to be dealt with by denunciations from governments. They would not tolerate it and that was assumed to settle the matter. Even to this day when a rate of well over a million unemployed has been endured by the country for two years, we are still told that any significant unemployment is 'unacceptable'. It was a step, an important step, towards the general feeling that the state was responsible for everyone whatever they did throughout their lives. It did not appear to demand any great activity from the citizens who composed the state. It was there to put right all troubles and take all blame while a growing army of its non-productive bureaucrats looked more and more to their own future and in pursuing the same aims of their particular organisations lost sight of the general good — or even common sense.

So we retreated, as I and many others have long since pointed out, not to a welfare society but to a welfare state, a condition in which people expected that the state would look after the unfortunate. Its resources were thought to be ample — the rich could pay.

Another feature of the Beveridge Report was that it did not contemplate that the recipients of its benefits would have the right to a say in what they wanted. They were not to be involved in the administration of the scheme. Benefits decided by a beneficent government passed by parliament, recommended no doubt by well intentioned advisers but not necessarily designed to follow any general pattern or meet any sharp felt need by the recipients, were handed out by methods of greater and greater complexity. It was tainted with corporatism and paid scant attention to the opinions and wants of people as individuals.

If it had been treated for what it largely was — a big extension of the social services which had been growing since 1906 and indeed long before — Beveridge would have done considerable good. But it wasn't. It was treated as a new departure, a departure made possible by the discovery of an elixir which enabled you to bypass questions of human nature and the resources available to Britain. So Britain stumbled into the post-war world. She was convinced that she had done conspicuously well in the war: Keynes had solved economic problems: Beveridge had eliminated poverty. It may have seemed odd that the Liberal Party to which both these great men belonged — for great men they were — should gain so little support or, alternatively, that these two had so little faith in the major parties. But that merely illustrated that British politics are not directed by logic or any consistent theory and were less so than ever after the war.

The implementation of the Beveridge Report did little to clarify the system of the social services. (As I have recorded, Neville Chamberlain in 1924 noted the difficulty of providing expert services in all-purpose institutions.) As far as services in kind were concerned, that is services by experts or officials direct to the recipient, it was eminently reasonable that the area concerned should be relatively large as the specialisation of their services increased. But this meant that the services became more impersonal and that local contact was lost. One of the principal disagreements between the Majority and Minority Reports on the Poor Law Commission still cast its shadow.

Two other heresies of the post-war world also cast their shadow across any reasonable development in the social services. The top of the civil service and most politicians, particularly Labour politicians, were enamoured of size. It suited the old craving for prestige. The fact that having larger offices has never led to economy was ignored, so too was the growing determination of professional bodies and trades unions never to shed a member. To take one example, Britain's influence in the world and her commonwealth responsibilities were both declining: the Foreign Office and the Commonwealth Relations Office were therefore combined. The new staff exceeded the old one.

The other prejudice or demand was for a career structure. This meant, and still means, that in place of attachment to the work in hand and to the people meant to be served, the individual looks to his trades union or professional body. And he looks to that union or body not to do a job in the public interest but to further his salary and perks. The social worker was indeed in a difficult position, as a girl pitchforked from the university into an unknown (to her) city explained to me. She was given a list of some fifty or more 'clients' all much older than her, all for whatever reason reduced to a state where they were incapable of running their own lives, all indoctrinated with the fashionable view that they were entitled to have someone to run their lives for them, some indeed almost proud of their inability and all resigned or determined to remain in this situation for ever. What was she to do? Doctors cure most of their patients or the patients die. Preventive medicine eliminates the cause of disease. But if the social worker remained loyal to the practice to which she had been introduced she faced thirty or forty years of going round the same treadmill with patients whose 'health' she could not improve — no wonder she wanted to move. Social work (indeed in my opinion any work worth doing) cannot be done by centralisation, computerisation or entirely within a career structure.

Nevertheless, social work became a popular career.

Beveridge and After

Sociology covering a range of subjects attracted thousands of students at the universities. In an age in which research was a growth industry, social research was a leader in the field. No student could listen to a blackbird or read Jane Austen without a special grant. Your grandmother could only be taught to suck eggs by graphs. The obvious, which illiterate yokels who could use their eyes had known for hundreds of years, was elaborately pursued by expensive research. Any community which was even comparatively remote from Putney and the outlook of London, W1, was examined again and again by universities and the BBC.

Meanwhile, not only common sense but judgement which cannot be quantified was at a discount. Meaningless statistics were worshipped like the images of Baal. If the statistics of production increased everyone was supposed to rejoice, though drink, tobacco and indeed, if known to the statisticians, heroin and arsenic would all be in the total, and the ruthless waste of energy and raw materials in running government departments with no benefit to the public were certainly included. The idea that moral values and human happiness or great art might be furthered by wasting less was laughed away.

However, according to the accepted statistics the GNP in 1945 was some £8,000 million. Expenditure by local government on the social services was about £272.4 million. In addition, housing took £43.6 million. By 1955 these figures had risen to £576 million and £133 million. The GNP at current prices stood at some £18,000 million.

Beveridge promised that for the first five years of the scheme the extra cost would not exceed £100 million a year. Keynes held that this could be supported. These calculations were based on insurance. Pensions under the scheme were to be 'genuinely contributary' as Beveridge said. Those near pensionable age were to be covered by 'assistance pensions' subject to a means test. Beveridge also produced on his own initiative, financed by Sir Kenneth Lee, David Astor and Edward Hulton, another report, 'Full Employment in a Free Society'. When examining his report on Social Insurance and Service it must be remembered that in producing it he was bound to have regard for the terms of reference given to him and that 'Full Employment in a Free Society' was designed by him as a complementary scheme of equal importance.

The six fundamental principles of the Report as defined by Herbert Morrison in the first debate in February 1943 in accordance with the seventeenth section of the Report were flat rate subsistence benefit, flat rate contributions, unification of administration, adequacy of benefit, universality and classification of benefit. It can be disputed whether these are principles. To some extent in spite of the clarion cries that the Report was new, a great break with the past and a leap towards better times, it continued many of the old methods. And the debate every now and then echoed many previous debates on similar subjects. Sir John Anderson, the first speaker for the government, warned, as members had often (and rightly) warned, against the increased costs. He pointed out that the charge on the tax payers would increase year by year and 'in the twentieth year will have grown by £168 million compared with the first year'. He stressed that the scheme's success would depend largely on Beveridge's forecasts of relatively full employment coming true. Every 500,000 off the unemployment figure, he said, was believed to mean £200,000,000 on the national income.

There were a few warnings about possible side effects. The plight of the middle classes (defined as those earning between £500 and £1,000 a year) was mentioned; the weight of contributions; the possibility that by lumping industrial risks in with other risks we should weaken the incentive to safety in factories. But the general effects on the economy and on the outlook of the people were inadequately discussed.

Nor was it mentioned that although the scheme claimed to be a unified system bringing together and superseding the piecemeal legislation in operation, yet it was far from being completely unified. And the relative advantages or disadvantages of direct aid rather than cash payments were hardly discussed though Sir John Anderson claimed that the provision of school meals, by then taken by one million children, had proved the most effective way of helping growing families. The standard of subsistence which the Beveridge payments were designed to achieve was related to the total of £35 million, paid out on proof of need (Public Assistance) in 1938.

The second world war gave an even greater push to the demands for government and public authority interference than did the first. The process is, of course, cumulative. As more people are absorbed into government service, more pressure builds up among them to extend their empires. As their clients come to depend upon public aid, so the appetite for it grows. The increase of expenditure on the social services both absolutely and as a percentage of government expenditure has been fairly steady since 1890. While often lines on graphs for other public expenditure jerk up and down, the line for the social services expenditure per head of the population runs fairly steadily upwards. As a proportion of total central government expenditure the social services share grew from around twenty-one per cent in 1890 to around forty-five per cent in 1955.

The Beveridge estimates, as was to be expected, proved far too small. The main increase Beveridge foresaw in social security expenditure was in retirement pensions and sickness benefit. During his transitional period of twenty years he expected the basic pension to rise from 70 pence for a single person and £1.25 for a married couple to 95 pence and £1.63 respectively in 1955 and to the full rates of £1.20 and £2.00 in 1965. As for sickness benefit, Beveridge reckoned that it was only deficient in that persons not previously insured would not have qualified for benefit if they were ill for long because they would not have paid their contributions for three years.

However, the future turned out differently: many new services and benefits were introduced, the assumptions were not fulfilled. Beveridge fixed his rates on the estimate that the cost of living would be 25 per cent above pre-war. By 1948 it was 94 per cent above the 1938 level. So far from declining as Beveridge thought it would, supplementary benefit increased. In 1948 3 per cent of the population was dependent upon national assistance (or supplementary benefit). The percentage rose to 5.1 per cent in 1954, declined slightly in the late fifties and then rose until in 1975 it was 8.1 per cent so that both in the rates of benefit which had to be paid to keep pace with the rise in the cost of living and in the numbers requiring assistance from the taxpayer, Beveridge underestimated.

Two lessons can be drawn from this. First, the folly of long-term estimating. Secondly, the failure of the Beveridge-type of traditional social services to 'work themselves out of a job'. It can be said that they were never meant to do so. But, as we have seen, enthusiasm for the Beveridge Plan seemed to rise from a belief that poverty could be reduced, if not ended, by a system of personal insurance; this has proved an illusion. In every field of social service except for unemployment insurance, until the last two years, the call upon the tax payer has increased — in many cases dramatically. The Beveridge estimate for retirement pensions in 1945 was £126 million: even that estimate was exceeded, the figure being £176 million, but the estimate for 1965 of £300 million was much more seriously at fault, the actual sum being £1,238 million. Of course inflation is chiefly to blame. But, nevertheless, there is something wrong with a system which results in more and more people living on the backs of each other while the standard of living as a whole either declines or rises very slowly. Advances in technology and education should surely have achieved a higher standard of life and political skill could surely have done more to ensure that it was earned and enjoyed by a greater proportion of the population without the proliferation of doles and services.

Yet the needs of different areas vary greatly which shows how ineffective this huge effort has been in establishing anything like equality of opportunity to lead a satisfactory life wherever a child may be born.

So we have arrived at the present. We have a huge cat's-cradle of services in cash and in kind. In 1977-78 it is estimated that £12,651,000,000 will be spent by the central and local government on personal social services and social security. Of this, by far the greater part will be spent by the central government on social security (£11,659 million). Expenditure by the local authorities will be largely on personal services (£980 million). This emphasises both how expenditure on these services has grown and how centralised it remains.

In 1973/74 expenditure per head for unemployment benefit varied from 186.4 per cent of the national average in the North to 63.2 per cent in the South-East. Disablement benefit was 209.1 per cent of the national average in Wales but only 63.2 per cent in the South-East and 70.7 per cent in East Anglia.

In 1973/74 supplementary benefit was running at 146.6 per cent of the national average in Northern Ireland, 123.1 per cent in Scotland but 67.5 per cent in East Anglia. In the same year, family income supplement was 143.1 per cent in Scotland, 135.6 per cent in East Anglia, and in Northern Ireland, which is of course a special case, it rose to 482 per cent; in the South-East of England it was 65.7 per cent. Health, employment and wealth are all lower in the North of England, Scotland, Wales and Northern Ireland than in the South of England. 'You don't need statistics to prove that,' you may well say, 'It is obvious and proving the obvious by graphs and tables wastes a lot of time nowadays.' I would agree. But statistics are thought to lend weight to an argument and a more serious reason for quoting them is to illustrate the huge amount spent on the social services and how little it has done to spread equality among the different communities.

A glance at the personal social services statistics published by the Chartered Institute of Public Finance and Accountancy and the Society of County Treasurers shows both the complexity of the personal services and the amount of resources they consume. In 1975/76 expenditure on the administration of the services run by the local auttorities of Hammersmith (which as appears from figures quoted above is a small proportion of the total) was £10,859 per thousand of the population paid for from the rates and the rate support grant. In Durham the net expenditure per thousand of the population in that year for residential care of the elderly was £27,482. Community care (meals etc.) cost £816,666 in 1975/76 in Cleveland or £13,258 per thousand of the population over sixty-five and £1,863 per thousand of the population. In Newcastle-upon-Tyne in 1975/76 13.8 per cent of the population under eighteen were in residential care, compared with 5.7 per cent in the Isle of Wight. And within cities there were, as one would expect, great differences. In the London borough of Haringey the net expenditure per thousand of the population under eighteen for children boarded out was £1,868 and in Enfield £430. In Camden the staff employed on the social services was 246 of whom 51 were senior staff.

Are we getting value for money? I would suggest not. We are certainly alleviating some of the hardship caused by the aftermath of the industrial revolution, over-centralisation, the decay of cities and other well known causes. But we are not making too much progress in eliminating the causes of poverty. We have come a long way since 1914 when state expenditure on the social services had just doubled since 1905 and when 8 per cent of net income went on taxes.

Undoubtedly in many ways we are better off. Services, some generally defined as social, some that I would include under that head though they are not generally so called, have contributed to this. The most notable advance over the last two hundred years has been in medicine. It has owed comparatively little to the state though I am an admirer of the health service. Pensions, unemployment pay and sickness benefit helped many people in severe need. Whether that need could be met in other ways than by state assistance should be considered. But though they are curative and not preventive they still are a necessary element in a good society. Several of the practical schemes for helping the disabled and, at least in their time, school meals for children, have been well worthwhile.

What the effect of even these payments and services has been on the life of the country is difficult to estimate. At one time, as I have illustrated, plenty of prophecies were made about the debilitating effect they would have. Now it is generally assumed that these prophecies have turned out to be false. For my part I would suggest rather tentatively that the services mentioned above, by themselves, have not resulted in any great disposition to dependence or idleness, at least up to now. But as part of a general tendency they may well have done so.

There are two points to be made in any discussion of the form in which the social services have grown up in this country. First, they have formed part, an important part, of the growing control which the state exercises over its citizens. Secondly, they may now have reached a stage when they are beginning to have a debilitating effect. This effect may be a delayed action. Many years ago the Webbs used a curious phrase when objecting to insurance against sickness, 'The state gets nothing for its money in the way of conduct'. In considering the Mondragon co-operatives the conclusion must be that the conduct of the Basques has been stimulated by the lack of state support on which they could fall back. Cause and effect are difficult to disentangle. We have become a bureaucratic country. Whether this led to the present form of our welfare pensions or how far it was caused by the welfare system is difficult and perhaps not important to assess.

At the back of these considerations lie deeper questions about human nature. We do not know how we may be able to change the effects of heredity or modify inherited characteristics. It would seem, however, that there will always be a proportion of the population which has difficulty in realising a reasonable standard of life whatever may be done for them by improving their communities or providing them with an income.

In this context the stimulation by advertising must be mentioned. The constant dangling of something new before the television viewer, the constant encouragement to demand more of everything, and to be dissatisfied with what you have, may boost the economy but may also teach people to believe that they have a 'right' to these goodies and that if they cannot get them, somebody ought to see that they do.

Unfortunately, a great vested interest in the social services has grown up. Social workers are organising themselves into a profession like lawyers. No doubt like lawyers they will persuade themselves that things can only be done as they have always been done in the way they have been taught to do them. No doubt the disappointing results of their methods will have as little effect as the results of the legal system and its failure to serve the public in a cheap and satisfactory way has had upon lawyers. So their activities will no doubt be extended still further.

But in a world where resources, by whatever schemes they are allocated, are so far limited this can only result in a misdirection of effort. I discuss elsewhere whether we need a philosophy behind the welfare state or society; I have suggested that such a philosophy cannot be separated from our philosophy of the state or society in general. But whatever conclusion is reached about the inadequacy of our general thinking or our theory on purely practical grounds, judging by the results and taking into account the resources expended, there must be something wrong with this vast network of services and subsidies which shows few signs of contributing further to the betterment of our country.

Let me say once again that I believe that it has contributed in the past but the wider hopes sometimes expressed for the welfare state or society seem to me to have been dashed. However, I do not want to exaggerate, if they have been dashed here in Britain, it is not clear that they have been realised much better anywhere else. Looking around and asking other people's opinions, it seems that we are a decent society. In statistical terms we are a lot better off than we were. The gross domestic product has increased by over a third in twenty-five years. Expectation of life has risen, especially for infants. Cars are more widely owned and, of course, television sets far more widely owned. The poverty line has been raised to a level where the ownership of washing machines, refrigerators and cars is taken as a matter of course even by those on public assistance. The British may be, as they are traditionally accused of being, a little self-satisfied. But in the ordinary business of life they are probably as decent, perhaps rather more decent, than other nations. If people leave Britain it is usually for tax reasons. There are plenty of people anxious to come here particularly from behind the Iron Curtain.

As I remember when I was Rector of Aberdeen University I obtained some money from my fellow directors of that admirable institution the Joseph Rowntree Social Service Trust to enable some students of the University to travel in various countries and report back upon how they liked them and what they thought of their welfare services and their success. The countries visited were the USA,

Sweden, Norway, Finland, Italy, Germany, Holland and Australia. I particularly did not ask for statistical research. I wanted not the figures involved, which I could get from libraries, but the impressions made on the travellers which I could not get from libraries, nor — being of a different age and experience — from my own voyages. The most popular countries were Scandinavian. The students were impressed by how hard the Swedes, and above all, Swedish women work. I, too, thought I detected the same disposition among shipyard workers at the Gotewerke Company. Germans are often built up as hard workers yet Germany initiated welfare services before we did. When one remembers the excitement, indeed the ecstasy of British visitors to Italy in the last century it seems surprising that the least popular country was Italy. It was found to be a country which tolerated, if it did not actually promote, extremes of poverty and wealth. My couriers did not want to be poor. Their standard of life included cars, travel and a considerable expenditure on drink. But they rated social services, which I suspect would not occur as a factor at all fifty years ago, as an important element in the country in which one might like to live. Too much weight must not be attached to this blissfully unscientific experiment. The experimenters were young, they were relatively well-to-do and successful. Though they were asked to consider in which country they would like to live, no one was going to compel them to live in the country of their choice. Nevertheless, for what you consider it worth, their reactions point to the value being now attached by the middle classes to the welfare state and certainly many members from this class look to a career in the welfare services.

The ambitions of the student travellers were modest. It certainly seemed that the 'Lad (or Lass) of Pairts' had departed from the Scottish scene. Students no longer wanted to be millionaires, Prime Ministers or even distinguished scholars. They did not hanker after richer pastures in other countries. Perhaps this was because careers such as that of Andrew Carnegie were no longer open, I think this is certainly part of the reason. But, equally, they did not want to live in Franciscan poverty.

One, if not two, cars, coloured television, foreign holidays, two and threequarter children (the average) were what they expected. All this seems to me perfectly reasonable, indeed creditable. But I have some doubts as to whether without other ingredients it will make a wholly satisfactory mix.

A satisfactory community must be a stimulating as well as a tolerant community. I don't myself think that tycoons are essential. But if a few people set a high standard they may open the eyes of their neighbours and among some students I felt that the standard they expected (relatively high to, say, the standards of Africa) was a lowest common denominator — or tolerable denominator — of their friends' way of life, assumed without much examination. Dr Leavis has pointed out that civilisation needs an informed and critical public, even if small in numbers, prepared constantly to examine the human condition, its art, and its way of life, to defend what is good and condemn what is bad even when it is fashionable. The universities should be providing this: I wonder if they are?

Certainly if there is to be any intelligent control of government expenditure, both the aims of our society and the methods by which it attempts to achieve those aims need constant consideration. A society not interested in the value of individuals or personal relationships cannot be a welfare society. And without the pressure of a public which knows the sort of society which it wants we shall continue to waste our resources. As Professor Peacock puts it in his essay on Economic Analysis and Government Expenditure Control (*Public Expenditure*, Oliver and Boyd, 1963): 'Only a major change in the attitude of the electorate to public spending will force any present-day government to take adequate action'.

8 The Urban Programmes

Even governments and the bureaucracy could not be blind to the comparative failure of their policies as regards industrial relations, the social services and planning. In spite of increased expenditure on the social services, conditions in the cities were very bad. So a programme was set up under the Home Office.

Notes on the Urban Programme ICR/728/2/1 make clear what sort of programme it was. It was a programme authorised by the Local Government Grants (Social Need) Act of 1969. The Act provided for payments to local authorities only. Voluntary organisations are not excluded but their proposals must be grant-aided by the relevant local authority; the local authority is then entitled to Urban Programme grant on approved projects. In practice this means that aid to voluntary bodies is limited to those which local authorities themselves support. There was to be nothing new about the administration of the grants. They were to remain firmly in the hands of the existing bureaucracies. They could only be expanded on projects approved by these bureaucracies. 'Local Authorities may only incur expenditure on projects for which they have a responsibility. For instance, a local authority can provide day nurseries and can propose them for grant-aid under the new programme; it could not propose a hospital as that would not be within the powers of a local authority'. How revealing. Nothing must be done to upset the correct channels. Nothing must be done to break the monopolies of the entrenched bureaucracies. A little competition for the Health Service from local authority hospitals might do no harm. But, apart from that, if a local authority wanted to establish a 'centre of excellence' which would raise morale and attract fee-paying patients from elsewhere perhaps by boosting its hospital, that would be forbidden. For new projects, even such as a day nursery, the permission of the central authorities must be sought.

'The Urban Programme' is not intended to do the work of the major social services like education or health. It tries rather to encourage projects which have a reasonably quick effect on 'special social need' which has broadly been equated with multiple deprivation. The notes recognise that troubles may be multiple by which I take it to mean that it was designed for areas in which say, housing, employment and income were all low. But it is confined to particular manifestations of the trouble and usually peripheral ones at that — summer projects, adventure playgrounds, etc. It is not that some of these projects are not wholly desirable and needed. It is that they go nowhere near the root of the trouble in such communities. Further, no attempt was made to encourage initiative by the people themselves, nor to create communities which would be attractive to the 'non-deprived' to coin a horrible phrase. The ghettoes were to continue, with some blemishes removed.

The notes go on to explain 'The Community Development Project, which is a national action-research experiment based in the Home Office, consisting of action and research teams working in selected urban localities to discover how far the social problems experienced by people in a local community can be better understood and resolved through closer co-ordination of all agencies concerned — central and local government departments and the voluntary organisations together with the local residents themselves. There is special emphasis on citizen involvement and community self-help. Good, if the terms of urban aid did not make it very difficult to enlist local initiative or break the hold of the centre.

An examination of the phases, as they were called, of the Urban Programme shows that they were too much confined

The Urban Programmes

to schemes of the provision-of-adventure-playground, decorating-the-houses-of-pensioners type to make any significant improvement in the community. In phases ten to sixteen, November 1973 to November 1976, bids were invited for the following types of project:

Easter and Summer holiday projects.

Play schemes, community centres, hostels, childminders, etc.

Projects designed to help re-settlement of Ugandan Asians and holiday projects.

Capital and non-capital projects.

School holiday projects.

Capitalised and non-capital projects, including non-recurrent holiday projects.

Responsibility for the Urban Programme was eventually transferred from the Home Office to the Ministry of the Environment signalling a diminution of its importance in the eyes of the government in comparison with the problems of immigrants and the increasing anxiety over the inner cities. It has now become part of the Inner City Programme. In 1976-77 and according to the estimates for 1977-78 it cost some £4½ million per year. Grants in 1975/76 varied from £374 paid to Somerset to £660,917 paid to Liverpool, £423 to Haringey and £577,690 to ILEA. Although in some ways it was intended to tread new ground, in fact it followed very much in the footsteps of the innumerable grants and services piled up piecemeal since the war. I doubt if it was effective and it failed to blaze any new trail in communal activities.

The mere recital of these projects shows how inadequate the Urban Aid Programme was to the problems of the cities. And, though the programme was confined to the cities, the problems were not. It would have been better to have concentrated the effort on one city. If £4½ million had been concentrated on a single area, it might have been a valuable example of what could be achieved. But that would have run up against political and administrative opposition. Convention demands that help from the central government should, at least to some extent, be spread; that it is often spread unfairly does not invalidate this. MPs will press the claims of their own constituencies and the government will be embarrassed if one is singled out for massive aid. Further, while governments do attempt experiments and pilot schemes they are seldom able to make them revolutionary and unless they are revolutionary and command significant resources they will seldom gain much attention. Nor will the lessons from them be learnt. If they are revolutionary they will cut across administrative channels. This, as we have seen, the Urban Programme was careful to avoid. They will also entail some change in the relations between central and local government. This will be seen by civil servants as setting a dangerous precedent, even if it can be done without legislation for which there may be no parliamentary time. It will probably not please the local authorities. If at the end of the experiment the verdict is against the change it will be difficult to reverse it.

Some time ago a Reith lecturer suggested that in a 'throw-away-age' we could use some 'throw-away-institutions', by which he meant both that there was room for experimental institutions and that some institutions should be designed for a short future. He saw no shame in admitting that they might have outlived their usefulness after five or six years. There is a lot to be said for his view but caution is necessary. In today's climate few things can be done simply and cheaply. An illustration of this which taught me a salutary lesson was an application from a doctor for a small parking space outside his surgery. His surgery was on a country road with open rough grazing opposite the surgery door. It seemed perfectly possible to cut a few square yards into this field, lay down a little tarmac and make a parking place for half a dozen cars. I wrote to the appropriate authority. Months later I got an architect's drawing which proposed to build up a quarter of an acre of the land on the side of the road next to the surgery where the ground sloped away, cover it with concrete, surround it with walls and erect a street lamp at a cost running into tens of thousands of pounds.

Any innovation will also set up a vested interest in its

future. Here again there was until lately a good example of this British disease. The Development Commissioners established before the first war were still in existence up to a few years ago despite the powers of the Board of Trade and local authorities to develop and the creation of such bodies as the Highlands and Islands Development Board. Indeed, the Commissioners for the Prince Consort's Great Exhibition are still with us. Nevertheless, if the Urban Programme could have concentrated upon a medium-sized town not yet laid waste by motorways, property developers and high flats, and if it could have tried out new forms of planning, education and transport in such an area I believe it could have been more effective.

I myself wrote a letter to the press in April 1972 — published under the heading of 'The Challenge of the Inner Cities' — pointing to what was happening in America and asking, 'Do we want to create deserts of dust, concrete, disaffection and violence?' I went on to draw attention to the departure of the middle classes and the presence of endemic unemployment:

> The method must vary, the aim must be to raise cities or parts of cities or rural areas to a standard at which anyone would be content to live. It is my belief that harnessing energies to community purposes we can at the same time release energies for initiative and self-expression. It is not only a question of ameliorating vandalism by clubs or simply digging the gardens of pensioners, admirable though these activities are. It is a question of curing the causes of vandalism and creating a community in which the old naturally find themselves well looked after. We should attempt to give practical expression to the desire for a culture counter to our present faceless and unequal society.

Then, and indeed long before 1972, what was happening was obvious without research. As I said:

> If we look at Dundee, Glasgow, Liverpool, Birmingham or part of London can we be altogether proud of what has already happened there? And if we look at some of the smaller communities of Central Scotland, the North East of England, the West Riding and elsewhere may we not be more worried still?

Indeed, we should have been. It has taken twenty years for the government to catch on to what they have done in collaboration with the local authorities to the centres of the cities.

Over the whole of the city or indeed the small town hangs the blight of some aspects of planning. The conception that you can gather up statistics which show the state of affairs at one point in time and from that draw up a plan for the future ignores the living and changing nature of the community. Planning must be a continuing process. There are then some particular aspects of planning which are harmful. One is zoning. Factories which emit unpleasant smells, or worse, need control over their siting. But the notion that all places of work must be in one zone, shops in another, housing in another, makes for an unsatisfactory community. It also means that more transport is needed and that local authorities are unwilling to spend money on housing in areas zoned for something else. It makes it very difficult for small businesses to find accommodation. Many small businesses provide services which people like to find near where they live. And often a neighbourhood of some diversity, with shops, restaurants, small builders, garages, craftsmen, is more interesting and lively than an area devoted to nothing but housing.

Inflation, which leads to speculation and enhances the value of real property, the rating system and the use of compulsory purchase by some local authorities make matters even worse. We all know of areas which have lain waste or buildings which stand unoccupied (Centrepoint) for long periods. Sometimes an area has been acquired by a local authority or speculator only to find that funds are not available for its redevelopment. Sometimes would-be purchasers cannot find the money. Instead of rating the site, which would encourage development, vacant land or unoccupied buildings escape high rating which is borne by improvements. Yet it is improvements we want.

Instead of striking at the root causes of the decay of the inner city and the lack of suitable employment (which can usually only be given by small enterprises) governments attempt to overlay it, in the true style of British governments, by granting special subsidies or setting up new boards. A researcher from the Department of the Environment has estimated that between three per cent and five per cent of the land in cities of the greatest value for community development lies idle. Three quarters of it is owned by local authorities or public bodies. Look out of any train window and you will see it, much of it in the hands of British Rail, despite their cries for more cash. In 1974 British Rail owned over 22,500 acres of 'derelict land'. The proper and full use of city land is of great importance in any attempt to promote community services in the sense I use the term.

Some rural areas and smaller towns have suffered equally from modern planning. Because an example often brings the lesson home better than generalities, let me recount the history of Kirkwall, a town of some six thousand inhabitants in Orkney. Across the harbour, on an excellent site facing the main town, an aerodrome with hutted camps was built in the war. After the war it was handed over to the local authorities. It was then zoned for industry. Too rigid zoning is pretty mad anywhere but to apply planning rules of thumb designed for cities to towns of a few thousand inhabitants shows how centralised, academic and inhuman government has become and how common sense has been expelled. As there was a need for housing after the war the huts, good huts most of them, were occupied. The local authority could not rehouse the occupiers but because the area was zoned for industry they would not look after it. The grass grew rank, rubbish accumulated, offal from a knackery flowed out of a sewer and the huts deteriorated into slums. A few local industries moved in but Orkney is not an industrial area and did not require an 'industrial estate'. In any case, it was a site crying out for a mixture of housing, shops and small industries and admirably sited for housing in particular. Though some excellent restoration has been carried out, for which credit should go to the Islands Council, much of the middle of Kirkwall has been gutted to make car parks. Parts of the town have thus been shredded and the whole is in danger of being reduced to a copy of some industrial city. This same tendency is to be seen in Stromness, an even smaller town and most satisfactory for those who live in it. Here at least the centre has not been desecrated, indeed praiseworthy attempts have been made to maintain and rebuild it. The old Stromness Town Council was in many ways a lesson in small being beautiful. But larger authorities which control education are determined to move the secondary school out of the town, thereby denuding it of life, making more cars inevitable and no doubt erecting a hideous enclave of new school buildings on agricultural land, while leaving good stone buildings to decay.

In developing communities the part to be played by voluntary associations is still obscure, at least to the government. In White Papers they are graciously mentioned, their co-operation is sought. But too many bureaucrats regard them as at best fringe organisations and at worst a hindrance to their tidy, office-based, career structure profession. It is true that most voluntary organisations are set up to do a particular job, which makes them unsuitable for use as the only instrument for the all-round development of a community, but it does not disqualify them from most useful work within the community. The Urban Aid Programme like the Inner Cities Programme was obsessed with the need for an 'over-all' national strategy. This was a product of the dominating fashion of the fifties and sixties. It was never clear what it meant. Sometimes by strategy the authorities seemed to mean an examination of how to get the best value for money. This was an admirable attitude as far as it went. It should have meant, however, monitoring how things went, stopping the unsuccessful and learning from the successful. But, once again, it all too often meant research in the sense of examining already well-known features of our society, reducing them to statistics and trying to deduce the future from them. At other times strategy seemed to mean the formulation of some scheme suitable for all the various communities in the country.

In 1974 the Home Secretary announced a 'new strategy' for tackling the problems of those living in the most acutely deprived urban areas. It involves the preparation and subsequent implementation by selected local authorities, in collaboration with all those concerned, of comprehensive community programmes containing an analysis of the

The Urban Programmes

needs of the area considered as a whole, and proposals for meeting them. This was indeed the curate's egg. Certainly the area should be considered as a whole. But 'the whole' should have included the better-off as well as the worst-off in the community. There was no indication of the standards at which the local authorities should aim, nor is it clear who 'all those concerned' might be. As might have been foreseen when the schemes under this policy were examined, it was found that the problems of urban deprivation cut across administrative boundaries and that the local authorities still operated the social services through separate services while any solution to the problems required a unified approach and greater co-operation between the various services. As the Home Office had an Urban Deprivation Unit set up in 1973 before the programme began this was disappointing. The Unit was divided into two parts, the inevitable research organisation and a section said to be concerned with immediate practical issues. But even this second section was not so much concerned with action as with 'examining the need to bring together the various activities of Government Departments'. In this it appears to have failed.

The tangle into which government policies have been twisted during the last thirty years can clearly be seen in the policies for the inner cities. There was a deliberate policy for excluding industry from the inner cities. They were deliberately bulldozed by the public authorities. At the same time national policy discriminated in favour of large monopoly or semi-monopoly industries. These deliberate policies led, as they must have led, to the decay of the inner city. As people and industry were driven out, they went, leaving in their wake those who were too poor or feckless to leave. Suddenly it dawned upon the government with a blinding flash of the obvious (only accepted of course after much research) that:

> Many of the inner areas surrounding the centres of our cities suffer in a marked way and to an unacceptable extent, from economic decline, physical decay and adverse social conditions. In some cities the process of clearance and redevelopment have got badly out of step.

The bulldozers have done their work but the rebuilding lagged behind. The inner cities have a higher concentration of poor people, shortage of private capital, prevalence of poverty, poor environment and bad housing conditions.

They might have added vacant land to the list. All these features, which were created by government policy and which can be noted by anyone taking a walk in the city, were only recognised by the government after four years of research.

We then come to one excellent piece of modern comedy. The Location of Offices Bureau which was set up to move offices out of the city is now directed to move them back. London Underground stations a year or two ago carried Location of Offices Bureau posters urging firms to escape the stranglehold of the city. Now the functions of the LOB have been reviewed and part of its new role will be to give particular attention to the promotion of office employment in inner urban areas, including London.

The government has even begun to recognise one of the main themes of this book. The urban studies of recent years have shown that urban problems cannot be tackled effectively on a piecemeal basis. I, and many other people, could have told them that without the expense of 'urban studies'. 'The problems interlock: education, for example, is affected by local conditions.' I should say it is. 'Social conditions which in turn are affected by housing and employment. . . .The best results are likely to be achieved through a unified approach in which the different activities and services of government are brought together'. But do not be misled into thinking that because after years of expense and delay the obvious is beginning to dawn, common sense will triumph and logical action will be taken — that would upset the dominant attitudes and interests.

The difficulties should not be underestimated. Central government and the local authorities are organised on a functional basis. Government departments are responsible for specific fields of policy and local authority departments with the provision of specific services. This is sensible and efficient for the most part [not two of the

The Urban Programmes

happiest adjectives to have chosen]. Where, however, it is necessary to adopt an area based approach to public sector activities, as it is in the inner city areas, it requires special efforts of co-ordination and joint working which cut across established practices.

This requirement is true of most fields of government. It should not be either surprising nor so difficult as is made out but various departments fight their own corner as rigorously as any prize fighter. It is only now proposed that the government 'will work in partnership with certain cities to develop inner area programmes. . . . Other cities will be free to prepare inner area programmes themselves'.

This new policy is to be implemented largely through an old and failed policy, the Urban Programme. Why did it fail? For the old reasons: it was too much of a 'handed down' paper exercise, it relied too much on the local authorities and it took little notice of the real conditions in which people live. The same objections, particularly the last, can be made to its successor. The inner city is not a natural area; it is not a community; few people think of themselves as citizens of the inner city. Both the Urban Programme and the Inner City Programme bear one mark of the poor law: they do not help a whole community, rich and poor, clever and stupid, to make the very best of themselves. They are remedial and only then up to a minimum standard. They do not take account of the differences, the inevitable and beneficial differences between communities. For instance, having changed — many people would say, wrecked — the centres of Birmingham and Glasgow with a cat's cradle of entwined highways, no one can now put them back as the living space for decent communities. Parts of the inner city in some towns should perhaps be abandoned.

The same criticisms can be made of the Comprehensive Community Programmes. Indeed, the very notion of a programme — so typical of modern government with its overtones of research, committees, paper plans, the shifting of people like sheep to new pastures, and finality (it's in the programme, it must be done) — is inimical to the proper and natural development of a community, which is never to be totally foreseen and is never finished. The

White Paper of June 1977 does mention that decentralisation is to be desired. It even mentions that there is some criticism by their clients of local authorities; but it gives no indication of how out of touch some of these authorities are, nor does it show any realisation that it is the people themselves, people of all sorts, who should be making the community. Surely governments should be a little humble. Since they are largely responsible for the decay and poverty of the inner cities, are they quite sure that they are the people to put matters right? The White Paper mentions that the Rate Support Grant provides £6,000 million a year to the local authorities. But it does not draw the obvious conclusion: if matters are so bad after giving £6,000 million a year to the local authorities, must not something be seriously wrong with this form of aid? Most people, if they find after laying out huge sums of money that they are not getting value for it, do not take pride in their mistake, they look to see why the results are so poor. I suggest it is not difficult to find out. But at any rate these programmes show a welcome, if insufficient, shift in government thinking.

9 Previous Experiments in Communal Planning

Why should the change be so slow? Is there nothing to be learnt from history? I found that there was — though sometimes in forgotten corners of history.

Some of the efforts made to raise the standard of life were ambitious for their time. Many of them were all-round efforts. Most were aimed at communities, seeking to improve the prospects and not merely modify the hardships of these communities. They were made by various individuals and organisations and go back a long way.

Those who think that the welfare state was invented about 1945 should consider what was attempted by governments for the Highlands and Islands in the eighteenth century. Most people now think of the history of the Highlands for the last two hundred years at least as a tale of neglect, oppression and brutality. Great cruelty was inflicted by the Hanoverian government after the Forty-five and no one will approve of the behaviour of some Highland chiefs who became absentee landlords living on the rents of tenants for whom they did very little in the early nineteenth century. The clearances were certainly brutal and so were many other practices of landlords and merchants (the kelp industry, for instance, was hardly a model of good wages or working conditions). But there has not been much publicity given to the programme of development in roughly the last third of the eighteenth century. These measures were partly, perhaps largely, directed at breaking the clan system and merging the Highlands into the rest of Britain. In so far as this was their motive I believe it to have been wrong, and indeed unnecessary, but there were other motives as well. The government made a genuine attempt to raise the standard of life of the area. The methods employed are interesting and of considerable relevance today. For a description of them in detail the reader should go to Professor A. J. Youngson's admirable and very readable book *After the Forty-five* (Edinburgh University Press, 1973) — to which I am much indebted.

After the Forty-five forty-one estates were taken over by the barons of the Exchequer in Scotland; most of them were sold to pay creditors but thirteen were annexed to the Crown. The Act of 1752, quoted by Youngson, provided that the rent and profit from the estates were to be used solely 'for the purpose of civilizing the inhabitants upon the said estates and other parts of the Highlands and Islands of Scotland and promoting amongst them the Protestant Region, good government, Industry and Manufactures and the Principles of Duty and Loyalty to His Majesty.' Youngson gives the Commissioners (who were unpaid noblemen, crown officials and judges) credit for consistent policies: 'The Commissioners dealt with many aspects of life on the estates, notably agriculture, communications, education, manufactures and the establishment of new towns.' It has taken over two hundred years for any such comprehensive approach to be even hesitatingly considered by governments.

The Commissioners themselves built schools, recruited school masters and in some cases paid the school fees of poor children. In fact, the government and the Commissioners were far ahead of the Urban Programme in seeing that the subdivision of community life is fatal to its true development, in accepting that there are various ways of educating and in seeing that education is not something which can all be organised centrally but that it is vital to the community. If the community wishes to undertake it and believes that it can add something to the national scheme, why not let it do so, so long as standards are maintained (and maintained better than they are in some schools now).

Previous Experiments in Communal Planning

Agriculture in the Highlands was exceedingly primitive. The main crop was the cattle driven down to lowland trysts or markets but many animals did not survive the winter owing to lack of feed and there are accounts of cows, too weak to walk, being carried out to the pastures in early summer. Many highlanders lived near to starvation. The arable land, such as it was, lay largely unfenced and the rotation of crops was unknown. The Commissioners encouraged enclosure, laid down some rules for husbandry. Tenants were 'bound to fallow annually not under five aikers of ground for each plow kept by them upon their severall farms and proportionally.' Two acres were to be in red clover, and two fifths of the enclosed arable land sown to grass. The prosperity of Orkney is partly due to the introduction of clover a century later. Foxes and eagles were to be kept down. The Commissioners also encouraged forestry and supplied tens of thousands of young trees. They appointed wood keepers to prevent the stealing of timber by man and its destruction by man and beast. The Highlands were becoming denuded of trees through these agencies before the introduction of sheep. They also improved the handling of timber. Some of the highland sawmills were said to be 'perhaps the most Gothic thing of their kind in the world. The saws are one fourth of an inch thick and at the most moderate computation destroy at least one fifth of all the timber manufactured in that way.'

Housing also commanded the attention of the Commissioners. They do not appear to have introduced new types of housing but to have concentrated on trying to get existing houses repaired, or new ones built in the traditional style.

In many ways the most interesting part of the programme for Highland Development was the founding of new towns and the development of the fishing industry with which these were connected. The latter half of the eighteenth century was a period of great intellectual activity in Scotland. In particular there was much discussion of political economy, a subject in which the Scots can claim to have taken the lead. Indeed, some would say that they founded it as a study. Adam Smith published

An Inquiry into the nature and causes of the Wealth of Nations in 1776. Its title was significant and Smith was instrumental in diverting men's ideas from the pursuit of wealth and prestige for the nation to the well being of the individual. Wealth up to the middle of the eighteenth century was seen largely as the means by which nations became powerful. The whole case for mercantilism was a nationalist case, looking ultimately to the armed strength of the nation state. But Adam Smith was not an extreme exponent of laissez-faire; he was very conscious of the community, its importance and the impossibility of considering individuals as isolated atoms. As a professor of moral philosophy he was much taken up with the moral and social aspects of economy. His economic theories are based upon moral and philosophical theories, they owe something to Hume and the other philosophers busy writing and talking in the Edinburgh of his time.

It is sad that lately economics have been so intermingled with economic theory and mathematical analysis that among professional economists the subject of political economy has been pushed into second place. Adam Smith and his contemporaries saw that many so-called economic questions were political or moral questions, as is inflation today. Whether we can afford to continue the policies of the enlightenment which he preached in an age now resembling the late Middle Ages remains to be seen. The political economy of the enlightenment assumed that output per man, per machine, per nation could be raised and so the national and individual wealth increased without seizing the product of someone's labour or the territory of another. In communist states this belief is abandoned as their economy staggers from disaster to disaster.

Youngson describes in the third chapter of his book the debate which took place about the 'Aims and Principles of Economic Policy' in the later eighteenth century and the discussion of their relevance to the Highlands. Those who regret the absence of any political philosophy behind the modern welfare state should remember that there was a discussion about the philosophy behind Highland welfare schemes as early as the 1770s. It took place largely between

Previous Experiments in Communal Planning

those who wanted to pacify the Highlands and absorb them into Britain so that the state of Britain would be strengthened, and those who looked at the miserable condition of the Highlanders. These latter were followers of the new individualist, liberal political economy which maintained that the human condition could be improved by freeing trade and raising output. Hume advocated that after the minimal necessities of food and shelter had been supplied, surplus labour should be employed in manufacture. Those who examined the economy of the Highlands found that manufacturers (using that term in a wide sense) were virtually unknown, owing partly to the subsistence level of life which in Adam Smith's eyes prevented the division of labour, partly to the absence of towns or villages, and partly to various policies, such as the imposition of a salt duty, which made the proper cure of fish unprofitable.

Some of the best minds of the eighteenth century gave thought to the development of the Highlands. They selected three lines of development, all of which have a strangely modern ring. The founding of new towns, the promotion of better communications and the promotion of fishing. They rightly saw that the three interlocked. Fish were a great resource to the Highlands as they should be today. In the eighteenth century huge shoals of herring came south from Shetland and some of those which passed the west coast came close inshore among the lochs and islands of the Minch. As I mention in connection with Shetland, fishing is an occupation in many places better suited to keep the population than agriculture, at least when practised on the soil and in the climate of the Highlands proper. It can also give employment in secondary industries, such as net making, curing, etc. The herring fisheries have played a major part in several European economies. One of the changes in European life was brought about by the departure of the herring from the Baltic. The Dutch for centuries prosecuted a huge herring fishery based to a great extent on Shetland.

It was obviously sensible, therefore, to base Highland development on the natural resources of fishing, livestock rearing and forestry. Fishing and the secondary industries which were to be based on these natural resources demanded small towns, and roads and canals were essential for access to markets. Restrictive legislation was repealed and considerable sums voted. Some of the Highland landlords were involved as Commissioners, as directors of such bodies as the British Fisheries Society, and also as individual developers. The admirable development of Inverary was carried out by the Duke of Argyll, and in some of the small towns of the Moray Firth (though outside the Highlands) the good effects of enlightened paternalism in town planning can still be seen. Ullapool was one of the most complete new towns. Laid out on a rectilinear plan, the stone houses and public buildings faced the sea. Behind them were built houses with individual gardens of a reasonable size and a pier and inn were included. The commission appointed to build the Caledonian Canal employed Telford as their engineer and he also improved the main highland roads from being largely tracks for cattle droving to a standard which allowed stage coaches.

The development of the Highlands as planned and indeed to some extent executed (everything as usual proved more expensive and took longer than estimated) was on soundly based lines which appear much in advance of their time. Why did they not succeed better? Part of the answer is that they did succeed to some extent and in some places. Several of the new towns flourish today. What increase there was in industry, agriculture, fishing and the standard of life was largely due to these developments. However, they met with formidable obstacles both local and national and there was probably insufficient effort to enlist the active sympathy of the Highlanders. How far this could have been done, or what the results might have been, it is hard to say. The existing lack of education, the difficulty of language and the remnants of the clan system made it difficult to find local men with either the training or the outlook to take a prominent part. The whole development was an imported idea. Most of the native landlords continued to look to their tenants as a source of the income they needed to enable them to live elsewhere. The area could not support, at any decent standard of life and in the existing state of technology, the population which already

Previous Experiments in Communal Planning 137

existed. The industrial revolution as it gathered pace drew labour to Glasgow and the Lowlands. In every slump, such as that of the kelp industry, the Highlands suffered severely and bad harvests still meant starvation.

The lesson must be that even well considered schemes for the all-round improvement of a community require support for a long period. Economic changes have an inevitable effect in the short run. The discovery of oil in the North Sea must today mean a recasting of plans for the islands affected. A balance has to be struck between the longer term requirement of keeping the fundamental characteristics of an area in mind, while adjusting to changing circumstances in the short term. There was not and still is not a political agency capable of doing this. We find again that it is attitudes which take longest to change. And, in spite of the good intentions of many of the bodies involved in Highland development, it was not until the Crofting Acts at the end of the nineteenth century that the Highlander had any security of tenure. These Acts, though they were a godsend in at least guaranteeing some rights to the crofters and checking the inhuman exploitation of many estates, to a great extent froze the rural economy. Here again we see the difficulty of balancing the conservative instincts, which are important to any community, with the need for innovation and change. In many unsatisfactory or impoverished communities, innovation for the individual prepared to innovate means removal from the community. In Britain this has often been too easy for the good of the less fortunate districts. It is the very difficulty of leaving places like Faroe which has forced the Faroese to make the best of their homes.

As there was no repetition of the Forty-five and no area comparable to the Highlands, the experiments were neither followed up nor repeated. But there were other experiments in building communities.

One of the most famous of these was New Lanark. Founded in 1782 by David Dale and Richard Arkwright, a mile or so outside Lanark itself, New Lanark was indeed a new community. The original workers came from the Highlands, from impoverished lowland towns and villages, and as pauper children despatched to the mills by the Poor Law authorities. Already in Dale's time New Lanark had some features which were an improvement on most satanic mills but when Owen took over it was a poor place — poor in wages, housing and the general conditions of life. He therefore had to start by attacking the causes of misery and stated in his 'Address to the Inhabitants of New Lanark': 'My attention was ever directed to remove, as I could prepare means for their removal, such of the immediate causes as were perpetually creating misery among you.' He enlarged some houses and built others. He improved sanitation and checked thieving. He had to behave in a paternal, indeed autocratic fashion. He was intensely unpopular but gradually his popularity increased and as the living conditions improved he unfolded his great design. This was no less than what he described as 'a fundamental reconstruction both of human character and by its means, of existing social and economic relationships'.

Like Arismende at Mondragon Owen attached great importance to education. Much (too much in the estimation of some of his partners) of the profits went into founding schools, including playschools for infants, and what we should now call further education. These schools had a practical and artistic bent. The curriculum included dancing, singing, nature study and military exercises. For adults there was accommodation for reading, writing, playing and talking. Lectures and concerts were provided. Unlike Arismende he was opposed to formal religion. In the mills themselves he no longer employed pauper apprentices, he raised wages and shortened hours. But even at work 'character building' went on. Beside each worker hung a tally with four sides each coloured differently, each colour told of the behaviour of the worker during the previous day. (He did not believe, however, in punishment.) When the mills had to close for four months owing to the high price of cotton all the workers were kept on full pay. Owen achieved remarkable fame in his day. He travelled all over Europe preaching his ideas and visiting schools. His doctrines were actually laid before a conference of the great powers at Aix-la-Chapelle:

The grand question now to be solved is, not how a

sufficiency of wealth can be produced, but how excess of riches which may be most easily created, may be generally distributed throughout society advantageously for all and without prematurely disturbing the existing institutions or arrangements in any country.

Owen and New Lanark still have lessons to teach us. The workers at New Lanark did not participate much in the running of their affairs, but much of Owen's popularity was due to his tolerance. No one suffered because they disagreed with him. He benefited too from the tolerance of his eccentricities and antipathy to religion, a tolerance which an aristocratic age extended more easily than our own. The Czar visited New Lanark and Queen Victoria's father, the Duke of Kent, was one of his staunchest supporters. Owen proved the importance of education. He showed that how people lived, what he called the internal character of the town, was important as well as where they lived and their conditions of work. The New Lanark workers preferred to work hard for shorter hours. They seem to have appreciated the care he took for their leisure.

The New Lanark experiment was in many ways behind its time. It was in some ways more suited to the idea of man held by the philosophers and political economists of the later eighteenth century, than to the industrial world of the nineteenth century. Owen may be seen as trying to do with his mills what the more enlightened eighteenth-century landlords did with their estates. He was also a genius, with many saintly qualities. He was defeated in the end by the climate of his world and the demand for the distribution of profits by his partners (not to mention some opposition by the clergy). But perhaps the wheel may turn again and his insistence upon play, self-expression, dancing, enjoyment and tolerance may once more be appreciated.

The most interesting experiments in urban planning from New Lanark to the Garden Cities were carried out by individuals. New Lanark itself and such other communities as Port Sunlight and the Rowntree village at York were linked to particular firms. But the structure of British government would have hampered similar experiments by the state even if the philosophy of politicians would have countenanced any such thing. In central government, work, housing, education, transport, were all in different ministries. At local level the authorities had neither the will nor the means to carry out this type of community development.

Yet it remains strange considering the success of various private experiments that little attention was paid to the way our cities were expanded in the nineteenth century. The century had before it the admirable examples of city extension at Edinburgh and Bath. The eighteenth century had developed a style of architecture beautiful to look at, easy to live in and simple to design and construct. What went wrong with the profession of architecture? The spirit of rational pragmatic enlightenment which was behind the reform of government should have been well suited to laying out housing with grace and simplicity. The terrace and the square were there for all to see and copy, yet in the last hundred or so years cities have been ruined by inhuman planning and made hideous with huge, heavy and shapeless buildings. If some of these were inevitable they need not have been erected on the corpses of their predecessors and not all buildings needed to be gigantic match boxes. Some of the worst architecture of all has probably been among the relatively small houses and tenements of the public authority estates.

The roots of the decline seem to lie in mass production, bad taste resulting in the training of bad architects, failures in education and lately in the gradual draining away of humanity and personal judgement. I regard this decline in town, village and country as important to a proper structure of social services for reasons which I will develop later. Here, all I want to note is that it happened and as it has happened we have to live with its legacy both in actual buildings and in attitudes. Towards the end of the nineteenth century public parks were provided, but even though some standards of drainage were imposed and some cleansing undertaken, the population lived in dank and cramped conditions, for the most part unable to reach the countryside, to lie on the grass, to play, to sleep in a deck chair or see new sights. No wonder then that the motor car was popular. Along with such shops as Marks &

Spencer and Woolworths, I regard Henry Ford and Lord Nuffield as great social workers.

I must remark at this stage the curious history of thought and art in the nineteenth century. The years which began the debasement of our cities produced many of our best poets and writers. If we had no artists of the standing of the French Impressionists, nevertheless our visual arts were creditable. This artistic success lasted throughout the nineteenth century and after the second world war: from Dickens to Graham Greene, from Turner to Henry Moore, from the makers of early nineteenth-century china to Mary Quant. In furniture and clothes there have always been some notable designers at work. Attention has been rivetted by the spectacular vulgarity of some Victorian design, the ostentation of the Edwardians and the ugliness of the later twentieth-century buildings and furnishings, but that has not been the whole story. Looking back, therefore, it would have seemed possible that a combination of the charity which the ages of reason and reform brought to bear on government, with the eye and heart of the romantics from Coleridge to Henry James and Yeats, might have bred a rather successful attitude to living. The hunger of the working man for knowledge, the high personal standards which existed alongside wretchedness and its companions of drink and squalor might have led to conditions, as the country grew richer, of considerable satisfaction. William Morris and the Pre-Raphaelites were well-known and exhibited different values from those of mass production or indeed early nineteenth-century Utilitarianism. The century and a quarter from 1800 to 1930 was one of great variety, indeed it was a century in which eccentrics flourished as profusely as ever in British history. Along with professionalism and the division of labour it produced unacademic artists of great ability such as Blake (and even Lear) and many academics of wide general learning.

To some extent life was much more satisfactory in the time of our great-grandfathers than is now supposed. But the satisfaction, though I suspect not by any means confined to the rich or middle class, did not spread through more than a small proportion of the nation. The social services were dominated, and as I shall argue to a large extent still are, by the successors of Bentham. I write as an admirer of Bentham but there is some truth in the saying that he was concerned with the mechanism of life rather than life itself. The 'greatest happiness of the greatest number' is an excellent idea. If politicians would only content themselves with working towards that they might achieve much more than they do by pursuing more high-sounding aims. But happiness does not only consist of the removal of grievances and the attainment of a subsistence level of life. The trouble is not that Bentham, Chadwick and Shaftesbury were in any sense wrong; it is that the tradition they started, while abundantly right in their time, persisted into times when it became inappropriate and when it led to a proliferation of acts and services which are unnecessarily complicated and choke the growth of new thought.

The force of the tradition which innovators in the field of community development and town planning had to meet is illustrated by the fate of Ebenezer Howard and Sir Patrick Geddes who, with others, produced valuable thought on the cities more than seventy years ago. Howard's book *Garden Cities of Tomorrow* (Ed. F. J. Osborn, Faber & Faber, 1946) has never received the attention it deserves. Its author does not even win an entry in the *Dictionary of National Biography* yet Howard can claim to be the father of the New Towns. He pointed out that the big cities were too large; he advocated dispersal into towns, big enough to support services etc. but small enough for people to walk to work and to reach open country on foot. A feature of his scheme was not only to supply space for gardens in the town but to marry town and country. The land of the town was to be publicly owned but every type of economic initiative was to be encouraged within, including co-operatives.

Another of his suggestions was that the bigger cities were to be divided into wards, preferably of around five thousand inhabitants who were to form communities of their own — an idea which might today be applied to such cities as Liverpool. In Howard's work can be traced many of the ideas which have been put into practice since the war: in addition to the New Towns he was also the first person to

Previous Experiments in Communal Planning 143

suggest a Green Belt and included re-cycling — for example the use of manure. As far as I am concerned what I find particularly sympathetic is his conception of the community as self-developing, his blending of different occupations and his desire to mix different classes as well as his treatment of the community in all its aspects, work, living and leisure. He was less paternal than Owen but then he was looking at the world seventy or so years later. His approach was both idealistic and practical. He was no admirer of the primitive state of man, though heavily aware of the importance of guarding the beauty and life of the countryside. Seeing the pass to which great areas of the cities had reached even in his time he did not propose to scrap the idea of a city but to give it new life. Some of his proposals do not now seem to me to be right but his approach with its blend of the over-all role of the community (which would, if he had his way, own the land) and the encouragement of freedom and individuality in commerce and art seems to me entirely right. Letchworth was the outcome of his ideas. He had, of course, collaborators and he and the other pioneers of the Garden City were lucky to be able to encourage such architects as Norman Shaw.

F. J. Osborn in his preface to his edition of *Garden Cities of Tomorrow* writes about the neglect of Howard by academics. He attributes this to the simplicity of Howard's use of English, 'His book avoids technical terminology, displays no great learning, contains little historical or demographical documentation'. I am afraid he is right and as language affects thought and thus action, the jargon of modern sociologists is a symptom and cause of some attitudes. We should heed not only the generosity, but the language of Swift, who 'Gave the little wealth he had to build a house for fools and mad.' I suppose Clare, Cowper and perhaps Blake were mad — but not mentally deficient. I doubt if St Francis would relish being called underprivileged or, worse, socially deprived. The word 'Community' itself has become tarnished, as has the word 'Society,' but I can think of no others to describe what I mean.

I do not share Howard's enthusiasm for driving wide

boulevards through the centre of the city. They make his aim of work, shopping and home (which I discuss later in this chapter) being within walking distance of each other more difficult to achieve. They are certainly unsuitable for some climates, nor does everyone want a garden. The Champs Elysées is exhilarating but I prefer New York to Washington and before it was over-run by strip tease Soho was one of the attractive districts of London. His suggestion that the centre of the city should be left open, might well be tried, perhaps in Liverpool: 'In the centre is a circular space containing about five and a half acres, laid out as a beautiful and well-watered garden and surrounding this garden, each standing in its own ample grounds, are the public buildings'. An ideal which ought to be considered, not for everywhere, but as a possibility for some inner cities.

I have seen it suggested that the scale on which Howard worked has been radically changed by the motor car. People, it is said, can now easily cover much greater distances. If we are due for scarcity of oil we may have to revise our thoughts about distance. But, even now, it is not always just a question of how far you can get in a given time, it matters how you cover the distance. Men can walk or bicycle no further or faster than they could. Walking is enjoyable in its own right. If you like towns, to walk about them, to look at the people and the shops is part of their attraction; it also enables the walker to talk to people and take an interest in what is going on. You cannot enjoy this pleasure from bus, train or motor car.

Howard was right to press for balanced communities and for freedom within the limitations of a unified city:

> This principle of freedom holds good with regard to manufacturers and others who have established themselves in the town. These manage their affairs in their own way subject, of course, to the general law of the land and subject to the provision of sufficient space for workmen and reasonable sanitary conditions. Even in regard to such matters as water, lighting and telephone communication — which a municipality, if efficient and honest, is certainly the best and most natural body to supply — no rigid or absolute monopoly is sought and if any private corporation or any body of individuals

proved itself capable of supplying on more advantageous terms either the whole town or a section of it with these or any commodities, the supply of which was taken up by the corporation, this would be allowed.

We have failed to draw a line between the general rules under which a country, a city, a country district, must operate and the free choice which must be left to its members. We have allowed the principles of liberalism as inherited from the eighteenth and developed by the nineteenth century to wither. We have failed to build on the work of the eighteenth-century developers in the Highlands, of Owen and Howard. We have called in the state, not as an impartial arbitrator, nor as the protector of the poor or weak but increasingly as the weapon of powerful interests, to take over more and more of our life. As a result liberals meet the dilemma: do they themselves form an 'interest', like a trade association, do they use the state to further their interests or do they persevere with the ideal of a liberal society even though their very liberation is exploited by those who would wreck a liberal community?

Howard also put forward interesting proposals for raising finance for his city by rent-rate. His ideas are similar to those of Henry George and the land-taxers. More attention should have been paid to the land-taxers but whether or not their policies should have been put into practice as proposed, there can be no doubt that our Rent Acts and housing policies generally since the first world war have been a failure. They have been more than a failure, they have prevented at least three generations from getting decent housing and they have contributed to the degradation of the cities. Howard was concerned primarily to reduce the size of existing cities and although his proposals were something like an admission of defeat they did — and perhaps still do — have something to contribute, particularly his suggestions on finance. His vision of a partnership between town and country may be realised, albeit in a small way, in Ed Berman's urban farms. Though for a complete range of activities, cities bigger than his are needed, he was right to criticise the size of some British cities and to point out the advantages of small towns.

Nevertheless, if Howard is to take some of the credit for

ideas in town planning which lately have received the serious consideration they deserve he must also take some of the blame for a pernicious vice of the planners. This vice is to turn their backs on living, existing communities and to evade the complexities of towns gradually built up by centuries of growth. Instead of grappling with the fascinating needs of existing towns, they either demand virgin sites or they ignore what is there — even when it is excellent. I am thinking of the ludicrous and barbaric proposal by a leading planner to carry a fly-over across Princes Street Gardens in Edinburgh and even, I believe, across the Royal Mile. On a smaller scale we have the sightless building for the Royal College of Physicians of London, blind as a prison to the view over Regents Park. Modern architects are accused of putting up buildings which are too big for their neighbours or which clash with them in style. Though accusation is often justified diversity is not always fatal: the campanile of St Mark's in Venice is out of scale with its neighbours and many agreeable streets have buildings of many ages. What is inexcusable is not only to put ugly buildings up but to make no use of the possibilities of their site and surroundings. It is a lack of imagination, or perhaps just an inability to look around them, which cripples so many planners and architects.

The Garden Cities, unlike New Lanark, were peopled largely by the middle classes (though Howard hoped for mixed communities) and they owed something to the ideas of William Morris. If only the Left in Britain had paid more attention to Morris, Ebenezer Howard and above all to Robert Owen, we might have a more satisfactory and beautiful country today. Though the chief claim of the Garden Cities was that they were pleasant to live in, they aspired to something more. Bedford Park, London, for instance, would become, it was hoped, a home for artists, actors and writers and indeed several, including Yeats, lived there. They were founded as communities, they aimed at a high standard of architecture, lay-out and life. Though it has been out of fashion, their architecture is coming back into favour. It has always, by its finish, the touch of individuals of taste, and a certain civilised arrangement, been superior to most building which has succeeded it.

Garden Cities included schools and, at Bedford Park at least, an arts college. In spite of Howard's hopes their main purpose was residential. The houses which employers, like the Rowntrees or the Levers, built for their workers were adjacent to their factories but the housing was to be separate from the place of work, nor were other occupations encouraged to set up in it. Commuting, the separation of living and leisure from work, grew with the growth of the middle classes, the expansion and degradation of cities, the unpleasant sights and smells associated with much Victorian manufacture and improvements in transport. The physical lay-out of the community now demands fresh thought, especially when, as I have suggested earlier, Owen's 'grand question' may need serious consideration, and when more leisure, which his workers so ardently desired, may be within the reach of those who want it.

While I believe in breaking down the division between work and leisure, to have a place of work is an asset. An office or workshop is a haven and to have a regular rhythm between home and place of work is satisfactory to many people. In fact many people, while quite capable of enjoying some leisure at their place of work, find it impossible to work at home. Lastly, companionship is agreeable.

I am not suggesting that a place of work should be far from home — walking distance is ideal. Nor am I suggesting that it should be a place for nothing but work — just the opposite. But what is the man or woman whose main employment has finished for the day, week or year, to do there? Of course, some people will be incapable of finding anything to do but unless the human race has lost all initiative, curiosity, skill and ambition — in fact, everything which makes us human — many people will find self-employment. Ed Berman's urban farms are a case in point. Self-employment must include, indeed may largely consist of, work for the community. We must involve far more people in building their own community. As I want to see every community not merely brought up to some minimum standard but aiming very high, I should like to enlist in community work experts and artists of high skill. When I say work for the community, therefore, I mean more than, say, voluntary assistance to the old, important as this may be. Unfortunately, the results of public patronage by local authorities and bureaucrats have been disappointing. Some great architecture has been bespoken under republics — though more often, as in Venice, by rich individuals or churches in the republic. But one only has to travel in Eastern Europe to see the sad results of state control on art. Inequality seems necessary to art.

In the visual arts Britain's reputation during the fifties stood as high internationally as it ever has done. Some credit at least for this should go to the art schools. They were a remarkable example of what can be achieved when energies are released and originality encouraged. For a time at least they escaped the bureaucratic straitjacket. They should have been, and still could be, brought into the stream of community development. For art is central to human life. They are one way in which we could maintain a streak of originality, of non-conformity. Their pupils could be enlisted to decorate and furnish many drab townscapes. Art transforms the way we see and feel things. Communities should not be allowed, but compelled, to draw up their own planning procedures and standards as far as the lay-out of streets, lamps, gardens, fountains and the facades of houses are concerned.

The embellishment of our surroundings must surely be reckoned a public good though often most successfully assisted by individuals. This requires public funds which are at the disposal of a community. It could be argued that the money for parks, galleries, libraries, even squares and promenades, could be raised by charging. Indeed, to many people these seem to be the activities for which charging is most appropriate. I am not so sure. I certainly would make some charge for the upkeep and running costs of libraries, museums and galleries. Public libraries are much taken up with lending detective stories and the like and most people at present rates of wages can well afford to pay for these. There is indeed no reason why novels should be on the rates any more than sweets but I do not believe that the capital cost of first-class buildings for libraries, museums

Previous Experiments in Communal Planning 149

and galleries could be easily met by charging in any form. And I regard the existence of galleries and theatres as public goods even, in a rather undefined way, for those who never visit them.

10 Theory and Practice — Greenock

In 1971 I got together a small meeting in London to discuss what the various community projects which had sprung up in the last few years could do, what should be their aim, how they might co-operate and how they might be financed. At this meeting Sir Claus Moser, who was then a statistician in the Cabinet Office, pointed out that though everywhere in the country conditions might have improved yet the poorer areas were still, compared to the rich areas, badly off. By every statistic — income per head, health, length of life, educational success, housing, etc. — the differences, say, between the Hartlepools and Bournemouth was very large and hardly decreasing. This we have seen is all too true.

This fitted in with my own feeling about the failure of the policies designed to improve the prospects of the depressed areas. Immense sums had been spent under various Acts on regional development, grants to special areas, the social and health services, housing and other policies designed to assist these areas. They obdurately lagged behind.

One of the main causes of this depression is obvious but seldom taken seriously as something which needs to be changed. I refer to centralisation of government. Wherever a main centre is set up it will attract people of enterprise and ambition, it will act as a magnet right through the country. This is true of any centre of government; it gives employment, it attracts business of all kinds. It is particularly true in a country which has become as centralised as Britain. Not only politicians and civil servants flock to the seat of government: everyone who wants or needs to be near the fount of power and influence settles near the government, everyone who must do business with the central authorities, everyone seeking prestige wants an address at the centre of decision-making. And, of course, at the centre things happen, life is more interesting, people feel close to important events. Entertainment, sport, new innovations, these happen at the centre. And so new businesses, new services, are sucked in.

A hundred years ago a city like Dundee was far more self-sufficient than now. Numerous firms had their head offices there, decisions were taken there. The city had its own social life, its own entertainment. Big ships constantly came and went from its docks. You only have to read the local paper to see how much more important were local events. If this was true of Dundee, how much more did Liverpool, Manchester, Birmingham and Leeds make their own lives and form centres of local attraction and interest? Once amalgamations of all sorts took place and the fatal fashion for bigger units took hold, the parts of Britain away from London were drained of their blood and indeed beheaded, as head offices left for the South-East. The peasant economy, as it has been called, was the result.

So the British proceeded in their usual way: instead of trying to disseminate power and encourage many centres of influence they allowed the cause of the trouble to continue but tried to off-set it or plaster it over. Grants were made to firms to counter the pull of the South-East. Firms were paid to do what they would not have done for their own advantage. But no effort was made to make dispersal more advantageous, no effort was made to disperse government or its main agencies. The headquarters of the nationalised industries, even of the coal industry, remained in London. The BBC in particular allowed television national news and commentary to concentrate not only on London but on the west end of London. The grants and loans induced some industries to set up in Scotland, Wales, the North and West but the factories were mostly branch factories. The pattern in the cities, encouraged by zoning under the planning laws, was to denude their centres of industry and head offices remained in London.

The depressed, development or special area policies also suffered from another general fault in British legislation: they did not attempt to involve the local people in shaping or operating them. They were themselves practising the very centralisation which they were trying to combat. The local authorities in the regions, of course, competed to attract industry but the grants were essentially handed down from London.

The social services were also handed down. Neither the recipients nor the local community were involved in their design. The social services, too, are a centralised operation and, with some exceptions, the same services are offered in Shetland, Worcester, London and Cornwall.

Ever since the first Poor Laws, the main object of these services has been to relieve or ameliorate conditions which have already arisen — before you can get the payments under national assistance you have to be poor, you have to be unemployed to get unemployment pay and sick to get sickness benefit, and so on. In fact, they are not preventative. One of the successes of medicine has been in prevention — in removing the conditions in which disease flourishes. Yet, as Sir Claus Moser pointed out, in facing the general conditions of life the chances of requiring help were much greater in some areas than in others. We had failed to eradicate the blacker spots in which social and economic troubles flourished.

Though I do not believe that equality of wealth for all is necessary or desirable I do believe that children, wherever born, should have a good start in life.

I am convinced of the need to achieve greater equality between different communities within the country. Here we run into the confusion between equality and similarity: because there should be greater equality in the sum total of what life has to offer in different parts of the country that does not mean life in each different part should be similar. A very obvious example is the difference between life in the town and life in the country. They both have advantages but cannot be made the same. However, from the point of view of a country trying to provide opportunities and decent lives for its citizens there are difficulties in treating different places in a different way. For instance, if densely populated areas have television, remote and thinly populated areas demand it too. They demand their share of public goods, education, roads, etc., and often go on to claim that if private undertakings will not supply other goods then the state should provide these as well. In some cases the problem can be solved by imposing standards which must be reached, for example in hygiene; yet even this, appropriate only in a fairly narrow range of cases, is not easy to administer in a way which allows the variety of different areas to blossom. However, while aware of the difficulties, I maintain that the characteristics of each district must be taken into account. The aim must be to allow each to reach its full potential. All cannot be excellent in the same way but all should be as excellent as their circumstances allow in the way which comes naturally to them.

I say excellent deliberately. Going back to the days when it was considered wrong for the Poor Laws to make people comfortable the social services have aimed at a minimum. They have been designed to keep people above dire poverty but below what they would reasonably aspire to, if lack of employment, health, or intelligence did not retard them. In so far as the social services are personal services this probably must be so, or at least in many respects it should be so. If I work hard I should be allowed to get both as an inducement and reward some things denied to those who work less hard or less successfully. Though it may seem harsh to impose this difference even on those who through no fault of their own work less successfully, the consequences of paying individuals out of work at, say, the top rate of wages of those who are in work, could be harmful to the country and unfair to individuals. The remedy is to make everyone's start in life more equal. Already by one of the countless side winds of galloping inflation we have what has been described as the poverty trap. The city centres and the housing estates are also poverty traps. At whatever level the personal services should be set, communal services should aim high. We do not want to perpetuate second or third rate communities. We do not want to drive people to emigrate from their home communities by deliberately keeping their standard low.

A further feature of the present social services is that it is only by keeping supplementary benefits or unemployment pay low that there can be any incentive to do without them. The health service cures patients in order that they may return to work and so better themselves, but there is little in many of the other services to help the recipients to help themselves.

All these considerations seem to me to point to the need for a new departure in the age-long effort to give better lives to the less well-off; and also to demonstrate that the well-off would benefit from such a departure. The departure should reaffirm that only individuals can have value but that individuals cannot be isolated, they are individuals in a community. Whether they can make good their latent potential and reach those states of mind which philosophers such as G. E. Moore, and to some extent most religions, claim as valuable, depends to some extent upon the circumstances of their lives and the communities in which they live. I must constantly make it clear that I claim neither that the community is the only influence, nor that its influence means that we can dispense entirely with individual social services. They should, after a national minimum income, be confined largely to services for the physically handicapped. I would hope therefore to reduce the need for them drastically. But I would claim that the state can act upon the community and it is in this direction we should now look.

It is in this direction that we may find an easier path to the reconciliation of the desire for equality and the obvious and decisive contradiction of it by the inequalities between individuals. For while inequality is in some respects innate and unalterable in the individual, this is much less the case in the community. We cannot create as attractive a life in the depths of the Antarctic as in the Mediterranean but communities have flourished in all sorts of conditions, geographical and cultural. Human beings are a mixture of contentment and discontent; they crave security and adventure; they are conservative and sometimes reluctant to move yet often restless. Communities, therefore, are unpredictable: we cannot control them but we can help them to make the best of themselves. We certainly should not try to confine people to the community in which they happen to grow up but by helping each community to develop itself as far as it can in the direction it wants to go we can offer individuals both a better chance in life and a greater variety of chances, so long as they can move between communities. Further, we meet the demand that children who are not responsible for the circumstances into which they are born can be more generously treated. While learning the lesson that a free market with proper rules is essential both to a free and prospering country, we should make its benefits more widely enjoyed. We should emphasise that within a good community economic forces should not be allowed to invade every sphere of life whether under the cloak of socialism or free enterprise. The money changers must not take over the Temple. Nor should we heed the advice of Belloc's Modern Traveller on the treatment of missionaries:

> The present way is an abuse
> of Economic Forces;
> They preach but they do not produce.
> Observe how I would change it.
> I'd have the Missionary lent
> Upon a plot of land,
> A sum at twenty-five per cent,
> An ever-present fear of debt
> Would make them work like horses.

With these considerations in mind I made a broadcast explaining my views on community development. I then asked for anyone interested in carrying out an experiment on these lines to get in touch with me. I had at once two responses, one from Councillor Ronald Young in Greenock and the other from Dr Dowle in the Northmavine district of Shetland. These seemed to me suitable places for an experiment.

Greenock is a city of some seventy thousand inhabitants with a personality of its own. It has its own daily newspaper. It has a variety of industries — sugar refining, IBM, shipbuilding and related trades, and a container port.

Yet for many years it has had a high percentage of unemployment so that it contains families which have been at best sporadically employed for two or three generations. Children all too often move straight from school to the dole. It has a marvellous site banked up above the Clyde facing the Highlands to the north and backed by moorland to the south but some of its housing estates perched on the higher reaches of the hill which runs down to the river for the most part lack beauty, convenience or suitability. Built either between the wars or soon after the second world war, they are a sad monument to the inefficiency of architects and the dead hand of professional planners. Some of these estates are well cared for with flourishing gardens but others are in a state of almost unbelievable dilapidation. Wages are high (particularly in the container port), everyone is now educated for at least ten years, every local authority has a large budget and a growing host of officials. It is not as though the Clyde valley was in one of the more impoverished parts of Africa. It is not as though the public authorities were entitled to only a miniscule part of our wealth. It is not as though the tenants were down-trodden, ill-paid serfs. Most of the richest workers in Greenock live outside the city but everyone today, even those on supplementary benefit, receives an income which allows them some luxuries.

If my idea was to become reality then the richer and more successful people who made their living in Greenock had to be lured back. Greenock schools must become so attractive that they would send their children to them. Life in Greenock must be made so stimulating that they would spend their time there rather than in Glasgow or London. I stress that Greenock already had much to offer. Its City Council attracted men of distinction; the Scotts, the Lithgows and other shipbuilders were among the best in Britain and in the case of the Scotts by far the oldest (the Scott family have been building ships at Greenock for some two hundred and fifty years). I stress, too, that neither I, nor Ronald Young, nor anyone associated with us, expected to be able to change it at once. All I hoped to do was to make a small indent on conventional thinking, to sound out how far our ideas had support.

Theory and Practice – Greenock

The Joseph Rowntree Social Service Trust generously granted us £7,500 a year for seven years with occasional increments for inflation. This was hardly enough to change one tenement, let alone a city. But the project was meant to be an experiment, we were dipping one toe into the water to take the temperature. Ronald, who in addition to being a local councillor, was a lecturer at the Paisley College of Technology, brought not only knowledge of Greenock but some resources from the College. We were also very lucky in engaging the aid of Mr Robert Winter, the Director of Social Work. But obviously we could only wield a teaspoon in our effort to shift a mountain of ingrained attitudes towards community life and the social services.

The first thing that became obvious — and it remained true throughout the experiment — was a difficulty I had often met before: stimulating people not only to air grievances but to innovate and improve, to take a positive part in political activity. It is almost impossible to get people in Britain to look ahead or to avoid repeating the mistakes of the past. The notion that community services should be as important to the rich as the poor is incomprehensible. The notion that they themselves could do very much is equally incomprehensible. We met with some suspicion: was not the whole enterprise a waste of money? Who were these Rowntree people or their local representatives, as we appeared to be? We were in fact nothing of the kind. But suspicion was not the most serious obstacle. In so far as anyone was interested in community work, they assumed that it must be for the poorest areas. Unconsciously it was assumed to be the successor of nineteenth-century charitable endeavour. It would be concerned with the raising of grievances with the local authority and other organs of the government. Its positive efforts would be directed towards such peripheral activities as organising play groups and tenants' associations, both then fashionable.

We formed a small committee. We advertised for someone prepared to live and work in Greenock and received a fairly large number of applicants. From these the local committee selected Miss Barbara Darcy. She was installed in a flat among the decaying tenements of

Strone-Maukinhill. So we started. And once it was obvious that we must make a start on a small scale, since everyone expected us to deal with the shoddy areas of the housing estates, we confined our efforts to Strone and Maukinhill and, as far as I was concerned, the grander vision of an all-Greenock effort was shelved.

I still believe that this decision was inevitable but mistaken. It wasn't even really a decision, the alternative could hardly be considered. As most of the lessons of the Greenock experiment were negative it is worth pausing and considering this first negative, unconscious assumption that such schemes are schemes for the poor, the inhabitants of the poorer parts of our cities, that they are in fact still tinctured by the assumptions that they can only be ameliorative, that the standard they aim at cannot be very high. Indeed, within Greenock the scheme failed to break away from those handicaps which I have tried to diagnose in the existing personal social services.

Why was this? We are all aware now that the new housing schemes of the last fifty years have created 'concrete deserts'. So they have. It needed nothing much else besides common sense to see this would happen. But common sense has been conspicuously lacking in the management of our affairs, squeezed out I fear by some types of education. As a result, any feeling of common interests is lacking. The people have no stake in their neighbourhood; they do not own their houses, they cannot even repair them — that is the job of the local authority (a job which in Greenock it was often incapable of carrying out through lack of craftsmen). The surroundings are rank grass and broken railings. The disastrous effects of current housing policies were clear and have been clear for three generations at least.

Almost every family which lives in Strone and Maukinhill wants to leave. They therefore have no wish to improve the area. Except that it provides housing there is no other reason to remain there. There are no factories and little work, few shops or places of entertainment. The need to take into account all aspects of life, housing, the layout of the neighbourhood, employment and education was clearly illustrated. Relief of poverty is not enough. Added to this was the lack of transport. Strone and Maukinhill lie to the south of the heart of Greenock up a steep hill which forms one of the banks of the Clyde Valley; although the distance in mileage is not great they feel removed from the centres of life and the seat of local government (this has probably been made worse by the creation of the large Strathclyde region). In physical terms the walk is quite tiring, especially for old people, yet there is little public transport. So here too we have another factor — transport.

The effect of raising the school-leaving age without providing adequate resources can also be seen. Indeed the difficulties of teachers in handling boys and girls from such a neighbourhood and keeping their interest for ten or more years are great. One day Ronald Young and I were contemplating a forlorn enclave in the area where a burn struggles through rubbish down a cleft too steep for housing. It could have been made an agreeable place but was, like so much else, abandoned to rubbish and neglect. In it there were a range of wooden sheds housing racing pigeons. As we wondered what could be done I noticed some boys and girls trying to set fire to these sheds by stuffing lighted newspapers under them. I drew Ronald's attention to this undesirable project. He pointed out that I was a bigger man than he was, shouldn't I remonstrate with them? In return, I reminded him that they were his constituents. With courage and public spirit he accosted them. When he did so they very reasonably agreed to desist — then asked what they could do instead. Some of them should have been at school for the rate of truancy is high. All were bored. The boredom of much life in areas such as this is pervasive and cannot be relieved by cash payments alone.

So this network of deficiencies in living conditions, workshops, transport, education and amusement interlocks to create thoroughly unsatisfactory living conditions as it does in parts of many other cities. Individual welfare services do not touch it. Protest, if it is merely a demand that someone else should do something, is not enough.

We had hoped that by putting Barbara Darcy at the people of Greenock's disposal to act, so to speak, as their civil servant, we might strike a spark. But the tinder was not ready. I see signs of a similar deadness elsewhere. The Young Volunteer Force met the same obstacles; from Liverpool and parts of Yorkshire came much the same stories. This is not to be wondered at, even in the most lively of communities the active participants are few. It is a Liberal delusion that the whole human race wants to sit around discussing how its work, or life, or the organisation of public services should be run. For many people the right to protest is enough. It was, after all, the basis of the English parliamentary system, one of the oldest and in many ways most successful. In communities long used to misfortune participation has even less attraction. The daily hazards and chores are enough. Dependence becomes a habit ingrained by the constant need to be a client of bureaux, social workers and housing officials, employers or union officials. All too often the rules of our society prohibit enterprises or co-operation. Tenants may not alter houses or even carry out major repairs. If you work you may be worse off. There is the 'we' and 'they' division. 'They' being the authorities in all their numerous manifestations. Often those who stand for office are met with the question, 'What is the good of voting?', 'What has the government, or the local authority, or a particular political party, done for us?' They have probably done a great deal but while 'they' are despised, 'they' are also expected to do everything and only their failures are remembered.

I started at the level of a practical experiment because, having been a politician for twenty years, I found that speeches and arguments seemed to be having less and less effect. Endless enquiries often dignified by the name of research are carried on by the holders of arts degrees. They are not intellectuals in that their general intellectual capacity is not always high. They are usually academic in the sense that they have no practical experience but, though many of them are attached to universities and polytechnics, they are by no means all qualified to be academics. Often such enquiries confuse common sense, cause delay and almost always end up by recommending the expenditure of more resources and usually the setting up of some new board, commission or branch of the civil service. I rather despaired of working from the top, so, start from the other end, I thought.

There was indeed some encouragement in Greenock. The local committee and their excellent workers were particularly successful over an educational experiment at the local technical college. There seems to be a healthy appetite for further education.

There also grew up a considerable degree of goodwill towards the project. I can't say that it was widely known nor perhaps understood. But I think a very small seed germinated. If it did, I believe the reason is the desire for self respect which is undermined by many modern ways of life. The social services themselves contribute to this lack of self respect. That they are sometimes aware of this is shown by such attempts at flattery as calling old age pensioners senior citizens — though this kind of nonsense is also the result of the absurd prestige seeking which insists that rat catchers are rodent officers and every secretary an executive. Anyway, it makes the situation worse. We did at least try to behave as servants of the community and not its masters. We left as much initiative as we could to the local people.

Another obvious lesson confirmed by Greenock is the danger of the career structure. As we become more and more divided into various bureaucracies, so each human being regards him or herself (and is regarded by bureaucrats) simply as a member of this or that profession or trade union. He or she is not expected to live and work and become attached to a community. They must be forever thinking about the next step up the ladder and their loyalty is demanded by their bureaucracy. Loyalty today is a horizontal affair all too often. It is not to a firm, a hospital, a neighbourhood; it is to a union which runs across many firms and institutions. This makes it all the more necessary to encourage local and voluntary participation. Social workers, I read, are to form themselves into a profession. I fear that means that they will be further divorced from ordinary people and increasingly taken up with the salaries, prestige, pecking order and public relations of their profession. The General Practitioner has no career structure. We must redouble our efforts to increase the democratic, voluntary, unstructured participation in local affairs and the running of community services.

The running of services was outside the scope of the Greenock project. We did not therefore learn how far the community was willing to undertake such services, nor did we get much information from local people about new services required. But some were obviously needed.

For the repair of the large number of flats and houses for which it was responsible, it was obvious that the Council had a quite inadequate team of workers. This seems strange when unemployment in Greenock is high. There appear to be three remedies, not mutually exclusive. One is to encourage the tenants to buy their houses and look after them. Secondly, to let them remain as tenants but give them some reward for keeping their homes well. In this age of 'Do It Yourself' many of them would have repaired and even improved their houses if given some incentive or indeed absolved from the ban which in some cases forbade them to carry out repairs. The third is that the community itself should arrange for the training of carpenters, plumbers, masons, bricklayers, etc. essential to its own well-being and become a co-operative. This could be done in a number of ways, by co-operation with the technical colleges, by a community or communities setting up their own training schemes, by enlisting the aid of local firms.

The surroundings of these particular housing schemes in Strone-Maukinhill are being improved but in so many estates all over the country the surroundings are deplorable. Even where they have been improved it should be asked why it has taken so long and what guarantee there is that the improvement will be maintained. So bad is the original lay-out of some estates, so poor their architecture, that to try to make their surroundings more beautiful or even less sordid is a depressing business. Uncut grass, broken railings, wind-tossed paper and old beer cans spread desolation. Again, a main cause is the lack of ownership: give people a garden of their own and many will make it attractive and productive but neither tenements nor blocks of flats allow for individual gardens. The next best thing would be for the community itself to look after them. If the community is too big then their

Theory and Practice – Greenock

control should be broken down into smaller units. Greenock was too big. I rather hoped to arouse some interest in getting children, students, particularly perhaps students of art colleges, to see what they could do.

As my belief is that we should not, as in the social services, aim only at the relief of poverty but try through community services to aim much higher and offer to all communities the chance to make the best of their education, work, etc., so it is not enough simply to tidy up the surroundings. The drabness of much public authority housing is proverbial. Why not murals? Although the streets are often mean, made meaner by concrete curbs, hideous lamp standards and the lack of any focus, anything on which the eye can light with pleasure, yet in nearly all housing estates there are corners, vistas, open spaces which could be effectively used. As I have mentioned, in Strone-Maukinhill there was an area of great possibility with steep banks and a burn. Grass and fountains add very marginally to the expense. There is no local authority which could not easily save the few hundreds required — for instance, if they stopped mowing the grass verges of open roads or erecting concrete curbs at the edge of roads where they are both ugly and dangerous. The difference between the gaiety which children show in their paintings at school and the dinginess in which they often have to live is striking.

But, here again, neither the habit of mind nor the machinery exists. It does not occur to people that they could and should do something about their surroundings. The surroundings indeed are not theirs. Nor have they any means of getting together to tackle such very local problems. Tenants' Associations where they exist are largely concerned with raising grievances — demanding that someone else does something. Community Councils in Scotland are likely to go the same way. Far be it from me to discourage protest — it is the stuff of politics, but it is not enough.

Then there was the crying need for transport. This is a feature of life common to many communities; so many people have cars that public transport does not pay. It was peculiarly serious in Strone-Maukinhill owing to the steepness of the hill. The community might have run their own but the licensing laws and the desperate anxiety of public transport undertakings to protect their monopolies are against it.

Transport is a good example of the fatal effects of some aspects of the modern state. First we nationalise and amalgamate. The resulting undertakings are often too big and nearly always too inflexible; they are top heavy with administrative staff; they are not responsive to public needs; they are neither a service under democratic command nor a commercial undertaking operating in the market. Local transport is much better conducted in small units. When I was in the town of Zagreb I was told that there were 140 bus operators driving in and into the city, many of them single buses driven by the proprietor. This shocked some of the more orthodox Marxist bureaucrats as much as it would shock our own, but it worked reasonably well allowing for adjustments to timing to suit the customers and tailored for every suburb and neighbouring village.

On top of rigid monopolies with schedules often determined by the wishes of the employees we have a system of licensing which greatly adds to the expense and is a final bulwark against any awkward competition in timing of services or price. One would-be operator in the west of England was only given a licence on condition that he did not charge less than the nationalised undertaking. He was later hauled up before some other commission for making excess profits. It is certainly necessary that all vehicles plying for public hire should come up to a certain standard and it may be necessary to limit the number of operators on some routes, but restriction has gone too far. Mini-buses, whether run by the community or by private operators, should now be encouraged.

This brings me to consider how far some jobs now considered to be suitable only for public operation could not be contracted out. So far from removing them from public accountability this might well increase it. For nothing is so effective as the direct impact of the consumer. Public authorities can become far removed from those they ostensibly serve. They stand in no fear of bankruptcy and have little incentive to efficiency or enterprise. There is a strong case for local services being provided by local entrepreneurs. Transport is one such job in some places. It is possible that refuse collection is another. Even where the service remains under public control there may well be an advantage in some minority share-holding held by individuals. If such individuals feel their own money is at stake they may take a salutary interest in the operation.

Local banks in Norway invest local savings in local industries and services. This is something we could well copy. At present the savings banks and the Post Office remove local savings from the community. They are then invested in government stock which over the years have proved a poor bargain while denuding home industries and services of much needed capital. I see no reason why the savings banks which now run unit trusts should not take local equity investments. No doubt there would have to be some guarantee by the central government. Perhaps the savings movement should be split so that those who wanted their savings to be invested as at present would be separated from those who were willing to use them in local risk investment.

Nor is it only transport that is lacking in some of the poorer housing estates. In Strone-Maukinhill there are very few shops. Indeed I thought at one time that the most useful activity we could back in the area was to give assistance to anyone who would open shops, hairdressers, small carpentry and repair businesses of all kinds. If we succeed in getting communities to consider these possibilities, local committees formed into co-operatives might well undertake such enterprises themselves. It would take time and there would be mistakes; expertise would have to be imported at first. We cannot be satisfied with the present arrangements; it is not as though we are faced with success by these arrangements — the state of many of the poorer communities is profoundly unsatisfactory.

Here again we come up against the need to change national attitudes and policies. Much of recent legislation, even apart from the high rate of taxation, is hostile to small businesses. The amount of paper work, the endless forms and returns that have to be completed, the restrictions and hazards imposed on the employer are a serious deterrent. In the project itself, for instance, while we were gratified by being chosen to run the local Youth Employment scheme, we viewed with trepidation the responsibilities thrust on us by the Employment Protection Act. Not only did we not have the staff to devote to form filling but we were nervous that once having taken on anyone to do a job we should have great difficulty in getting rid of them if either they were unsatisfactory or the job was finished.

Another source of difficulty for many small firms is the jungle of regulations, for example the fire regulations. No one would advocate the use of dangerous premises or unhealthy premises. There is no doubt that a century or more of legislation in this field has greatly improved working and living conditions but are we not in danger of going too far? There is now a strong vested interest in extending such regulations. There have been horrible accidents through fire and no doubt we have continually to watch the effect on health of inadequate sanitation, but some recent requirements are immensely expensive and in their more extreme forms unnecessary.

Of course, the Greenock experiment took its own course and was very different from, for example, what happened at Northmavine. Had this not happened I would have been disappointed. Such success as it achieved was very largely due to Ronald Young who gave it a quite extraordinary degree of attention and to the invaluable support from the local committee, from Barbara Darcy, Bob Winter and Joe Brady. One service he provided which would not have been otherwise available was the writing up of the project in various articles: another was a link to local government practice. I do not know what circulation the papers of the Local Government Research Unit of Paisley College of Technology have achieved, but I hope it is wide. Some of his conclusions in an article published in *Social Work Today*, Vol.8, No.9 emphasise points which I believe to be important:

> I am bewildered by the apparent wholesale conversion of politicians and professionals alike who some five years ago wouldn't even concede the existence of such things

as poverty and alienation let alone contemplate some of the programmes favoured by those who think in such terms. To be perfectly frank, the concern currently expressed for poverty seems more like a smokescreen behind which, if one listens carefully, one can hear the sound of groups grinding their own professional axes. 'Deprivation' is now a useful, indeed necessary, word to use to governments and civil servants to show that you deserve extra money or rather that your authority or department should be shielded from too severe a cut back! Penetrate a little through the smokescreen and you will however stumble across some familiar animals — the view that it is by and large the poor themselves who are to blame — that only economic growth will change the situation — that better management, more staff etc. are the panaceas to mention but some of a variety of different explanations.

How true. Once again we meet the expulsion of common sense, the shutting of eyes to obvious results of fashionable but mistaken policies and the sudden and wholesale switch to other policies which in turn require careful watching rather than swallowing in a gulp. He pinpoints the appetite of the vested interest in ideas as well as careers. If you think of how tinkers in Scotland or gypsies in England have been treated (see Report No. 14 of the Minority Rights Group 1977) you can detect the censorious frown which still greets some of the poor. And from Northmavine experience we can learn that growth — an increase in wealth — will not of itself benefit a community, necessary as it is. In the same article, Ronald Young goes on to give good advice, 'First, understand the process by which such multiple deprivation has occurred . . . secondly identify the contribution of local authority policies and procedures to that process and its amelioration'. Here I would interpose that local authority policies are very much influenced by national policies and the procedures of the civil service. 'Thirdly clarify the precise role of local government'. In one of the papers of his Local Government Research Unit (*Positive Discrimination – Notes on Greenock Experience 1972-73*) Ronald has this to say about the response of central government civil servants:

Central Government should be readier to respond to initiatives, to test conditions at their best rather than their worst: they make in relation to research two false assumptions: first that monitoring can only be done by outside centralised units, second and more profoundly, that research has a rationalistic bias — precisely because it is within the civil service or civil service controlled programmes it abstracts from politics and political processes; it is technocratic in its assumption that the problems are 'given' and objective and that the issue is which mix of local authority policies is most 'effective'. To put it in personal terms, the very existence of the project — let alone the various community initiatives it enabled — created a Strone-Maukinhill focus which I had never — as a member — had before and forced me (a) to look at the impact of local authority services in the area and (b) to question their effectiveness and helpfulness to the people, not only of that particular area but others like it.

Indeed, as quoted in an article in *The Times Educational Supplement*, 'The majority of citizens in the area [Strone-Maukinhill] are in a dependent relationship to the dominant culture and their perceptions and aspirations are under-represented in the decision-making relevant to their lives.' The Strone-Maukinhill Information Education Project which sprang from the wider project was one of the most successful offspring, bringing education nearer home, making it less imposed and alien, giving the people the sort of education they themselves wanted and stimulating co-operation between the local authority and the local technical college — the James Watt College — to which much gratitude is due.

I would make only two comments here on the views expressed above. I do not believe that local authorities any more than national authorities are fit for all the tasks now heaped upon them (not that I am suggesting Ronald Young necessarily thinks they are). And, once again, I repeat that I do not believe that it will be enough (though it will be a great deal) to raise unsatisfactory communities to a decent minimum standard. We should be helping them to achieve the highest standards they are capable of reaching.

Theory and Practice – Greenock 169

In its latter stages those involved in the Greenock project became much interested in communications. This is a very important subject for a community. Greenock is lucky, as I have said, in having a lively, daily newspaper, the *Greenock Telegraph*. The part played by weekly newspapers in their communities all over Britain is sadly underestimated. They have successfully for the most part resisted the debasement of news which is constantly threatening broadcasting and the national press. By the space many local newspapers give to local events, the news from different neighbourhoods, and the views of their readers on local matters, they are a rational force for the good as well as being an essential link. So far the barrier of information or publicity officers has not shut them off from local decision-making. They will report honestly, accurately and at length about local events which are without the attributes which will make them national news, for example exotic triviality, violence, personal offensiveness or the involvement of some figure or place which London, SW1 considers of importance. In Orkney and Shetland we also have local BBC radio largely owing to Alastair Hetherington, the Scottish Director of the BBC. These stations are proving a great boon. Praise for this must go to the two men who run them, Howie Firth in Orkney and Jonathan Wills in Shetland. They both know their constituents intimately, they are both receptive and enterprising.

But despite local papers, and even in places which have local radio, the need to interest and inform the community remains and how to do it has not been resolved.

11 Practice — Northmavine

I had thought it would be interesting to carry on two experiments, one in an industrial area and one in a rural area. For one thing, as some rural areas have not been so affected by the segregation of rich from poor as have the cities, it might be more possible to encourage developments by and for the whole community. I was lucky in getting an enquiry from a rural area.

A response to my broadcast from Aberdeen came from the doctor in Northmavine. Northmavine is the most northerly district of the Shetland mainland. It is almost severed from the rest of the mainland, a narrow isthmus only being left at Mavis Grind about twenty miles north of Lerwick. It is indeed remote but has none of the glamour which attaches to separate islands. Shetland on a small scale carries with it some of the centralisation which is such a feature of Britain as a whole. Those in the country districts are apt to grumble that Lerwick pays little attention to them and sometimes profiteers at their expense. Lerwick was stationary or growing in population when the whole of Shetland was declining — thereby being blamed for sucking the life-blood from the rest of the country. All the officials have their offices in Lerwick. Many Lerwick people seldom, if ever, visit the islands and only tour the mainland for a car expedition on a fine Sunday. There has always been a considerable commuter movement from outlying areas on the mainland into Lerwick which is not always welcomed by the local crofters. This anti-Lerwick feeling

Practice – Northmavine

should not be exaggerated and, of course, there is another side to the story — Lerwick's side. But whether justified or not there has long been a feeling of neglect in areas such as Northmavine.

As in most of Shetland, the land in Northmavine is poor. It is let out in crofts. Crofting tenure means that the house belongs to the crofter but he rents the land at low rent from the landlord. The landlord has few responsibilities and the tenant has security. To the croft is usually attached a right to run a number of sheep on the common grazing or scattald as it is called in Shetland.

Most of the landscape is desolate and craggy moor. On a fine Summer day it can be very beautiful with the sea a blue never matched by the Mediterranean and the glowing luminous twilight of the far North. It is indeed by British standards a long way north, some three hundred miles north of Inverness, as far from the north tip of Scotland as London is from Darlington, and almost on the latitude of Leningrad. While, therefore, there is light all through the night in summer, the winter day at its shortest begins about 9.30 a.m. and is closing in by 3.30 p.m. Children go and come from school in darkness. The climate is as you would expect in a northerly island enclosed between the North Sea and the Atlantic. Ferocious winds blow from all directions. I believe the highest gust recorded by the RAF in Shetland was around 170 mph. Certainly winds over 100 mph occur from time to time and 50 to 70 mph gales every winter. It is also extremely wet. The dampness of the atmosphere, the wind and the lack of sun make Shetland often feel very cold. It is not so much that the watery sun sits low on the horizon in winter as the absence of real warmth in the summer. Even on the finest day there is always a cool air off the sea; it is hardly ever possible to sit outside in shirt sleeves and crops and fruit ripen slowly and late.

I mention the natural conditions of Shetland at some length because I believe that climate and landscape are very important in community development and seldom taken into account. At the beginning of the last war I served with a squadron from the Fife mining villages. For a time we were stationed in Sussex. The eyes of the young miners were opened to the bland, warm life of southern England. They saw regency Brighton and compared it with Cowdenbeath. They drove over the Downs and enjoyed the gaiety and entertainments, the sun, the beauty of the south coast. Human beings, like plants, need some sun, or most of them do. They need some assistance from nature. If this is not forthcoming the compensation must be large.

In Shetland there are compensations. The chief of them is the character of the Shetlanders themselves. They are peculiarly fitted to run a good community. They are tolerant, helpful to one another, not greatly impressed by grandeur, not particularly avid for prestige, versatile and, considering their small number (some eighteen thousand), skilled and constantly throwing up men and women of ability. They are not as quarrelsome as the Scots nor as censorious. Their native character, strengthened by a long history of having to cope with a top layer of landlords, ministers of religion and officials largely drawn from Scotland, has led to a pleasant ability to laugh at pretension, a skill in keeping out of the way and an ability to make the best of things. It has also led, perhaps, to a comparative lack of personal ambition. Equality comes naturally in Shetland. There are few very rich people and few desperately poor though until the advent of oil the wages were low and most people had to be, and were, contented with little. Class distinctions, of course, exist but not with the severity of Scotland. Most Shetlanders are extremely handy in boats. Agriculture was traditionally left mostly to the women who stayed at home while the men went to sea either as fishermen, merchant navy sailors or whalers.

This brings me to the second advantage of Shetland. It is in the middle of some of the best fishing grounds in the world. And here again is a lesson for those interested in communities and why they succeed or fail. Fishing is a risky business which over the centuries has never on the average yielded a high income to fishermen. It has mainly survived outside Lerwick in three islands notable for their rocky, barren landscape — even in a land notable for barren rocks — Whalsay, Burra and Skerries. No doubt the inhabitants of these islands continued to fish through the vicissitudes of the industry and the bad years because there was nothing else they could do. Run a few sheep perhaps but crofting even of a low standard was impossible on any scale so the people fished. Today these three islands have roughly the same population as a hundred years ago, all other Shetland islands have declined. Fetlar, three times the size of Whalsay and much more fertile, has around a hundred inhabitants, Whalsay around a thousand. Why?

It cannot be that fishing over the last hundred years has proved a conspicuously safe, comfortable or profitable occupation. But it does answer some human needs and it answers them in a way that agriculture does not. It is a gamble; men and women like a gamble. Crofting is dull compared to it, often a species of drudgery. Fishing is dangerous and exciting. It is like hunting, indeed it is hunting, hard exertion and then times of relaxation. It gets the men out of the house. It enables the women to live in villages; crofts dotted about the hillsides, perhaps half a mile from one another, can be lonely places. The would-be improvers of the Highlands in the eighteenth century were right to promote fishing if they wanted to hold and increase the population. Fishing (until now at least, and unlike agriculture) needs a lot of hands.

But fishing, skill in a boat, the curious habit of life and the hardness of the life have to be bred in the bone. Once it has died out it is difficult to bring back. A fishing village like a mining village has a strong personality, a unity, a sense of suffering and triumphs shared and a fighting history against the elements. You can train fishermen but they must want to be trained. The yearning for the sea comes on some Shetland people and they make good skippers. I knew a Shetlander, a gentleman farmer, who took to fishing in his forties and skippered his seventy foot boat with great success for the rest of his days. But it is rare to find men taking to fishing successfully from a wholly land-locked existence.

Fishing depends on good skippers. There is all the difference between a good and an average skipper; only a good skipper will keep at sea in rough weather or find fish when they are scarce and it is when the weather is stormy and the supply poor that fish fetch high prices. Finally, share-fishing, and all Shetland fishing has been share-fishing for the last seventy years at least, is a co-operative effort. Life on a fishing boat is of necessity co-operative, it must be friendly. Sharing the profits adds naturally to this way of life.

Apart from lobster catchers there were no home-based boats in Northmavine ten years ago and fishing had almost died out, though a few boys went off to fish from other places. However, there was in the sixties a remarkable upsurge of local fish processing in Shetland. Before that the only market was Lerwick and many boats 'tripped' to Aberdeen where the prices were better, though it entailed a waste of fishing time and often a dangerous passage. The credit for the rise in fish processing and concurrent increase in small knitwear factories must go primarily to local initiative, though access to loans and grants helped. Again there is a lesson here: initiative will erupt in small communities, it does not seem to depend upon direction from above, nor on education, nor on the provision of capital. As I say, the latter helps but I suspect that many of the fish processing and knitwear plants would have come to life even if only ordinary commercial sources of capital had been available.

Dr Dowle had already started a small processing plant in Ronas Voe. Though occupied by his medical practice and with no experience in business he had with great energy and hard work got it off the ground. He was anxious to make it the nucleus of a wider effort in rehabilitating the area and stopping further depopulation. He had also started a development association with others. Now with funds from the Joseph Rowntree Social Service Trust we decided to appoint someone to live locally and be the 'civil servant' of the local people. For this remote, not unduly well paid post, with no hope of a career structure, we had around a hundred applicants. Eventually two were asked to visit Northmavine and there the local committee chose Miss Jane Sampson. There seem to be plenty of people anxious for such a job. It was also interesting that the unanimous choice fell on a girl as against several well qualified and more experienced males. The choice was admirable. Miss Sampson settled so well into Northmavine that she married a local man and now lives there. From the first she won everyone's confidence: she took to Shetland and the Shetlanders took to her. Sailing across the Atlantic in her father's small yacht and walking in Nepal proved better qualifications than most degrees.

Much of Jane Sampson's time was taken up in dealing with individual problems — whether this should be so is very much open to question. Since the reorganisation of local government and the abolition of one local authority in Shetland (the Lerwick Town Council) the number of local officials has at least quadrupled and so have individual salaries. Of course, the discovery of oil and the spate of legislation pouring out of the Westminster parliament have very greatly increased the work but Welfare, Youth and Recreation offices now abound over the country where there used to be none. The eighteen thousand Shetlanders have well over two hundred officials and secretaries in the Islands Council offices alone, besides the increased staffs of the Health Board and other public organisations. As might have been expected, this has led to proliferation of paper and complication of administration rather than any comparable increase in helping individuals to help themselves. I used to advocate a counter-civil service to be at the beck and call of the citizen and to monitor and criticise the working of government. I am impressed by the distrust of the governed for any and all manifestations of government including the public boards and the nationalised industries. Now I am frightened both by our experience of how governments make a hash of any innovation and by the likelihood that any new body or service will not only itself become dropsical and bureaucratic but will lead to a fresh all-round increase in the size of the conventional public service. Some of the duties which seemed appropriate to a counter-civil service are no doubt now the job of the Ombudsman — but some only. I fear that it is too much to expect the entrenched vested interests of the bureaucracies to change their ways or suggest any slimming cure for themselves. The need for a counter-civil service remains but its creation could now only be justified if accompanied by a general change of attitude, an increase of the democratic as against the bureaucratic element in our lives and a drastic reduction in orthodox administration.

Jane Sampson then discovered the gaps in community endeavours. All over Shetland there is a demand by those between twelve and eighteen for more amusement. This may seem strange as there exist many voluntary bodies, clubs, the Boys Brigade, etc. In Lerwick there are many halls and every parish has a community centre. But youth rightly asks for a chance to run its own affairs. Some voluntary bodies are not keen to promote dancing and discos. Transport is a difficulty. The problem seems to be worse in spite of the appointment of three full-time youth officers.

Miss Sampson began to work on a number of possibilities, improving transport, a show, various ideas for assisting crofting. Her resources were, as they were for Greenock, tiny. No one suffered from false optimism about what might be achieved yet interest was aroused. The community was small enough for one person to know many of her neighbours. There was a nucleus of younger crofters who wanted to make their farming a full-time job. They wanted to stay and make their lives in Northmavine. For generations crofting had been eked out by other work. The croft was a home, a part time occupation. The more ambitious took it for granted that they would have to leave. The less ambitious hoped for work on the roads, occasional fishing, lorry driving and so on. And still many men went to sea.

Then oil struck. Just across the isthmus of Mavis Grind on the southern shore of Sullom Voe the largest oil terminal in Europe was to be built. Two pipes were to bring oil from the fields east of Shetland. Huge tankers moving down Yell Sound would load it from gigantic storage tanks. In time, if oil was found west of Shetland a pipe might be brought across Mavis Grind or another tanker anchorage opened to the west of it at Swarbacks Minn. To build the terminal great numbers of unskilled workmen were needed. Most were imported, many from Northern Ireland, and housed in camps. One of the two main camps alone held more men than the whole population of Northmavine. Houses were built just to the south of Mavis Grind, quarries were opened, the road to the north was doubled almost in width, waitresses and cleaners, taxi drivers, subsidiary workers of many kinds were demanded. Wages were high, astronomic by Shetland standards. Where a few years earlier twenty pounds a week had been considered a decent wage, the building labourers now earned a hundred and fifty pounds a week and more. Those in the camps had everything found for them, food, accommodation, sport (squash courts and indoor football), entertainment. Boys fresh from school could take home eighty pounds from their first week's work. Maids in the camp earned seventy pounds and their keep and transport. It was a boom time. Many men and girls from Northmavine drove the twenty miles or so every day to the oil sites. The hours were long and generally a six-day week was worked. New houses, a few of which were just being built in Northmavine and which had no land, were rapidly snapped up by people working at Sullom or Lerwick.

This is not a sociological treatise on the effect of oil on Shetland. There are going to be all too many of them. Already, researchers of every kind and from many climes have descended upon the islands. Indeed, providing material for sociologists, naturalists, journalists and television teams has for many years been a Shetland light industry. Agreeable up to a point, this is now becoming irksome to some Shetlanders, many of whom, having sailed the world, are more sophisticated than their examiners and some of whom are growing weary of being photographed and asked the same questions. But the effect of oil construction on the Rowntree project in Northmavine is very germane to this book.

The young men who left at, say, seven-thirty in the morning returned at six in the evening tired with heavy labour and disinclined for much exertion after tea. No Saturday, not even Saturday afternoon, was a holiday so football, visiting, even dances, languished. One week in five was a holiday and then many of these men left Northmavine altogether to spend it in Scotland, or even the Costa Brava. Nor was much of their money spent locally. What are called consumer durables consumed much of it: furnishings, deep freezes, gadgets of one sort or another, coloured television sets (when the service came) and cars.

All this was perfectly good. It should not be considered strange that the less well-off Joneses want things their richer namesakes have long possessed. But along with it went some disruption of community life. Though commuting is a standard feature of the Western world and had long been the practice in Shetland, this mass commuting six days a week from dawn to dusk was something new. Admittedly it took the men out of the house, as fishing did, but it took many of the women too, and it was irreconcilable with the development of crofting. Further, when money began to flow suddenly on this scale, it was spent not on community affairs, nor even for the most part on improvements to the croft land and stock and the recipients looked outside their native districts for their recreation.

Had we known when the Rowntree experiment was started that Sullom would offer the wealth it has, we might never have begun it. For what has happened is not surprising. It should never be assumed that by raising the income of a place you will encourage people to stay there. One of the curious sights of the North is the island of Stroma off Caithness. From the air you see what appear to be some twenty or thirty well-roofed, comfortable and tight stone houses. Not one has been inhabited for some thirty years. I can remember visiting Stroma as a boy. Then it had an apparently happy population of perhaps eighty souls. All they wanted was a pier. At last the public authorities provided a pier — it was used for little less than the shipment of the Stroma folk and their furniture and gear. On the other hand their remoteness, the hardness of their lives and the existence of their own language has been a factor in the success of the Faroes. The oil construction boom makes it all the more necessary to provide for the time when it is over. The decline will begin quite soon and much of the unskilled labour be out of a job in five years and there are lessons to be learnt from it for the future of social and community services.

Although many of those who live in Northmavine have taken to a new way of life, and most of these are the younger men and women, many have not. The fish

Practice – Northmavine

processing plant still gets workers. Its wages have risen but not to oil construction levels, neither, however, have its hours of work. Those who have gone to work on building, shovelling concrete, driving lorries, show an appetite for hard labour which we used to be told most of the British have lost. Admittedly, this may need qualification: an American oil manager in Orkney who had no reason for national bias told me that the Northern Irish made good workers, the Scots not too bad and the English much the worst. Both Sullom and Flotta in Orkney were well behind schedule but the Italian firm in Orkney was well ahead. Nevertheless, big money incentives seem still to work. A surprising number of people in these inflationary days want to save money but, in Shetland and Scotland at least, rather for a car or a new carpet than to set up in business, improve a croft or even buy a house, though in this latter regard several building societies have opened in Shetland — rather, I fear, to take money out of the islands than to put it in.

It seems all too likely that when the construction boom ends there will be a number of young Shetlanders used to high wages but with no particular skills and with no jobs which will yield the return to which they are accustomed. This, you might think, will be a proper field for some planning — that is to say, for some action now. Training should be available within the islands. By the time it is established the number of unskilled workers may be declining. There never has been a sea-school and agriculture training has been largely a failure. The construction companies should be asked to co-operate in this, as should the oil companies which will be at Sullom for a generation at least. I have already suggested that the Savings Banks should become one means of channelling local wealth into local industry. The new rich of Shetland have no means of local investment so their savings go into government securities or southern housing. The Jane Sampsons of this world should be retained where possible against the time they will be needed.

If this book is not a treatise on the social effects of oil neither is it a programme for the future of Shetland. However, the experience of oil in Shetland emphasises certain general truths, indeed Shetland can be treated as a laboratory. There, the effects of some modern trends and fashions which flourish outside it can be seen all the more clearly because the scale is small. The discovery of oil has shown the futility of elaborate, static planning. Some half a million pounds must have been paid to the planners and consultants by the public authorities to draw up bound tomes on the future of the Islands replete with statistics, graphs and jargon. Much of this has been done by young men and women from the South who spend a few weeks in the islands and pick the brains and books of people who know more than they do. Oil has made much of this work valueless, it has completely changed the economy and outlook. Oil, of course, was a dramatic intervention but all life is full of unexpected interventions; the coming of oil to a small community is merely a rather extreme example of what is going on all the time. The social and community services must not be tied to a rigid plan, they must be adaptable. The new generation in Northmavine will have learnt needs and will meet problems not dreamt of twenty years ago. In the meantime, plans for the future are not enough. We must keep the native industries going now, improve and cheapen transport, maintain confidence.

Fishermen face a future which may turn out like that facing oil workers. Fishing in Shetland has done very well in the middle seventies by historical standards. But the North Sea may soon be fished out. Fishermen, some of whom have taken sea jobs associated with oil, may then find their profession in decline. This is a national problem with particular local effects — quite a common combination. It can best be tackled by a joint effort between local fishermen and the makers of national policy. But the machinery for such an exercise barely exists. Although fishermen's associations, community and welfare workers lobby the government they seldom feel it to be their job to take action in accordance with local initiatives. So long as things are reasonably good, it is difficult to get much action; when they turn sour the action is too often borne of panic. We watch the inner cities decay owing to policies which could easily be seen to promote their decline and then we try to counter their decay by measures which pull against

Practice – Northmavine

the policies which have made counter measures necessary but which are still in force. In an area such as Northmavine it may make sense to carry out a holding operation in regard to the fishing and fish processing which Dr Dowle and his associates have encouraged and think of what new employment is likely to attract the displaced construction workers. This may entail providing money now, if necessary from the oil revenues, to the fishermen, even though they are doing well. It may also mean considering what new amenities are necessary in a climate such as that of Shetland. But even funds drawn from oil revenues which sound large will be of no avail if industries decline and communities disintegrate. Oil money will nowhere near compensate for disruption.

As in Greenock, we come up against the all-important question of the attitude of the people. This, as everywhere, depends a great deal on local education. Education in Shetland has been of a high standard, teachers have taken a deep interest for the most part in their communities yet it has been a factor making for depopulation of the rural areas. Secondary education for the more academically successful children has been concentrated in Lerwick — with a population of some eighteen to twenty thousand this is not surprising. Further education has meant leaving Shetland and for those with a university degree there is little work to bring them back. So the rural districts have their best brains skimmed off and sent South. This may be partly inevitable but it is also partly due to the British reverence for the professional man and the bureaucrat as against the entrepreneur, be he in business, fishing or farming. Further education adds to the general indoctrination by television, advertising and fashion which is largely controlled by urban minds in the South. Of late Shetland has felt some of the reaction against the way of life to which this has led. There has been a small drift North, sometimes of hippies or near hippies, but not to be sneered at. But on the whole the pressures of conformity, and education, added to the inhospitality in some respects of the climate, have pushed towards the city and the South.

Are these pressures worth opposing? And, if they are, can it be done with the co-operation of the local people?

There is little point in driving people to live in Northmavine unless life there can offer something worth having and which people want. If they can find the life they want elsewhere then by all means let them go and leave Northmavine to sheep. A population kept there by subsidies, but by subsidies which really tie them to a low standard of life which, if they had the means, they would abandon, would not be worth preserving.

What Jane Sampson did discover in Northmavine before the advent of oil was a number of young men anxious to live and work in their own native district. The desire still exists and may well be stronger once Sullom has settled down into an oil village with some stability. It may then form a focus and rival attraction to Lerwick. If this happens it will be an asset to Shetland as a whole. It will mean providing the community, at least in the early stages, with some of the amenities to which people have grown accustomed and fitting these to the traditional and attractive way of Shetland life. A good restaurant or pub may be as necessary as a public hall. Shopkeepers may be as worthy recipients of grants as fishing boat builders or crofters. If some of the oil could be supplied at a cheap rate to provide central heating this would do more good than the 'landscaping' with which we are constantly threatened, to conceal the oil tanks. Public parks and adventure playgrounds are neither suitable nor necessary. The Rowntree project considered providing the money to keep the one dairy farm going. In the end this was not necessary as a farmer appeared willing to do it. The community should be assisted to provide its own transport.

In many places, not least Shetland, there are local people with taste and an interest in the historic buildings and landscape of their home country. The last twenty years have seen the rise of the Civic Society and numerous local preservation societies. So far, these societies have been mainly occupied in dissuading the public authorities and private speculators from destroying good buildings and beautiful country. The next step should be to interest their members in creating and improving agreeable surroundings. Yet in Northmavine the new houses are mass produced, not particularly suitable to the climate and set down in the nearest lay-out the planners can achieve to the suburbs of Cowdenbeath. All over Shetland there are springing up miniature city housing estates without beauty or imagination, replete with sodium lamps, curbs and concrete walls. Most serious of all perhaps, these houses have no land. They therefore divorce their occupants from Shetland tradition. We must develop loose villages in which housing, land and sea are entwined.

But, above all, we must take the opportunity which some temporary influx of money presents to encourage the community to do what its individual members want. The spirit of the times must cease innoculating people with acquiescence in alien fashions and with the belief that only remote authorities can take effective decisions. For all the talk that can be found in every district of Britain about local pride and the peculiarity of their own place, there is so far insufficient will to build on this and exploit it. As a politician I have been to many bye-elections from Devon to Inverness and I am always met with the warning that the particular constituency is indeed unique. I have heard it in Hull and Liverpool, as often as in Lochaber or Saffron Walden. And in a sense it is true. There are signs, too, that some places are drawing the obvious conclusion and breaking away from the herd.

Another lesson from Northmavine is the importance of working with local entrepreneurs — and the difficulties which arise. Local merchants have for the last two centuries played an important part in the Shetland economy. They ran the local shops, arranged to have the local wool spun, and marketed the knitwear, often paying for it with goods from the shop. They were also involved in the fishing along with the lairds (several of them were lairds) and later owned shares in many fishing boats. They were bankers and organisers, sometimes tyrannical, often unpopular but essential to the economy. To this day much of the organisation of the knitwear trade and fish processing is done by local individuals. The expansion of these industries in the sixties owed a great deal to a small number of such people.

The fish processing plant at Ronas Voe, essential to the general schemes of the area, ran into a period of trouble. A

Shetland entrepreneur, Johnson of Vidlin, who had already started at least two fish processing plants and a lobster pond, offered to take shares in it and manage it. A conflict of an all too common type then arose: the local people who held shares in the enterprise were reluctant to surrender control to an individual, an individual who was not from Northmavine. The factory had been started as a community effort, a co-operative with the aim not so much of making a profit, though that was necessary, as of giving employment. In the end Mr Johnson took control and it is probably due to this and to the unremitting efforts of Dr Dowle that the plant is still very much in operation. Much ot its output is loaded on a boat which calls regularly at Shetland on its way from Faroe to Massachusetts and is sold in America, particularly the Middle West. It is an operation requiring considerable commercial skill. A large percentage of Shetland knitwear is also exported. Thus, if the units are small, the expertise needed in running them is not. I have no doubt that the right decision was made.

To marry entrepreneurial ability to local development is one of the most important and difficult tasks for the community. Expansion, the pursuit of prestige, the amassing of power and money, these are not the aims of such development; if they are the by-products, well, they can have advantages and must be used intelligently.

Further, it is highly necessary that there should be greater sympathy and exchange of views between officials and entrepreneurs. They are too far from each other. The increasingly horizontal loyalties of men and women to their union, rather than to their place of work does not make for interest in the locality where many of them regard themselves as only temporary residents and to which they do not look for the advancement of their interests. We have in Shetland been lucky in finding a number of first class officials or perhaps credit for this should go not to luck but to the Shetlanders and their elected representatives. One of them was Bob Storey, a man extremely sensitive to human values and to the possibilities, desires and troubles of small communities. The least materialistic of men himself he was nonetheless very much aware of the benefits to be conferred by commercial ambition and acumen. He proved

Practice — Northmavine

a most valuable catalyst in many Shetland situations. How do you produce the Storeys of this world? Certainly not by the orthodox methods of educating planners, social workers, etc. Perhaps there is no recipe. All I want to record here is that in the particular context of raising the economy of a depressed area they are invaluable. In this context too, small businesses are essential. There is no substitute. Certainly the branch factory is not a substitute though it may have a part to play.

An interesting example of a break from the herd and indeed a most interesting experiment in many other ways is what Iain Noble is doing at Eilean Iarmain in Skye. This experiment has succeeded in at least three of the directions which I believe community development must follow. First it is an all-round experiment. Iain Noble having bought an estate of around twenty-five thousand acres in south-east Skye has set to work to develop the farm, which is in his own hands and amounts to some twelve thousand acres, the crofts, which compose the rest of the land, and the hotel. He has also set up a small knitwear factory employing some dozen people and is in the process of starting fishing. Secondly, the standards are of the highest. There is no question of bringing a somewhat depopulated and depressed area up to some minimum standard. Iain Noble aims much higher than that. There is no question of tinkering with adventure playgroups or a few seats for the old. As soon as you approach the village you are struck by its appearance of well-being and by the beauty and suitability of what has been done to the buildings. Thirdly, it is a local co-operative effort. Iain Noble is, of course, the inspirer and indeed the paymaster. But Iain Noble is not a feudal landlord of the old type, some of whom indeed were and are very good but some of whom were a dead hand on their estates, absentee, unable or unwilling to supply capital and with no intention of taking their tenants into partnership.

An interesting and unusual feature of Eilean Iarmain is that its affairs are as far as possible conducted in Gaelic. Before I went there I was rather hostile to this idea. The promotion of Gaelic struck me rather like the revival of thatching or Morris dancing but a short visit to Eilean Iarmain changed my views. Iain Noble has converted a farm into the germ of a Gaelic College. The insertion of this centre of academic learning and the speaking of Gaelic in the everyday life of the estate give the whole experiment point and interest. Gaelic is not pressed upon the visitor. Since everything that is done is done at a high level of efficiency, there is nothing olde worlde about Eilean Iarmain. The use of Gaelic emphasises that you are in Skye, that the experiment grows out of Skye and is not a hobby of a rich man from the South, nor an exotic transplant by some government body. Gaelic also seems to have been a factor in bringing back one or two graduates to work in the area. This, of course, is greatly helped by the existence of the college.

Iain Noble's emphasis on Gaelic and indeed his whole experiment has met with some opposition. If he were to insist upon Gaelic as a qualification for work or housing this could be justified but he does not do so. Some people are suspicious of any individual attempting this type of project; in their view only public authorities should do this sort of thing. Others have suggested that it is a purely money-making venture, that it is dictatorially run, etc. It is interesting and alarming, though not surprising, to hear these reactions. They are likely to meet anyone who breaks the orthodox and largely collectivist pattern anywhere in Britain. The introduction of Gaelic seems to have exacerbated the suspicions held by some of the authorities: the Inverness Council turned down Noble's application for permission to put up bi-lingual road signs. One or two firms or authorities have refused him grants from fury at the Gaelic revival. I regard these reactions as wholly satisfactory from his point of view. If local communities are to develop along different lines, and I fail to see how they will develop at all as local communities unless they do, then they are bound to irritate the centralised conformist bureaucratic outlook of the age. If they fail to do this their development must be in jeopardy.

What are the economics of Eilean Iarmain? Iain Noble told me that between the capital he has put up and various grants he has obtained, probably somewhere around

£750,000 has gone into it. If you consider that for this sum he has greatly improved the farm and hotel, set up his knitwear unit and started a college, it would seem that he has got excellent value for money — much better value indeed than has been obtained under such schemes as the Urban Programme.

It can be said that Eilean Iarmain is too easy — that it is one thing to revitalize a very beautiful corner of the beautiful island of Skye, which has escaped the industrial revolution and is virtually free from the diseases of modern technical society, quite another to repeat the experiment in, say, the town of Inverness, let alone in Manchester or Bristol. This comment I accept. But though the same type of experiment may be impossible in a city, some features of it may be relevant to other places. There is the high standard aimed at, the all-round nature of the project, the idiosyncrasy of Gaelic, the marriage of entrepreneur and co-operative. Also there is much room in Britain for rural experiments of the same kind.

A more intractable difficulty in repeating some of the features of Eilean Iarmain is the shortage of Iain Nobles. There are no doubt plenty of young graduates who would leap at the chance of doing something similar if they were supplied with the capital. It is tempting to think that capital-providing bodies such as the Highlands and Islands Development Board should devote more of their resources to this kind of project and set up these young enthusiasts all over the Highlands. But I fear that would not work: Iain Noble had been a successful business man before he bought his Skye estate and we must not delude ourselves into thinking that because he can do it anyone else can make a success of this kind of adventure. Then too, it is his own money or part of it is. And, above all, the imagination which is both the making of his triumph so far and the temper-raising goad for some authorities, is not usually produced by modern education, particularly not, I fear, by the study of sociology as taught in most universities and polytechnics. Iain Noble is in close contact with the outside world, he is interested in Faroese enterprises and ship brokerage as well as the promotion of fishing in Skye.

Eilean Iarmain has its own whisky blend as well as its centre for Gaelic studies.

Communities wax and wane in a changing world. Growth in numbers is reckoned a success in such places as Northmavine but the methods by which it is achieved, and its effects, need attention. One of the attractions for some people of such places as Northmavine (and there are many, many similar communities in the North of Europe and America) is some self-sufficiency. But incomers naturally bring with them the habits they have learnt elsewhere. In my experience, though some may arrive proclaiming how happy they are 'to be away from it all' they are apt to start demanding that the public authorities do this and that for them. They bring with them foreign habits. If they are housed in new housing schemes, however small, they are marked off from the old inhabitants. As Jane Sampson pointed out in a report she wrote:

> There has also been a large increase in the number of new people living in Northmavine this year (this was due to oil developments at Sullom). Both medium-stay families, usually living in house type accommodation and short-stay families, young people, etc. in caravans. This has had a very large social impact; no longer do we live in a community where everyone knows everyone and everyday happenings are of concern and news to us all. There are serious indications that the incomers are not being assimilated into the old communities and even in a village as small as 140 people two communities can exist which leads to minor, but irrevocable, misunderstandings and resentments on both sides.

Another gap in the community is that between the younger people, more concerned with material domesticity, and the older people, more concerned with community shared activities often based on crofting. Here the gap is particularly wide among the women, where very few younger ones are involved in crofting though the older ones are almost without exception. This is also connected with the great reluctance of young people to take responsibility for any community activity or function.

There are several points in this quotation. 'Everyday happenings are of concern and news to us all.' I find that very noticeable and agreeable living in the community that is Orkney. In spite of all its beauty and distinction I found Edinburgh a dull town to work in. Although it is a centre of finance, law, education and government nothing ever seemed to happen. The citizens pursued their work behind drawn blinds, so to speak. Go away from Orkney for a fortnight and you will find all sorts of things have happened. That everything should be of concern to everyone prevents boredom and also absorbs energy; life in Orkney is in many ways more hectic than life in London. Tourists are under a sad misapprehension if they think our days (or indeed nights) need filling.

Again it is true but curious that the young are less interested in shared activities. To listen to academics talking, notably elderly students and sociologists, you might think that the notion that neighbour should see and help neighbour was a recent discovery of scientific research. You might also think that they were active pioneers in this revolution — this is not so. It is partly a class or educational delusion. The poor and those who have gone straight from school to work co-operate more naturally and more fully than middle-class intellectuals. But it is a disturbing comment on the way children are brought up that so many should turn out more selfish than their parents. It is another reason for considering the course further education is taking and for giving a higher value to productive work. 'Often based on crofting'; that comment should move us to do more to spread the methods of crofting, that is co-operation of individual small scale and independent workers living in communities where they work and play and where social activities are closely knit. It should also be a reminder that productive work is not only essential to the country but often breeds a sounder outlook than is likely to be propagated by a country which rates academic qualifications too highly. 'The reluctance of young people to take responsibility'; this confirms my view that one reason for some socialists' distaste for the market is that its operation demands individual responsibility.

In 1976 Jane Sampson attended a conference at Vannoyin

in Norway at which, among other subjects, the importance of education to the local community was discussed:

> The impact of standardisation was often out of harmony with the periphery, for example emphasis on the need for single age classes leads to pupils having to travel long distances and the time this consumed may exclude people from other relevant community experiences. More serious was the standardisation of curriculum as lack of local knowledge and experience orientates the wrong people to look away, especially the brighter ones, who are particularly educated to leave by accepting the urban values of the school and through qualifying for further education and thus disqualifying for local work; above average pupils are very likely to migrate and even a limited number leaving can have great impact.

In this conference the central importance not only of work but of the type of work available in a community was emphasised. When people lose control over their work, for example when they become roadmen rather than crofters, when they cease to have any say in what investment takes place in their home district, then the roots wither.

At 1976 prices the cost of maintaining a community worker in Northmavine was about £5,000 a year including car and minimal equipment. It was found an asset that Jane did not have an office but lived in a croft house, indeed she indulged in some crofting herself. Community development must be spontaneous but it must also be backed by some organisation. This organisation, however, should spring from the community. Ideally, it should be staffed by part-time native workers. It must be, and be seen to be, indigenous. It certainly need not be expensive or elaborate.

In some communities a much larger investment of outside capital might be rewarding. In Northmavine there was at one time a chance that we might have influenced some of the big oil companies to undertake an agricultural scheme such as they have backed in Southern Italy. They did not do so partly owing to the growth of the oil terminal at Sullom Voe; had such a scheme come to fruition I would have hoped that it would have meant a marriage of outside capital to local skills. It would, I trust, have been an adaptation not supercession of the crofting system. Had it come about it could also, apart from the intrinsic value it would have had for Northmavine, have taught lessons about co-operation and local initiatives by big companies which might have been copied elsewhere. In Greenock we had the great advantage of help from IBM.

Over the past twenty years many groups have been got together to undertake various forms of what is often described as community action. I have, I hope, made it clear that to me the development of the community must mean much more than the organisation of protests, tenants' associations, play groups, the Samaritans etc. — excellent and important though many such activities may be. I have also, I hope, made it clear that I do not believe that economic opportunity is the only opportunity which needs to be increased, nor indeed that a higher standard of material life should be the only aim. I have stressed too that democracy means more than political democracy.

Central to my notion of community development is art, expression, play; central to these activities is individual choice, individual effort. Yet this is often squeezed even by well-meaning bodies, ostensibly sometimes designed to encourage individual expression. There is an irreconcilable difference of purpose between the bureaucratic attitude and self-expression. It is therefore to artists themselves, to spontaneous outbreaks of imagination, to those who enjoy art in all its forms and indeed enjoy play and games, neither as a means of making money nor as subjects for a thesis, that we must look for the promotion of this side of the community.

Of all the outbreaks which have waxed and waned since the last war Ed Berman's Inter Action seems to me one of the most interesting. Mr Berman's activities are manifold. They depend upon enlisting voluntary local support, they are part of no empire, they do not despise economy. One of his projects is the setting up of farms in cities. He seems to me to be on to something here which no one except an eccentric (to the bureaucracy) would have dreamt up. These farms and the method of running them have proved attractive to children and adults who appear to have adopted them as their own.

The comparative results between one such a farm in London and a local authority playground are interesting. The farm occupies approximately three acres near a housing estate, so does the local authority playground. The farm being built partly by voluntary labour cost £5,690 and contains stables for nine horses, tack room, workshop, youth club, community garden for the elderly, greenhouse, twenty allotments, caretaker's house, storage block, indoor riding school (the only other one in London belongs to the Queen), repair shop, farmyard for eighteen animals. The local authority playground cost £75,000 and contains play hut, football pitch, kick-about area, three mounds containing slides and nursery area. In the first year after this playground opened the building was destroyed by vandals, the whole affair had to be closed for eight months and £24,000 spent on refitting. The total cost of vandalism in the first year that the farm opened was £20. The running costs of the playground when operated by the local authority were £10,176, of the farm £4,200. In one year the playground was visited by some thirty thousand children, the farm by thirty thousand children and fifteen thousand adults. Five city farms have now been set up.

Another of Inter-Action's activities is Dogges Troupe which tours the country giving plays without theatres. Another is the Media Van which tries to draw out people unused to older fashioned means of expression by using a mobile cinema.

The premise behind the Community Media Van is that all people are subject to the influence and professionalism of the media. If people are expected to involve themselves in their community and leave their television sets, then they must be competed for in the new media languages everyone has learned to 'speak' — T.V., Sound (radio, telephone and tape recorder) films and photography. The function of this unit is to visit neighbourhoods, market places, street corners (where people are as part of their communal lives) and show brief films, slide shows and video tapes with accompanying music of an appropriate nature. After this initial attraction the important step of people voicing their own constructive ideas about their situation can take over.   (Ed Berman)

It is not my business to write a prospectus for Inter-Action. Ed Berman, though a man singularly free from material ambition of any kind, is well able to do that and indeed has done it. But the successful activities of Inter-Action are very important to my contention that if individuals are to have the chance of growing up in communities which not only offer help if they have misfortune but give them every help not only to avoid misfortune but to make the best of themselves, then we have to think in terms of all-round improvement, covering work, art and every aspect of living.

12 The Big City

I have suggested that experiments in new community organisation and community services in smaller towns or country districts may be very valuable. It is reasonable to try out new ideas on a smaller scale first: it is easier to see how they work and what their results may be in conditions nearer to those of the laboratory than is possible in big cities. For this belief I would certainly have the support of Howard. I believe that if the changes I propose were found to work in smaller communities this would be evidence that they would work in larger communities. Smaller communities and country areas, however, give a better life to most of their members than do large conglomerations. Vice and crime flourish in the big cities, so, often, do dirt, disease and cruelty. The big cities certainly present extra difficulties and I am aware that most people will think that the test for community action lies in them and that, however sensible a scheme appears in a smaller community, if it turns out to be impractical in the larger community it will be of little value. I do not share this view though I accept that as most of the population live in large conglomerations (many of which, however, have ceased to be cities) on numbers alone they are an important test.

On of the most baffling areas in post-war Britain has been Merseyside and in particular the great city of Liverpool. It is a city of vitality, as a seaport it seems more cosmopolitan than Manchester. Even today it has world wide connections and not so long ago its sea front with its triumvirate of great buildings was one of the best known facades in Britain. No city in Europe has built two gigantic new cathedrals in this century. It held the head offices of great shipping empires, independent banks and merchant businesses. Its football teams won the cup. It was the birth place of the Beatles (at least as a band). Yet its morale has suffered a sharp decline; much of it is forlorn, apparently abandoned. Waste paper and dust blow around the steps of its spendid eighteenth-century houses.

Liverpool is no worse than many other big cities — or if it is, it is only because the bones of its grandeur are more evident. The centre of Birmingham is a nightmare, Glasgow looks as though it has been bombed and laced up again by mad giants working with concrete. In most of our cities architects and planners have done more damage than Hitler and it is the damage which first strikes the visitor — the ugliness, the heaviness, of much of their architecture. What is even more alarming, and more destructive of decent values, is the pessimism which seems to have engulfed cities. They struggle manfully against it and nowhere has the struggle been carried on more courageously than in Liverpool. But in cities where pride, indeed arrogance, flourished not so long ago there has been a sad loss of confidence. Some years ago I visited Hull, I was hospitably received by the acting Mayor. In the course of conversation my hosts were bemoaning the neglect of Hull. 'No one ever comes to Hull' they lamented, as though Hull were Timbuctoo. On looking through the visitors book I discovered that Sir Alec Douglas Home had recently visited them. He was then Leader of the Opposition. I pointed this out. 'Ah,' they said, 'and look what happened to him.' I cannot believe that Sir Alec's displacement was due to his rash act in visiting Hull but that was the implication. The decline of confidence and vitality in many cities matches the state of their streets; indeed, they clearly go together. But there are signs of revival in some of them and I like to think that the resurgence of Liberalism in Liverpool under Councillors Carr and Jones has something to do with it.

It is not only in Britain that a disease as bad as Dutch elm disease has struck the city. The big city in many countries seems to be in danger of collapse. A few years ago it seemed that New York was almost beyond redemption. I spent a scarifying day talking to the director of its social services and going round the city with his officials. In some precincts the roads were pot-holed, buildings deserted, schools closed. Before going into administrative offices visitors were examined by armed guards. I was told that you could hardly leave a typewriter on a desk without it being stolen. In the evening when I arrived to dine with the director in an apartment block in a fairly expensive part of the city I was not allowed to go up in the lift until he had vouched for me. I was told that in the previous week a girl had been murdered in the lift. The main cause of the violence, I was told, lay in the army of drug addicts who were largely incapable of earning but must have money for their drugs. They were driven mad by addiction. The fear of punishment was no deterrent so the ordinary belief that criminals could be frightened by fear of detection and sentence was invalid. Yet New York, though its problems remain huge, survives. Other cities which passed through a time when their outlook seemed bleak, to say the least of it, seem to be recovering, shaking down to a more satisfactory life. So to talk of collapse may be to exaggerate though their state must still cause concern. Why did this happen? It is not certain that people all prefer some other way of life to that of the city, or at least if it is, it is a very new turn of events. It is less than forty years ago that the wartime evacuees clamoured to be allowed to return, even to cities under bombardment.

Why has there been this loss of confidence in the once-proud cities? Some of this loss of confidence was caused by atitudes of mind of people who did not belong to the cities themselves. Cities were subjected, by the prevailing failure of thought among officials, big business managers and so on, to tighter control combined with neglect. A more damaging combination cannot be imagined. (Mondragon in Spain, where the big co-operative movement started, was subjected to some neglect, even hostility, from Madrid but the founders of the co-operatives were left free to take their own initiatives.) After the second world war city budgets, for instance, were tightly circumscribed. At a time when Liverpool had 91,000 unfit dwellings and 64,000 families on its waiting list the government rationed the number of dwellings which would be built in any one year by the authorities or private enterprise. New initiatives from Whitehall went to the New Towns. When the university expansion began much of it went into new universities in the smaller towns. I am not saying this was entirely wrong but it was accompanied by some lack of attention to the cities. They were too big, no doubt, and could have been slimmed with advantage but in slimming them the bone and muscle, the more enterprising and able people, were too often removed. Nor was it foreseen, in spite of the American experience, that their abandoned centres might be taken over by immigrants. The alternative to this was too often to board them up or bulldoze them. The cities suffered too from amalgamations in industry and the loss of independent firms.

As well as the external factors from which they suffered the cities were also experiencing the effects of new ambitions, new desires. Every survey has shown that people would most like to live in single family houses: the central areas of the city were often dirty, the motor car opened up new possibilities and so surburban life was becoming more and more attractive to many people who could now afford it. The prevailing planning doctrine was too inflexible to allow the city to adapt to what people now wanted.

The buildings of the big cities deteriorated. The inner city housing was replaced by tall blocks or housing estates — both built by edict of the public authorities, poorly designed and contemptuous of their tenants' wishes. Above all, they were filled with tenants who had little incentive to improve or even maintain them. Neglect and bad housing led to violence. Rateable values fell, services deteriorated but the money was not available to improve them.

The new roads in the cities throw the most distressing light on the minds of the planners. They illustrate the inhumanity which underlies their treatment of the places where human beings live. The centre of Birmingham is knitted into a cat's-cradle of roads, centring round the railway station. The greatest need, so it would seem, was to get into or out of Birmingham — but what became of Birmingham in the process? You can motor through Glasgow — but where to? Motoring for many people is an enjoyable pastime but for most traffic it is a means to an end. If it is not, it might as well be practised on a closed circuit. The motorways were perhaps justified between cities but to push them through the middle, thereby ruining the place they were supposed to lead to, seems the sort of decision which is taken on paper, not in terms of flesh and blood. It also shows the dangers of piecemeal planning. The roads, housing, health, were treated as separate units. The unit should be the city or the rural community. Many warnings were given by Lewis Mumford and others. But our political system did not permit them to take effect. As Mumford said:

> The real alternative to the empty political patterns of the nineteenth century lies not in totalitarianism but in just the opposite to this: the restoration of the human scale in government, the multiplication of the units of autonomous service, the widening of the co-operative processes of government, the general reduction of the area of arbitrary compulsion, the restoration of the process of persuasion and rational agreement.
> (L. Mumford, *The Culture of Cities*, Secker & Warburg, 1945.)

I suspect that Mumford might have proved no better a practical planner than those he rightly criticises but he said many wise things about cities.

More important even than the psychological assault on the cities, their housing and roads, was the lack of employment. This was not helped by zoning. It was not helped by the influx of unskilled immigrant labour. To some extent, given the refusal to work at a wage or salary justified by the market, it was inevitable. Nineteenth-century mistakes were repeated, for instance, by encouraging large-scale factories on Merseyside producing goods for which the demand was likely to decline: that is to say, the demand for such goods on the conditions and at the price they were produced in Britain. However, I am not dealing here with changing conditions of employment,

The Big City

what I am emphasising is that in the big cities and their urban margins work is even more important than elsewhere. I should be a prime concern of the community. It is central to community or social services. Though subsidies, protection, feather-bedding may tide over short-term unemployment in industries such as steel or aircraft which have been formed into large state monopolies, in the long-run we must look to private enterprise, including co-operative enterprise, to offer new jobs. The local authorities should have been encouraged therefore to plan for an increase in private enterprise but very little new private investment has gone into cities such as Liverpool.

The cities have made great efforts to tackle their problems and the government, by its present partnership proposals, is trying to assist them. What can be done to make these efforts successful? Local government reforms appeared to downgrade the city. It may be of symbolic importance only but symbols are important and Liverpool was right to retain its Lord Mayor. But it does not seem to me that the Local Government Act tackled the changing pattern within the city — a pattern which was changing, as I have said, in response to internal as well as external pressures. The district councils of the cities were responsible for most of the traditional areas of the city and sometimes more. But the city was no longer one community. The council could neither draw it together nor set up some new division of administration. Various services were taken out of municipal control but were not put under democratic control of any kind. They were part of a nationwide network to which their members looked for guidance and promotion.

We see here, once again, the decline of loyalty to an institution. Elections to the city or district councils were on party lines. Far be it from me to deprecate political argument where it is about issues and not merely about office. In the running of a city of a million or more inhabitants there is room for some political ideology. The drawbacks are that the parties no longer correspond to the main divisions in the electorate and they are inappropriate to many city problems. Councillor Cyril Carr in Liverpool has constantly called for co-operation on a council where no party has an over-all majority. The committees require such co-operation. Cities are run by committees with corporate responsibility, not one-party cabinets in which ministers have individual responsibility subject to the cabinet. I believe that the committee system is the more appropriate for local government. But it has meant, as Councillor Carr has pointed out, that owing to the membership of the committees in Liverpool, committee decisions taken by a majority from one party are apt to be reversed in a full council by a majority from other parties. If, as I would advocate, large grants were given to the cities to use at their discretion for their all-round betterment and the attainment of the highest standards of which they may be capable, there would have to be more emphasis on consensus not confrontation.

I have suggested that the bigger cities are ceasing to be a community. If this is so are they to be allowed to split up? And, if so, are funds to be provided for each of the communities into which they split? Enthusiasts for community development such as myself must face the difficulty that fragmentation may go too far. It is central to my theme that rich and poor, able and stupid, native and immigrant, should all benefit from the community services and that the schools, art, and general life of the community should be of such a standard that all will feel part of it and participate freely in it. But there are in Liverpool 173 community groups. A remarkable flowering of democracy: but hardly designed to create the type of community I have in mind. I would guess that most of these groups have sprung to life because the city itself has not been able to provide a satisfactory over-all community. I suspect that many would gladly dissolve if the city council were given greater autonomy and resources. But some might well remain to the enrichment of Liverpool. I repeat that all sorts of different development must be tolerated, indeed encouraged. If these community groups can run housing, co-operatives or indeed industrial co-operatives and services, they would inject a democratic element and involve people in undertakings in which they had a particular interest.

The Big City

The Liverpool City Council, I think it is fair to claim, at the instigation of the Liberals, led by Councillor Carr and Trevor Jones, have initiated more democratic involvement in the city's affairs and have made a valuable contribution to housing policy. They have improved many houses instead of demolishing them, they have built houses for sale, they have entered into partnership with private builders to provide houses. A considerable amount of agreement seems to have been reached in the city over housing policy, showing that in spite of ideological differences co-operation can be achieved. Some of those who put their names down to buy houses have not actually bought them when offered. I do not see that this shows that the policy is unsound — many have bought them. But it shows what is indeed obvious, that it takes time to break habits — and Liverpudlians have been used to regarding housing as being provided by the local authority for tenants. In the years immediately following the war the rates of council to private house building was 10 to 1. Over the last ten years the City Council have built 23,571 dwellings, the vast majority for letting, and private builders 3,016. There has been a ready demand for the houses built for sale and this was welcomed by the Labour housing committee Chairman when the first couple moved into their new home in 1976.

But the inner area of Liverpool presents great difficulties. In the partnership scheme started by Peter Shore in 1977 (similar schemes have been offered to Birmingham, Newcastle, Manchester and some London areas) the government, the local authorities and the health authority are preparing a programme for the improvement of the city. The Government will provide seventy-five per cent of the costs of improvement schemes in 1978-79, up to £2.5 million and £30 million later. The scheme assists in other ways. But it is apparently to be run largely by bureaucrats. The committee, with Mr Shore as Chairman, which is to draw up the plan had only met once by March, 1978. One difficulty seems to be the relationship of this committee to the City Council. Once again, it does not seem that this is an effort to stimulate local initiative. Once again, it seems it will be help handed down. However, it has been argued that in the first stages, at least, of any such programme this may be essential. Mr Steen MP, for instance, who has taken a deep interest in the problems of the cities and most especially Liverpool, inclines to the view that a special corporation may have to tackle the innermost area. The amount of finance needed and the decay of such areas make their reclaim an operation more like building a new town rather than a normal task of local government.

Though there is an argument for a special corporation to handle some innermost cities, I would reject it. I am against setting up more corporations. It would add further to our already top-heavy government; it would apply conventional methods which have failed. I am not enthusiastic about the lay-out and architecture of several of the new towns. The idea of new towns had merit; some, or rather some parts of them, have been successful but on the whole they are not where I would like to live. A special corporation would be under little or no democratic control. Most important, who would set its aim and what would that aim be? The inner city is an abstraction: the inner city of Birmingham differs from the inner city of Manchester; in Liverpool it could be said that there is an inner and an innermost city. We must not repeat the mistakes we have made by thinking in abstractions. There is a danger that governments will now attempt to turn the cart round and attempt to populate the inner city, just as governments depopulated them thirty years ago. Some parts of some inner cities might well be left depopulated (see Howard's plan for a garden city).

Fifty, even thirty, years ago parks, open spaces, green belts and so on were greatly admired. I notice that in many cities the parks are not now much used for walking, games or even letting out children to play but quite small spaces — for instance Lincolns Inn Fields in London — on warm days are full of people eating their lunches or feeding the birds. The motor car may have drained off the city dweller who used the big provincial parks. He or she now either lives in the suburbs or goes to the country or seaside at the weekends. Perhaps, too, some of the Victorian parks are a little staid and dull for modern taste, though not necessarily for mine. Surely if some derelict areas in the cities were grassed over, the occasional holding left for some communal purpose, some imaginative items (by which I do not mean adventure playgrounds) introduced, it might well be as good a use as any. Ed Berman with his urban farms and other inventions might help. Some parts of the inner cities might be leased or sold to private corporations. I remember an interesting letter in *The Times* some years ago suggesting that areas in the East of London might be made free of the planning laws. We could then see what individual enterprise would do for them.

None of these suggestions would be much help to making a better place to live for the people who are already living in poor conditions in many parts of the city. Their troubles are often simple ones, poverty and hopelessness. The first of these can hardly be cured by any local council. To cure poverty the economy must be improved and people given a better chance of earning. (I have explained how I believe this can be done.) New housing policies would do something to dispel hopelessness which is often bred not only by sheer bad housing but by the fear that nothing can be done about it, that it is no one's responsibility and no one cares. Steps could be taken to get back shops of all sizes. Oxford Street in London may owe much of its vitality to foreign visitors but though the American habit of siting supermarkets in the suburbs may have advantages in a car-using age, it has disadvantages too. The old market place as well as the supermarket has its devotees — look at the Portobello Road. But, above all, the site of the city should be considered in all its aspects and neighbourhoods. It was the fashion to disapprove of suburban sprawl. Instead of the old town wall, a green belt was to confine the city and prevent it spilling over the neighbouring country. In some places, particularly those where the bounds of the mediaeval city could still be traced, this was desirable. However, many cities did not grow up as fortress towns, in these 'ribbon development' may be a virtue. Tongues of houses stretching into the country can be matched with tongues of country stretching into the city.

The troubles of Liverpool are a particular facet of the troubles of Merseyside. The financial problem of running the city is, as in New York, often acute. The suburbs and surrounding estates are unwilling to pay for an area of small rateable value to which they do not feel much neighbourliness. In cleaning up the mess we have made of some of our cities far more assistance than has so far been forthcoming will be required from the Exchequer. But it should be expended by local people in what they see as the local need.

Unemployment on Merseyside is in some places as high as thirty per cent. The results of unemployment today may not be so serious as they were fifty years ago — we have noted the luxuries which those on national assistance can enjoy. But in loss of self-respect the results are serious, as they are in breeding apathy and vandalism. The rubbish dumped on some urban railway lines is a sad illustration of what little pride people take in their neighbourhood.

Members of all political parties in Liverpool have suggested that some part of its docks should be designated as a free port. Raw or semi-processed materials can be landed in a free port, manufactured and exported without going through the customs. Shannon in Ireland is a free port and so are several ports in Europe including parts of Rotterdam and Bremen. It is not only freedom from customs dues but freedom from all the documentation and delay imposed by customs clearance (even if the dues are ultimately not levied) which is such an attraction to industries and merchants in a free port. The Customs and Excise have raised objections to any such scheme and so far have been supported by government ministers. No doubt the control of a free port gives extra work and expense. It has to be fenced off and other special arrangements made. But the most serious objection would seem to be that if Liverpool can have a free port, why not Bristol, Southampton, London, Newcastle, Glasgow, in fact, all maritime cities in Britain? There is also the complication that the EEC is supposed soon to become a customs union. An extension of the free port proposal was to make Liverpool–Hull a main route into Europe. A similar proposal was made for a Clyde–Forth gateway to the continent with a barrage across the Clyde. The strength of Liverpool's reply to this argument against a Mersey free port seemed to depend upon how far the Mersey is a special case and with thirty per cent unemployment it is certainly above the national average. Of course, it can be said, why not set up a series of free ports? Why not indeed? But you would then dilute the attraction of the Mersey for new business.

Whatever the merits of the proposal for a free port on Merseyside, it is a suggestion by representatives of a community for helping it in a serious situation. It would affect the rest of the country but then so does any discrimination. If some regions are marked out for treatment as special areas others may be deprived of industry which would have gone to them, that is the purpose of the measure. The difference is that the designation of special areas is done by the central government. In this case, though it would have to be approved by the central government, the suggestion comes from the area concerned. I consider this a considerable advantage. But we should have to arbitrate between areas making such suggestions if this type of local initiative became common: just as liberal doctrine accepts that the government by legislation must draw the line between the actions of individuals which may impinge on one another. This is not an impossible task.

The best way to reconcile such desirable initiatives would be to allow authorities such as Merseyside or Liverpool greater elasticity in arranging their affairs. If they were allowed to raise local taxation other than rates, this would be an important step. If the Merseyside authorities were entitled to a share at least of the customs duties on goods landed on the Mersey, they could choose to forego some of these and take instead the advantages of a free port. I appreciate in this particular case it may be the freedom from regulations rather than the dues which are important but the principle remains valid I believe: communities should retain a greater share of their own resources. The badge of independence and the spur to action is power over finance and responsibility for raising your own money. If then you want to tailor your budget to your needs no one has a right to interfere. This is not to say that there should not be aid from the central government and it would also involve a shift in emphasis from individual to community support.

The other schemes by which the government has attempted to mop up some unemployment are the job creation proposals. I say mop up because these schemes, for instance the help given to finding employment for school leavers, are short-term palliatives. I make no complaint about that in itself. It can, however, lead to dangerous consequences: it can be accepted as adequate and become a permanent policy. It is quite inadequate and in some respects is little more than relief. It can also divert attention from consideration of the factors which create unemployment and the need for a change of outlook in this country. In so far as Liverpool has a high proportion of unskilled unemployed and a great deal of work to be done in rebuilding the city, such schemes might be of particular advantage to her. I am not sure that they have worked out as well as they should. The resources devoted to them have been small. The question of wage rates is thorny. Nevertheless, the state of the cities offers ample work, and work which might be seen as yielding results which the local inhabitants can enjoy. It would indeed be work by and for the community. It could also give scope for constructive activity by the numerous community groups.

It seems to me, therefore, that it is in the big cities that community development may have most to offer. They are big enough to support first rate schools, universities, theatres. They can offer a variety of living conditions from the centre to the suburbs which could be knit closer together. If heat, light and energy are to become extremely expensive then to be within walking or bicycling range of shops and neighbours may once again become desirable. They could raise and dispose of their own revenue to a far greater extent than now. They could not only encourage but actually import entrepreneurs. They would be large and strong enough to start co-operative banks and enterprises. Under the umbrella of the general authority districts could be encouraged to improve their own surroundings. Associations could run their own transport or start their own enterprises. If the cities are to regain their confidence they must be free of too tight control and they must be spared the impact of theory and ephemeral and centralised fashions. We cannot alternatively decant people out of them and then attempt to rebottle them. Planning must be under their control and sufficiently loose to take account of human preferences, once the external pressures have been reduced.

Within the general community of the city, smaller neighbourhoods should be allowed to run their own affairs so far as they can, groups should be encouraged to co-operate in the provision of services and the management of business. Richer and more enterprising families must be attracted back by the bait of satisfactions other than purely monetary. The segregation of the poor into housing estates where up to seventy-five per cent may be on national assistance must be stopped.

13 The Community

In advocating a step from the existing social services to community services I am running counter to the fashionable trends in our world. De Tocqueville early in his *Democracy in America* wrote:

> The principle of the sovereignty of the people governs the whole political system of the Anglo-Americans .... In the nations by which the sovereignty of the people is recognised every individual has an equal share of power and participates equally in the government of the State. Why then does he obey society and what are the natural limits of this obedience? Every individual is always supposed to be as well informed, as virtuous and as strong as any of his fellow citizens. He obeys society, not because he is inferior to those who conduct it or because he is less capable than any other of governing himself, but because he acknowledges the utility of an association with his fellow men and he knows that no such association can exist without a regulating force.

'Government,' as Burke said, 'is a contrivance of human wisdom to satisfy human want'. De Tocqueville goes on:

> He is a subject in all that concerns the duties of the citizens to each other, he is free and responsible to God alone, for all that concerns himself. Hence arises the maxim that everyone is the best and sole judge of his own private interest and that society has no right to control a

man's actions unless they are prejudicial to the common weal or unless the common weal demands his help.

I would agree with this though I would maintain that a man's wants are rather greater than what Burke had in mind and that the common weal was rather more important to a man than de Tocqueville supposed. The above passage is taken from a chapter in which de Tocqueville is describing the townships of America, a description of interest today:

> In the township as everywhere else the people are the source of power. Municipal institutions constitute the strength of free nations. Town meetings are to liberty what primary schools are to science; they bring it within people's reach, they teach men how to use and how to enjoy it. A nation may establish a free government but without municipal institutions it cannot have the spirit of liberty. The townships and institutions of New England form a complete and regular whole; they are old; they have the support of the laws and the still stronger support of the manners of the community.

He goes on to describe how New England was divided into townships of two thousand to three thousand people, how they discharged numerous duties, their policies being settled at public meetings and put into effect by 'selectmen' elected annually, 'In this part of the Union political life had its origin in the townships'.

How far away this all sounds. The state is being once again endowed with quite inappropriate qualities and saddled with inappropriate jobs. The modern government is very bad at performing its essential tasks: it is weak in the face of determined disruptive interests; it is not a reliable guardian of the general interest and yet it is asked to extend its activities further and further. The maxims of Burke, de Tocqueville and indeed J. S. Mill are forgotten. At the same time as modern states are seen to be failing in their main purpose we are returning to eighteenth-century paternalism. Our obsession with such abstractions as the Gross National Product is like the belief of our ancestors that somehow the state must be made strong and therefore mercantilism (common today) was the right policy at the expense of individual welfare. As for the township, the bureaucratic centralising attitude of our times has done its best to destroy it.

I have talked a lot about communities. But what is a community? The word is much bandied about, not least by me. How do we define or recognise a community? So long as the community is seen as a negative or critical organisation, the difficulty in defining it does not matter because the complainers, the critics, define themselves by their grievance or demand in relation to the public authority which wields the power. The community councils as envisaged under the recent local government legislation in Scotland are intended to have little or no executive responsibility. They are designed to make known the views of a neighbourhood to the local and other authorities. It is true that most of them are attached to definite areas but at one time it was suggested that the whole mainland of Orkney might be represented by one community council which would be available to make representations on behalf of any area, parish, or group on the mainland.

In my view we should try to encourage more positive action by the community. I am not advocating simply the agitation of grievances which was the hallmark of the community politics fashionable a few years ago. I must therefore attempt a somewhat tighter definition of the community than would be sufficient were it to have no executive powers. It is not easy. If it were only a difficulty of definition, it would matter less. If we all knew a community when we saw it, as we do an elephant, recognition would be enough and definition unnecessary. But the difficulty is not merely verbal or intellectual. It is important to my argument to identify the community. What is it, for instance, in London? Certainly not the area of the GLC, nor can it be equated with the old or new London boroughs. In some ways the City of London remains a community and in others some of the housing areas to the east, but neither to my mind is complete.

The essential features of a community would seem to be first that most people in it feel it to be their community. Secondly, that it is not entirely of one class or income within an area in which other classes or income groups are

The Community

involved. This is important if a community is to offer a high standard of life. For this reason I rule out both the City of London and some parts of the east of London though in both there are some features of a community. Even more definitely would I consider the whole of most towns and cities, except London and some of the very largest, to be communities rather than divide them into housing estates, suburban areas, office and shopping areas. If the community is to reach a higher standard people will want to remain in it rather than hiving themselves off to the suburbs or further afield. Thirdly, where possible it should be able to support some of the institutions which offer opportunities and may reach excellence in schools and a fair range of social life. In considering Liverpool we have seen the danger of too much fragmentation. We have also seen the danger of communities becoming pressure groups joining the general clamour for 'more'.

Taking the requirements together it will be obvious that communities will be of many types and sizes. Nor will they all meet each of these requirements. There are some towns where the sense of community has sunk so low that some of the inhabitants would be hard put to it to say to what community they belonged. There are communities such as the individual islands of Orkney and Shetland where a nearly classless society already exists and there are country villages or townships where strong communities thrive without being able to support even a secondary school.

Of late, communities have been looked at solely as areas of government. And commissions dealing with government have started by accepting the need for existing services and then tried to define the areas in which they find it easiest to operate. This rapidly leads away from any organic view of a community. I remember being told that Shetland could not retain its own police force because it would be too small to offer a career structure. So for the purposes of police the whole north of Scotland is treated as one area, one community. In Scotland the method of defining units of subordinate government, which are often equated with communities, has led to Strathclyde, which has caught in one net of services highland and lowland rural communities, small towns with a long tradition of local independence and the large city of Glasgow. Some communities have been split by the new district boundaries.

There are demands which cannot be met by small organic communities, but we should at least start from the bottom, so to speak, and work upwards. We should ask what the people themselves feel to be their community — by organic indeed I do not mean to imply more than that. The community to which people feel they belong, in which they are interested, the neighbourhood in fact, is for my purpose organic. If the test of a community is to be that people should regard it as a community, most geographical communities would be small. Children might regard a few streets as a community. Villages certainly feel themselves to be a community. Even in London there are small districts, perhaps particularly those with a high proportion of immigrants, which feel themselves to be communities. But if we are to start by identifying quite small communities in most cases we shall have to embrace bigger areas — for the sake, as I have said, of covering within the community a spread of occupations and incomes.

Apart from geographical communities we should always be open to consider communities of other kinds, for example, co-operatives. Uniformity must therefore be shunned in drawing the community map. Bradford should probably be treated as one community, and the islands of Barra and Wight. Living communities will come in all types and sizes. Further, they will change, expand and contract. Once we get away from centralised statistical, tidy and bureaucratic thinking this should not be impossible to handle. There is no reason other than indoctrination with unreal paper-and-mathematics-bound prejudices why life should be truncated to conform to charts.

Some communities will not be able to supply all their own services, for example secondary and further education. Such small communities should become groups acting for certain purposes within larger communities (Ebenezer Howard's neighbourhoods), or they may be linked together.

Planners and researchers would like to reduce the community to a tidy single object which can be analysed, treated as a whole, and planned for from without itself. It is of course no such thing. The impossibility of speaking of a community as a whole, as wanting that, or disliking this, underlines the advantage of using the market whenever possible so that the multitude of individual choices can be expressed. Nevertheless, so long as we do not fall into the heresy of over-simplification, we must grapple with the need, the essential need, that human beings have for a group, or rather series of groups to which they belong. The ties which bind us together are not simply economic.

Having considered the attempts, old and new, to help people to run better communities, and the mushrooming of the personal social services which we have seen over the last thirty years, I come now to the main plea of the book: that we should develop co-operation in and by communities to offer their members the best life of which their circumstances permit, with variety of choice, the least compulsion and the maximum amount of room for self-expression.

I have suggested when discussing how we can define the community that it must to a great extent define itself. We must accept that people belong to many communities, for instance, their family, their neighbourhood, their profession or work, clubs, associations, etc. Not only must we accept this fact but welcome it. We must welcome too that people move from community to community. I have said that the hallmark of a community is the voluntary acceptance of it by its members. It is the voluntary adhesion to a group, a country, a town, a street, but also to a hospital, a firm, a club, that makes democracy possible. It is not in itself all that is needed for a satisfactory democratic life but once corporatism takes over, even by the most benevolent of bureaucrats, democracy becomes impossible. Conservatives are right to stress the importance of institutions and of loyalty to them, for institutions are the instruments of the community and their multiplicity a guarantee of choice and freedom. But how can we say that a child born in a many-storied tenement, a worker on the conveyer belt, a pupil in a school torn by discontent and truancy, has either chosen his community or has any chance of choosing? The answer is that we can't as things are at present.

If such people are not members of a community because they have not freely accepted their surroundings, how can we make them members of a community? Are we not all born into circumstances we do not choose and forced to accept the way of education, work, play, life, these circumstances dictate? If these circumstances are to be changed, has not the change got to come from without? To some extent the answer is 'yes': given the conditions we have now reached, help must come from outside the community. But the question of the type of help and the method of giving it is all important. In 1976-77 the National Insurance fund received around £9,300 million and the Consolidated Fund expenditure on benefits it financed amounted to around £2,800 million. In 1977-78 we are spending £7,403 million on the Rate Support Grant and nearly £348 million on regional aid to industry. The central government's housing and rent rebates subsidies were running at £1,500 million per annum in 1976/77. To this should be added the other subventions to industry, nationalised and private, now to be further increased by National Development Corporations.

In addition, there is the cost of the services directly provided by the state. This enormous operation is, as I have pointed out, manifestly failing to achieve its purpose. Nor can we be confident that if the state handed over more of the wealth it draws from the tax payer to the present local authorities the lot of the people would be much improved. There is some evidence, however, that local decisions at present give better results than those taken by remote, centralised authorities. Of course, we must allow for the way that ability has been concentrated over the last half century. We must take into account the highly distorting background against which the local authorities have been forced to take decisions. But it is, as I have said, no good pretending we start from a clean sheet. The reception of the Layfield Report shows that many local authorities would prefer to depend upon the central government to make up their minds on how to raise and spend their finance. Local authorities are infected by bureaucratic attitude, beset by vested interests and enmeshed in corporate conservatism to an even greater extent than the state itself. The story of how the Berkshire County Council which under the leadership of Mr Lewis Moss and a Conservative majority built a grand Shire Hall at an eventual cost of £27 million should be told in every school.

It is not easy, as my experience in starting community schemes taught me, to rouse the public at large to press for reform. The public is so indoctrinated that the example in their different ways of the Isle of Man which raises most of its own revenue, which runs its own services and where the top rate of direct taxation is twenty-one-and-a-half per cent of income, and Mondragon is met with incredulity: 'It can't be true. There must be a hidden hand'.

I believe, therefore, that any move to shift the emphasis of our public spending must come from two directions. Paradoxical as it may be, one move must be national. Before local communities will sort out their responsibilities and assume them, we must have a shift in national attitudes. This entails a political policy. With this should coincide demonstrations of what is possible. These have to some extent been made and I have described them, they are to be found in such experiments as Eilean Iarmain and the projects of Ed Berman, the work of Robert Oakeshott, Ronald Young and in the success of some local experiments by local authorities, such as those in Liverpool. At present these are regarded as peripheral and seen as the work of eccentrics. The lessons learnt we are told cannot be translated into large-scale practice. It must be said in parenthesis that even if this were so it would be better to have a few peripheral successes than none. In any case I dispute the thesis. Some small scale experiments which can be examined under almost laboratory conditions may be of great use.

In the opening chapters of this book I outlined the changes in our political institutions which would be necessary if we are to found a welfare society. Unless these are made we shall add still further to the excessive amount of government from which we already suffer. As we dismantle the central bureaucracy and its counterpart at local level we shall release a number of highly intelligent civil servants for work elsewhere. Even more important, we shall divert the growing streams of graduates which flow into the central bureaucracies.

Having taken some steps to remove the obstacles to community development, experiments which have been made in this field should be widely publicized. It should then be made known that any group of people who wanted to get together for community purposes would be entitled to a starter grant (quite small) to enable them to take the initial step, so long as they fulfilled the minimum qualifications I have outlined and undertook to raise an increasing proportion of their finance themselves. Or better still, in as far as they would be liable for taxation, they should have relief. How they fitted into the general pattern of communities would be a matter for negotiation.

At the same time existing local authorities — one tier of government having been abolished — should be required to prepare for their assumption of new responsibilities. The last ten years have seen a huge burgeoning of plans. But these have been static collections of statistics largely concerned with the existing features of the area concerned. To these snap-shots of the present is added a projection of trends according to the conventional fashions. I do not mean that we should embark on a new generation of structure plans or anything like them. What I have in mind is that the local authorities should consider first how democracy can be made more effective in their area. Secondly, how once they are more effective institutions of democracy, they can pinpoint and tackle the obvious sources of dissatisfaction, such as the housing estates. Thirdly, how they can prepare themselves for the task of raising as high a proportion of their own revenue as possible, and in the case of the poorer authorities, how they can cope with grants from central government which will be general, not hypothecated to particular purposes.

The block grants should in due course become the main method by which the state assists its poorer communities. To begin with, these will no doubt be a main source of their revenue. But a glance at the deposits in local branches of the Savings Banks or in joint stock banks for that matter shows that even in time of inflation there are considerable sums in the hands of individuals available for investment. The

The Community

existence of such savings points to a capacity even in poorer communities which is greater than is generally realised. As I envisage a minimum income, or a reverse income tax, taking the place of much of the expenditure now required by personal social services, and that this would be centrally financed, much of the expenditure by the communities would be self-financing through charges.

In Faroe, even when the population was around twenty-three thousand, the community took over responsibility for much that is at present done on a national level in Britain. The Kommunes or local government districts into which Faroe is divided were allotted a considerable share of income tax. This they could use for roads, piers, school buildings, and part of the salaries of doctors. Both the Faroese government and the Kommunes gave priority to development, particularly in fishing, but in agriculture and industry as well. As Smith and Cluness point out, 'The corner stone of private finance in Faroe is the local banking system, consisting of two joint stock banks and three savings banks, together with an insurance company'.

This bears out the lesson of Mondragon that the investment of local savings by local institutions is important in the running of the community. The Faroese government as well as supporting health, welfare and education services provides loans (in addition to those available through the Kommunes) for such purposes as fishing, ship-building and electricity. I cite the Faroese example as showing what a small community can do. For those who want to examine the Faroese economy I recommend as a starting point *Finance and the Small Community* by Hance Smith and Sandy Cluness — a study which I arranged these two Shetlanders should undertake, once again with finance provided by the Joseph Rowntree Social Service Trust. The study is some eight years old and the Faroese have their own characteristics not found in many other places but I quote them as showing what a small community (with backing and financial help from Denmark) can do. Faroe has been free to fix its own priorities and pursue them in its own way.

In Britain we should have to advance by steps. The parish councils in England and the Community Councils in

Scotland could form the nucleus of new communities. Some cities have a long tradition of supporting their own activities. I would hope that they might put in a claim for some allocation of finance to develop whatever the community felt to be its chief needs in employment, education, housing, transport or amenities. Other activities might be started in the community by groups founded for the purpose. As people became used to running more of their own affairs changes would be needed in the geographical limits, scope and organisation of communities. These changes should arise from the natural growth of confidence, rather than from preconceived notions about the size or nature of a community.

I am not greatly worried about the standards attained by different communities once it has been accepted that every community should aim at making the best of itself. The need for inspectors might persist for a time. But an inspectorate is largely the child of a climate which only leads people to expect minimum standards. Its unspoken reason for existence is that failure is likely — failure even to reach a minimum.

Nor am I worried by the difficulty in quantifying what resources might have, at first, to be supplied by the national government to local communities. It seems to me obvious that there is huge scope for saving in the administration of the state. The change-over to charging and to a minimum income, and the abolition of numerous special social services would increase this saving still further. No doubt communities at first would put in heavy demands for subsidies. No doubt we should have to be vigilant in case new bureaucracies with old habits sprang up. I do not underestimate the lengths to which corporatism, the bureaucratic attitude, and indeed the flight from democracy to disruption and violence, have gone, but the experience of running a different sort of life will breed a new outlook. What can be estimated is what has been provided, how much of that has come from the central government, how much could be saved and what lessons can already be drawn. The estimates cannot be precise and the results cannot be applied everywhere but they are some indication of what should be possible.

14 The Future

Each community or at least class of communities will require different treatment. However, they must all be able to make their own way with help and to some extent at least run their own affairs. But their resources will vary greatly. There is no reason why the communities in, say, south-east England, and in many other parts of England and around Edinburgh, should not use their own wealth; in the poorer parts of England, both urban and rural, and in many parts of Wales and Scotland they will need assistance, and initially assistance on a large scale, from the Exchequer.

Public finance has been complicated by the demand for it to fulfil two functions. Taxation is levied to remove purchasing power from the pockets of individuals and companies so as to leave room for government demand. If it were simply a question of finding money to pay for government services the government could print it — many governments more or less do print it or create it, hence one great cause of inflation. For taxation to meet this purpose it must result in a fall in demand. Unfortunately, many taxes have no such effect. The rich may sustain their demand out of savings. The well-organised obtain higher wages to off-set taxation and the government off-sets its effects on the poor by subsidies and other payments.

Public finance has other objects and effects. As it operates between central and local government it is a transfer of demand. In the process of transfer choice and responsibility are distorted. Ratepayers, for instance, clamour for bigger Exchequer grants although this may to some extent simply result in the individual or company paying out as a tax payer instead of a ratepayer.

Some may be better off, some worse off as a result but most are under the blissful illusion that it is better to pay out of the right pocket instead of out of the left; the effect on the management of the economy is nil. Instead of the comparatively ineffective efforts to redistribute wealth between individuals it might prove possible to make a more effective transfer between communities. This could either be done by direct exchequer payments by way of equalisation grants as at present or by relieving some communities of some taxation. I have long felt, for instance, that it would be more sensible to release the Highlands and Islands from say twenty-five per cent of income tax than to set up the HIDB or to replace regional subsidies by a variable pay-roll tax, higher in the south of England than the north. The drawback to subsidies in addition to the waste and expense of taking money from the community and then paying it back is that they do not necessarily encourage initiative from within the community nor tempt outsiders to migrate into it. Their main effect seems to have been the setting up of branch factories. Bodies such as the HIDB and the Crofters Commission are vaguely charged with social responsibilities but there is an inherent difficulty in trying to discharge community responsibilities from outside the community. The community however will not be — or more important, will not feel — responsible unless it pays a considerable part of the expense of its own development.

Any overhaul of our methods designed to produce a better country through changing the system of social services should start with the provision of minimum income. This should be the modern 'net'. Everyone should be guaranteed a sum of money sufficient to support the minimum standard of life as appears reasonable to the majority at any given time. It should not matter whether he or she is in difficulty owing to unemployment, sickness, general incapacity or any other reason. I prefer the phrase minimum income to reverse income tax or other descriptions though the system might well be worked

The Future

through the income tax arrangements after simplification. A minimum income or reverse income tax depends upon taking the tax returns of each tax payer (not his wages only) and using his return to calculate what he or she should receive to make their income up to the agreed minimum.

If this were accepted we could greatly simplify the complicated regulations and different scales of pay which have now to be administered by an army of officials. The whole tangled system of rent rebates, cheap tickets, heating allowances and concessions and claims of this sort and that could be abolished. Pensions should of course be raised to the minimum income level. It is much better that pensioners should be provided with cash to spend as they like rather than be offered reductions here and there in the prices of various purchases they may not want to make. Of course, such a scheme would impose a universal means test for income acquired from investments or employment should in my view be taken into account.

There are now several schemes for instituting a minimum income. One of the earliest and most interesting was devised by Lady Rhys Williams and explained in her book *Something to look forward to* (Macdonald & Co., 1943). The advantages and some of the drawbacks of her scheme are considered by Professor James Meade in *Planning and the Price Mechanism*:

> It is suggested that a straightforward monetary payment or allowance or 'social dividend' should be paid to every man, woman and child in the country . . . this would take the place of all social security benefits . . . . There would be no means test and no tests whether a man was seeking work or whether a man was genuinely ill. Doctors would stop writing out health certificates. Employment Exchanges would stop fussing about employment insurance. The Ministry of National Insurance would be closed down.

To my mind to pay a 'social dividend' to everyone regardless of their income from other sources is carrying the idea too far. But I am sure that we should pay a minimum income at one rate (with addition for children, disablement, etc.) to everyone whether they are unemployed, sick or poverty-stricken. I recognise that such payments may deter them from working but I have three comments on this. First, most people like to have a job and will always try to get one, especially as it will increase their income. They should not complain too much if some people want to live a more 'idle' (but not necessarily useless) life on a lower income. Secondly, all social services can be enervating but I suspect that the present system is worse in this respect than would be a minimum income. Thirdly, as I have suggested, we may reach a stage when we shall not require everyone to work. Those in interesting or highly paid jobs will accept as a permanent feature of our organisation that they carry some of their fellow citizens who make their contribution to the community in different ways. For further comment on these proposals which I regard as central to any improvement in the community see Milton Friedman's articles in *An Economist's Protest* (Thomas Horton, 1972).

It is arguable that such a scheme would encourage extravagance and discourage savings — less so, I would have thought, than the present rag-bag of special grants, rebates, etc. for particular purposes. Already national assistance may discourage saving yet savings remain astonishingly high especially when inflation can make them such a bad bargain. Taxation both on earned and unearned income should be reduced to a level at which saving becomes well worthwhile. The national minimum income should be fixed at a level adequate to relieve poverty but below the standard which people would want. And, of course, I am assuming a very different atmosphere from the present in which the state more and more dominates our lives.

Finance for the community from within its own resources could come in several ways. One of these might well be the revenues from oil and gas; that this will not last for ever is a reason for using some of it in this way. For if it is allocated for local development that should ensure that it is used for capital purposes with an eye on the long term and on the future when the oil boom (if it materialises) is over. Otherwise, it will simply disappear down the insatiable throat of the annual national budgets. A local income tax, that is a proportion of the general income tax allocated for local purposes, is another possibility, as is some revenue from excise duties and land taxation. The hope, too, must be that if greater equality, though not similarity, is achieved between communities, then once this has been achieved it should carry forward of its own momentum.

Certainly we should reform local government finance. If any such reform is attempted the guiding lights must be the need on the one hand to decrease the total burden and complexity of taxation and, on the other, to reduce the unfairness of the rating system and to replace it with a system which does not penalise improvements and enterprise.

If prevention of hardship is successful then less people will be in need of doles and benefits of various kinds. This will help to achieve the necessary economies in running the personal welfare services and release resources for community purposes.

The local communities can, I believe, make a much bigger contribution than is normally accepted. One of the curious features of the post-war world has been comparative buoyancy of savings. Of course, the value of savings is less than it seems because of the deadly erosion of value by inflation. Nevertheless, even in the poorer parts of Britain they have been considerable. In Norway local savings banks invest in local industry. They are backed by a central government guarantee but they provide genuine new risk capital for their locality. Our savings banks, on the other hand, draw capital out of the provinces; they are positively harmful to local initiative. Local banks, drawing on local savings for local purposes could be a vital element in community development. Their managers should know who is credit worthy, their customers should take a near view of their investments and follow their fortunes with a practical interest unknown to ordinary shareholders. It may be objected that to find capital for local enterprises is the job of the joint stock banks. But joint stock banks are themselves now becoming increasingly centralised. Their business is to lend short term. They are not in fact providing risk capital on a sufficient scale at local level. Perhaps they could be associated with the new type of savings bank which certainly should be free of government control. Nor do the merchant banks fill the gap. Other institutions set up to meet the need to some extent acknowledged since the Macmillan Report have also proved unsatisfactory. Apart from other objections they are not local and do not mobilize local savings.

The Savings Banks, therefore, should once again become local banks. They should be run co-operatively under the aegis of the local community. At the start, at least, the depositors should be guaranteed by the central bank. A high proportion of their funds should be available for local industry. And like the Caja Laboral Popular at Mondragon, they should provide advice and management and accountancy services. Holding as I do that a prime task of the community is to encourage wanted production, at a price people are willing to pay, I see the mobilisation of local savings being largely for local enterprise. Milton Friedman in an essay 'What is killing the City' points out that when it is said that expenditures for 'social services' in New York have tripled (leaving New York in a perilous condition) this may be misleading: 'Money has been collected off the citizens of New York, a substantial cut of it gone to the bureaucrats and the rest then expended in New York. But if it had been left in the citizen's pocket he or she might have expended it (plus the cut) more effectively'. But this criticism of the collection of money for social purposes is not wholly relevant to the thesis I am putting forward. Given the condition to which we have reduced large areas of the country, considerable aid will have to be supplied to these poorer areas by the national government.

If the history of the democratic nations had taken a different turn it is possible — to judge from Mondragon — that state social services might by now be, if not unnecessary, at least declining instead of increasing. The increase in wealth might have made it possible for people to look after themselves. As I have said, the Basque co-operatives run their own welfare services and support schools and hospitals for which people pay or subscribe. Even now those who favour a free society do not, surely, rule out the possibility that as it grows richer we should all be able to make our own way, except for those born crippled in one regard or another. There is no reason why class distinctions should survive for ever even with economic inequality. While, therefore, in the short run, state services may be supported on the ground that they make for basic equality, in the long run, except for Socialists, this should not be a convincing reason for their indefinite survival.

Further, even if some services are necessary over and above those offered to the handicapped, there is even less reason why they should be provided by the state. There are many other possibilities. They could be run by the local community, or by voluntary bodies, or through insurance schemes — to name a few alternatives. These considerations should be kept very much in mind, as should the aim of all welfare provisions.

History cannot be ignored, we cannot make a fresh start from scratch. The state of the public's mind is a fact. We have to work from the existing situation. Even if revolution were in itself desirable, which most experience shows it never is, it would certainly end by increasing rather than diminishing the power of the state. In the stage of evolution which Britain has reached it is going to be difficult enough to alter course a few degrees. Austria and Spain in the days of their decline as empires became increasingly conservative and bureaucratic. They never mustered the energy to throw off the inefficiency of the government under which they laboured. It is a sufficiently daunting task, therefore, for us to attempt to curtail the fashions with which we have been indoctrinated in the last thirty years: that the state must do more and more, that taxation must grow, that bureaucracy must swell not only by spawning innumerable public corporations, each intent on empire building, but by invading every walk of life, and that although they are so palpably inefficient nothing can be done to reduce the waste engendered by the nationalised and semi-nationalised industries and other public services. An effort to recast the dominant thinking of Britain must be made but it is no good pretending that the slate is clean.

One move I suggest should be to strengthen the family. For many purposes the family is a better instrument for helping its members than is officialdom. At the very least a choice should be offered. At present some services are only available from officials. In general, responsibility has been lifted from the family; children can be bred and the public authorities requested to look after them. If they turn out badly the blame is often put on schools, or television, or the neighbourhood. The factors external to the family may in varying degrees bear part of the blame for disruption, truancy, hooliganism etc. but external pressures are in many cases a bogus excuse. When it comes to battering either wives or children this is even more patently so. I reckon that these are crimes which have gained more attention because they are now more often recorded. In the tenements of nineteenth-century industrial cities I suspect that such assaults were common — and largely unrecorded. Nevertheless, considering our comparative affluence their prevalence is alarming. To some extent it certainly seems linked to the decline in personal responsibility and to frustration with a world which on the one hand flaunts extravagance to which all may aspire and on the other offers little satisfaction to many people. Much of this missing satisfaction has to be looked for in the community and work, but some in the family.

With the strengthening of the family should go an increase in the influence of women. Given modern weapons of war, and modern means of repression, the male virtues may prove destructive. Lust for prestige, aggression, power could end civilisation. Women to some extent at least, might bring a new and more humane element to the running of our affairs.

After finance there remain the other areas in which the central government exercises more and more control without conspicuous success. How far can a community control its own education? On the surface it does so now; in practice it does not. It is largely the instrument for carrying out government policy, it must be guided by directives from the centre. In the practical matters of salary, appointment of teachers, school meals, entitlement to school transport and so on it is bound by nationwide settlements. So while the central government disclaims responsibility for the curriculum, the local authorities feel their hands are tied. In the end vital decisions are made by a strange undefinable compromise between government directives, the examination system, the views of teachers and the fashion or constraints acting upon directors of education. The result has been poor, in so far as any generalisation can be true of such a variety of results. Some schools are good, others are very bad. I am not here concerned with the shortcomings pointed out in the series of Black Papers and now overwhelmingly documented to the discomfiture of the complacent educational conservatives of ten or twenty years ago. But I am concerned with the part which education must play in any change-over to preventative communal services in which local people take part and which aim at a high level of opportunity for each community.

Education is vital to the community in many ways. First of all, it teaches children the attitudes and skills which will partly determine what they do in life. Secondly, parents with ambition for their children or indeed normal concern for their welfare will not subject them to bad education. Thirdly, children are essential elements in the community. Their removal for educational purposes has been a serious blow to many rural communities. Their irritation at a prolonged education which many find uninteresting has led to juvenile crime and played its part in communal disruption. At the moment I doubt if many communities are capable of completely controlling the content and administration of teaching. To hand it over to them at once would be to instal the directors of education in a position of even greater power than they occupy at present. If I am right, too, in believing that communities should be of different sizes, some quite small, then co-operation between the smaller communities will be needed over education. It has been apparent since at least New Lanark, and become even more apparent to me after the experience in Greenock, that education is a vital element in community life and that local communities must become accustomed to playing a greater part in directing it.

The need of each family for education can be foreseen. No one perhaps should embark on a family without considering how the children are to be educated nor can anyone pretend that the present state of education has not in some places and for some children failed. I am, therefore, well disposed to any suggestions that might improve it, as well as giving back more choice to parents. The most widely canvassed radical reform is the voucher. Every family would be provided with vouchers equivalent to the cost of educating their children and they would be free to spend them at any school of their choice. There are variants of course. Some have suggested an element of positive discrimination, that is to say, some families who are considered to have a particular need for a good education, immigrants, for instance, would get vouchers for a higher value.

The first question which arises in my mind is, if every family could afford to educate their children up at least to the present standard required by the state, would we expect them to do so? The state doesn't feed their children for them (school meals excepted), so why should it educate them? The state could still insist on all children receiving education up to the prescribed standard even if the state no longer used the tax payer's money to pay for such teaching. I am rather inclined to think that in a world much more nearly approaching the ideal this might be done. The middle classes and a great many members of the working class have shown a commendable and determined willingness to pay for the education of their children. This, as I have said, is confirmed by the experience of the Mondragon co-operatives. To suppose the present British working classes would not do so is either to take a very pessimistic view of the effect of the welfare state upon the country or to take an extremely supercilious view that the existing lower paid are incapable of helping themselves; I don't believe either view is true. Nor would the system be divisive if everyone paid for their children's teaching.

If then it is granted that were all parents sufficiently well-off they should pay for the teaching of their children, should we advance towards this goal through the voucher system? Let me in passing say that while I have some sympathy with the feeling that bachelors and spinsters might contribute to the upkeep of those who are essential to the continuance of the race, I don't consider this a compelling argument for paying for education out of taxes.

The Future

There are several difficulties to be met before a voucher system could be introduced. If you take a large city, divided into poor and rich areas, London for instance, there would be a rush for the schools to be considered the best. It might be an advantage of the voucher system that the whole standard would rise. Good as are some of the existing state schools, the private schools (in which I would have included the largely defunct grammar schools) give on the whole a better education — more cheaply. This is at least partly due to the demand by the parents for value for their money and this would be to some extent carried over into state education by vouchers. But at the start of the voucher system some children would be left out of the rush and condemned to inferior schools. Further, how would selection be made? In country districts where there might not be so much difference between schools would there be any great advantage in carrying children criss-cross between parishes? The general advantage that parents could follow what results they got for their vouchers would result but the cost of administrating education might rise with no very great resulting improvement. At least in some places, original sin or original fecklessness being what it is, I can foresee some trouble at first in getting parents to work the system.

So long as the actual schools, staff, buildings and administration were supplied by public authorities the authorities would have to gauge the likely demand for different types of education in different places — not a task for which they are necessarily well suited. Further, the removal of children from rural (and no doubt urban) communities is harmful to such communities. The voucher system might well increase such movement and further damage community life. Nor, we must remember, are we giving choice to children — vouchers give choice to parents. Though on the whole I am convinced that parents are the best people to make such a choice (and certainly the rich have never doubted this), there must at first be some safeguards.

My conclusion on education, therefore, is that we might experiment in one or two places with vouchers, though the areas would have to be fairly large and the lessons to be drawn carefully considered. But before the system becomes anything like universal the type of general community development I have in mind should be carried out. To experiment with vouchers in a community in which the inhabitants were deprived of work, good housing, good health and optimism about their future would be putting the cart before the horse. It would also seem to me that the case for vouchers grows stronger as the child grows older.

This raises the question of loans. Many continental countries, some of which had long periods of democratic socialist rule, finance university education by loans. There seems to me much to be said for this and in the case of post-graduate work the arguments are particularly strong.

Who should provide education is a separate question from the question of how it is to be paid for. I accept that the community will still have to provide some schools even if the voucher system were introduced but a major advantage of the voucher and loan system is that it would encourage diversity in the provision of education. I consider this the argument which clinches the debate in favour of some experiments with vouchers and loans. I cannot believe that it would be good were the state to become the sole authority providing education yet that is the direction in which we are moving. Luckily we have not gone too far. The private and public schools outside the state system flourish; they flourish largely because most of them offer a higher standard of education. Egalitarian socialists confirm this by sending their children to them. A wider system would open these educational avenues to less wealthy families. There are also Catholic schools within the system.

Nevertheless, there is an element of compulsion growing up in education which is undesirable. As Colin MacLean pointed out in an interesting series of articles in *The Times Educational Supplement*, the state's position today is somewhat like that of the Scottish Church in its heyday. The parallel is not exact: far more individuality can be expressed in schools than the Presbyterian hierarchy would have countenanced. But he is right to question the authoritarian nature of education. This shows itself in many ways: in the claims by the bureaucrats to take precedence over the teachers; in the insistence on paper qualifications and membership of unions before anyone may teach; in the fixed terms, the universal ages for starting and finishing education and in the small choice left to most families or children.

Of all the menaces which we face from creeping bureaucracy, the advance of the bureaucratic outlook into education is one of the most alarming. As Mr MacLean remarks, it is indeed odd and significant that the only excuses accepted by bureaucrats for slipping out of their embrace are religious. Why, both in the context of the closed shop in industry and education, should conscience be equated with religious belief? Why cannot I be treated as a full human being entitled to my opinions, why indeed cannot I have a grievance unless I belong to a religious sect? I agree with Mr MacLean when he writes: 'I do not see why other groups (besides Roman Catholics) should not be allowed to choose other kinds of formative education'.

Mr MacLean discusses the effect of the compulsory nature of state education on the family — how it undermines the relationship of child and parent. He reminds us of the sad circumstances by which education is now beset, treated as a means of keeping down the statistics of unemployment, or a way of looking after children so that their mothers can earn money. Above all, he reminds us of the sorry conditions of which it has become a part: the smothering of originality in older children, truancy and failure. As he says, 'Government is tending to unify all things under its control. Such unification is at its most intense in some of our immense housing schemes where perhaps parents, far from owning their own homes have not chosen them and cannot change them, where all the services of transport, power, medicine, education, social welfare, rubbish disposal and to an increasing extent employment are run more or less by remote government'. As he says:

> The most important thing a child must learn is sensitivity to difference and diversity, yet, after about five generations of compulsory schooling and after two generations of welfare state, socialists have come to advocate a smugly benevolent egalitarian, centralised despotism with the schools as the major agency for its

promotion by manifesto and mandate, those twin bastard sons of democracy. Education is not now handing on the torch of a traditional culture, on the contrary, with the ample pocket money supplied by distracted parents and with the absence of teaching in which they can feel much interest many children now support that massive industry of pop entertainment which in turn bestows upon them the moral role of a generation apart with its own culture.

The case for diversity in the provision of education is overwhelming. It can best be met by allowing parents to choose and pay. If, as a gesture to dominant fashion or as a means of finding work for its bureaucracy the state insists upon making a contribution (say, by the provision of school buildings) though I believe that in the long run may become unnecessary, it may have to be accepted but should be available to all schools which attain some minimum standard. Poor communities anxious to promote experiments or offer special inducements for teachers with special qualifications will need special assistance.

As vital as education are good houses in good surroundings. Social services, attempting to give the individual the means to pursue a decent life, are frustrated at the start if he or she lives in bad housing, as do an appalling proportion of the population. It may well be increasing, for a great deal of new housing is bad. A few years ago although there were long waiting lists there were thirty thousand flats or houses more or less permanently unoccupied in Scotland because no one would have them. Scottish housing is a disaster. The whole waiting list mentality is a disaster. The new housing estates are indeed too often 'concrete jungles'. The tall, flat blocks are inhuman and hopeless for the old and those with young families. The local authority tenant system with its insistence on low rates and big subsidies has meant low standards and a drying up of any initiative. That we should tolerate policies which can be seen to lead to such bad results astonishes other countries. Scotland has deplorable housing policies partly due to political self-interest. The housing in England is on average better but it exhibits some of the same failings. Housing estates have for the most part been ghettoes of Labour voters, though the Labour Party is at last beginning to change its views as can be seen in the 1977 Green Paper. I am not writing a treatise on housing policies, but housing is central to one of my themes: that the shift of emphasis from social to communal services should aim at preventing ills from germinating and raise the all-round standard of communities to as high a level as they can attain. The lessons of Greenock made it very clear, too, what a fatal blight is spread by bad housing.

It is often argued that bad housing is due to lack of money. I question this. To begin with, the repair of old houses is often cheaper than building afresh, yet acre upon acre of useful housing has been torn down. Secondly, the cost of new and inferior local authority housing is as high, or higher, than superior private estates. Thirdly, much of the drabness of the new estates is due to bad lay-out and the failure to use natural features or provide reasonable 'street furniture' which could have been done at no extra expense. Here again, a great factor has been lack of consultation with the community. Too much is done on a drawing board, too little on the ground.

It is typical of much that is wrong with recent legislation that house planning has been removed from an obvious and historic community such as St Andrews in Fife. Ownership of a home, the base of life, is a widely felt human desire, almost an extension of personality. That is not to say that houses to be let are not also needed, whether provided by public or private landlord, but I find it difficult to believe that a community largely composed of weekly or monthly tenants will be a satisfactory society.

Contrary to some views now being aired, I regard the health service as having been in many ways a success. It is a pity that the old voluntary service within it has been reduced, and as with so many other services its administration seems to have been unduly expanded. The health service shows many of the faults on which I have commented but the important questions relate to its future.

There are many of its specialist services which must be handled over a considerable area. I refer to Neville Chamberlain's view that modern medicine demands some specialisation. It would not be possible for the smaller communities each to support such services — any more than it would be possible for them each to support a university. But I would like the community involved in its medical services and I see no reason why small communities should not collaborate over the provision of such services. Nor do I see any reason why, if they so desire, they should not run hospitals or clinics of their own. Once again, I am in favour of decentralisation and initiative, indeed competition, wherever possible.

A strong general case has already been made out for charging recipients for the social services. See, for instance, Arthur Seldon's book *Charge* and many writings by economists such as Alan Peacock. So far, the main hope has been that these writings will stir up a general debate of the kind frequently demanded nowadays and seldom accomplished. To lay down exactly the bounds of how far charging can apply would be premature in the light of public opinion. So far charging, which has been quite common in the social services, has usually been introduced apologetically and met by the parliamentary opposition with cries of derision. However, if we are to disentangle the present confusion and find public money for community purposes charging ought to be rationally considered and to this consideration Mr Seldon's book is a valuable contribution.

From my point of view to stimulate the individuals in a community to make up their own minds and make their own decisions would be excellent. If they had to choose what school their children should go to, they might become more used to choosing and more independent. I accept too that if people had some choice and were directly charged for services, they would be more likely to insist that they got better value for money. They would assail official waste with a good deal more venom as purchasers than they do as tax payers. And the present arrangements are extremely haphazard. We are still expected, for instance, to insure against having our own houses burnt down though this can be as serious as an illness. I therefore welcome attempts to introduce some order and logic into the present extravagant and often ineffective network of services.

When Professor Peacock asked in 1963 why the excellent public library in Edinburgh considered it one of its functions to provide *Lilliput* free of charge, he was asking only one of innumerable questions which could be raised about the provision of particular services.

It may be asked why vouchers should not be introduced for medicine. The difficulty would seem to be that while the demand for education can, so to speak, be quantified at least as far as primary and secondary education are concerned, demand for the services of a doctor cannot. We can lay down that all children must be educated between certain ages or up to a certain standard but we cannot foretell what medical attention anyone may need. How then do we determine the value of the voucher? If it is then said that we should give vouchers to the amount needed, who is to determine this? The doctor will have to be called in to decide which would impose an additional administrative burden on GPs.

Mr Seldon makes a formidable criticism of the National Health Service. He points to the dissatisfaction among doctors and nurses. He reminds us that we alone among western industrialised nations have a national health service but that the other industrialised nations with their mixed systems channel more resources per head to medical care than we in Britain. In Europe, North America and Australasia six-and-a-half per cent to eight-and-a-half per cent of the GNP goes to medical care: in Britain it is barely five-and-a-half per cent. He concludes that apart from environmental and preventative services (common goods) we should introduce a voucher system as a half-way house to full charging, 'In medical care it would cover not fees, as in education, but insurance costs, or a proportion of them. Topping up the vouchers out of pocket would be a source of additional finance for medical care'. The topping up would seem to concede part of my argument — that heavy unforeseen expenses could not be left to insurance. The crux of the matter is how much this topping up would amount to. If other countries have devised a more satisfactory and sophisticated system, by all means let us examine their methods; I would like to hear further argument before going as far as Mr Seldon.

Another suggestion is for a system of insurance against illness. There are differing views as to whether insurance should be compulsory or voluntary and whether, if compulsory, it should be against all risks, even the most dire and the most unlikely. Mr Seldon in *Charge* writes: 'There are some catastrophic risks against which it is very costly to insure and people may fatalistically prefer to run risks rather than reduce their standard of living'. Others might feel that these are exactly the risks against which they would like to insure. This is one example of the difficulties which, however, may not be insuperable. If insurance is to be compulsory then it will not make much of a contribution towards spreading self-reliance for the insurance premiums will be taken off us whether we like it or not, though I suppose we can then take the money to the doctor of our choice. Nor, I would have thought, would it reduce unnecessary calls to the doctor. On the contrary, every time we pay the premium we may be tempted to get value for it. It will be like a hypothecation of taxation for which there are arguments but of a different kind.

If insurance is to be voluntary it is going to be a very hard-hearted society which allows the sick to suffer — particularly, say, sick children, because they or their family are not insured. It isn't only inequality of income which stands in the way of access to medical care by charging for it. If it were, then inequality might be corrected, special arrangements could be made for the poor, etc. It isn't that health in all its forms is a public good — though some forms of health and certainly preventative medicine do benefit everyone. It is that the community cannot assume either that we are all rational, capable beings or that Calvinism should be our guide. When the sinner found himself in hell fire he looked up and expostulated, 'Oh Lord, I didna ken', to which, according to the apocryphal Presbyterian Minister, the Good Lord replied, 'Weel, ye ken the noo'. Such a reply would not, I hope, be given to the uninsured sick. It seems to me to be reasonable to accept something less than optimum value for money rather than penalise or even cause avoidable anxiety to people when they can least cope with it, that is when they are ill. As I have said, I have never believed that a very small increase in general welfare or efficiency justified causing a serious unhappiness to a small number of people.

I would be in favour of keeping private practice. If people want to spend some of their income on health to ensure that they are treated in the way they would like, I see nothing which would justify forbidding them. I am not impressed by the argument that no one should be allowed to buy medical attention either because it is inegalitarian or because it diverts doctors to attending on the rich. If there are failings or shortcomings in the Health Service they are not likely to be cured by forcing more people to use it. The existence of an alternative for which people are prepared to pay may provide a useful comparison.

All the major personal services could be better administered under local control. We should get better service if charges were made for the services rendered. By this means, too, larger resources would be made available. The recipients could be given more say in the sort of services they want. This would certainly entail a change of direction but can anyone be satisfied that by ambling forward in the direction in which we are now going we shall get the best country possible, value for money, or satisfaction for those who need assistance? If anyone believes this let him or her read the demands of the social service bureaucracies for more resources. And then let him consider, if more resources were made available to them on the present pattern, what reason there is to suppose that better results would emerge. The fault has not been any over-all lack of resources. On the contrary, resources have been poured into the public services. Considering the performance of the economy we may have spent too much on the social services. But it is the method of the expenditure rather than its absolute total which has been wrong and this can only be put right by allowing the individual or the community to choose how they will deploy the resources available for community development.

However difficult it may be to define the community this, nevertheless, requires to be done more satisfactorily than at present. It will mean accepting that communities may differ in size. It will mean that they overlap. For some purposes people may belong to one community, for others to another. It means that communities should not be of one class; it means that they must be flexible. All this will certainly entail a change in present attitudes. It may seem difficult to accomplish but it is certainly no more difficult than continuing within the present system. And it holds out far greater hopes for the future.

Epilogue

The economist and sociologist look at the welfare services from a point of view different from mine. This book has certainly not set out a party programme. It is, in the words of Mr Culyer, (to whose work along with that of others carried out under the aegis of Professor Peacock at York University I am much indebted) a tract. That is to say, I have in Mr Culyer's words 'evaluated policies according to my conception of how things ought to be'. Mr Culyer (in accepting a principle laid down by Pareto) says as far as his studies are concerned, 'we shall judge any course of action to be good if those affected by it agree that it is good'. The truth of this phrase must depend upon what is meant by 'those affected by it'. The peddling of drugs to drug addicts may be held to be good by those immediately affected by it, for the community it may be bad. But even if you define those affected in very wide terms I could not accept it for my purpose in writing this book.

I can also see that from the economist's standpoint it is sensible to describe 'the optimal allocation of resources' as a position in which no individual can be made better off without at least one individual becoming worse off. But as Culyer himself says this must depend upon an initial distribution of income very much fairer than at present. At present comparisons between better and worse off are difficult to make because a little extra to the very poor is worth the equivalent of a fortune to the well-heeled. I have watched governments, including socialist governments, allowing public authorities (not corporations out for profit for their shareholders) to introduce more and more gadgets at airports which yield only a marginal increase in satisfaction to the traveller. At the same time they piously cry for help for the poor and the poor countries.

The allocation of resources for the attainment of what I believe should be the aim of the social services in any case seems to me far from the best possible. Mr Seldon in his book *Charge* shows that the present activities of large numbers of tax collectors and welfare officers results in households of two adults and two children with an income of between £1,749 and £2,115 at 1974 prices (much less than the average income) receiving £658 for £685 paid out by them in taxes.

I would like to see us think of welfare in a much wider context as embracing employment, education, health and architecture, and the other activities of a healthy community and, secondly, embracing all the members of the community and not only the poor or incapable. And, of course, I would like the communities or groups of communities to take charge as far as possible of their own affairs. Within the community much more should be left to individual choice and voluntary collaboration.

I see co-operation in the running of commerce and industry as intimately connected with a new and wider notion of welfare. While co-operation should by no means be the only way of running industry, I believe that it can bring new motives to industrial life. It would help to solve many of our major problems such as inflation, unemployment and the friction between management, ownership and labour. As the shareholder becomes both less appropriate and less well rewarded in many industrial activities, the co-operator should take his place and play a more active part in the running of the business. Industrial democracy like the community has become a hackneyed phrase — but there is truth in the contention that political democracy is not all. I see co-operation as giving rein to those instincts to which guild socialism drew attention but which have been smothered by state socialism. It can be controlled by the market and through the market the consumers' freedom and indeed freedom in general can be protected. In some cases a community should band together to have an entrepreneur — as in some sense happened in Northmavine.

I hope that the tools which science can provide will be used to build more variegated societies with plenty of room for individual eccentricity but with an appreciation of the golden rule and the common good. If anyone contends that these aims are contradictory I deny it. On the contrary, just as freedom depends on order, personal choice and expression and play can only flourish in a community which has a common loyalty among its members.

We must reassert the twin legacies of the eighteenth century, the legacy which gave us Mill, Ricardo and the liberal tradition of political economy and the legacy which inspired Owen, Howard and indeed G. D. H. Cole. Having reasserted these traditions we must encourage the new building which is growing on their foundations. Freedom will not prosper in sterility.

Index

Index

Aberdeen 170
Aberdeen University 116
Aix-la-Chapelle 138
Althorp, Lord 87, 88
Anderson, Sir J. 110
Arismende, T. 74, 138
Artisans' Dwellings Act 1874, 89
Arkwright, R. 137
Asquith, H.H. 93, 95

Barra 212
Basques 73-75, 224
Beatles, the 195
Bedford Park 146, 147
Belloc, H. 155
Berman, E. 145, 147, 191, 193, 203, 215
Beveridge, Lord 49, 70, 95, 100-118
Birmingham 123, 151, 195, 198, 203
Bradford 97
Brady, J. 166
Breed 88
Bristol 187, 204
British Leyland 28
British Rail 125
Buchanan, J.M. 32
Burke, E. 19, 208, 209
Burns, J. 91
Burra 172

Caja Laboral Popular 74, 75, 78, 224
Caledonian Canal 136
Camden 114
Centrepoint 124
Chadwick, H. 142
Chamberlain, J. 55, 70, 85, 90, 91

Chamberlain, N. 96, 97, 100, 107, 233
Charity Organisation Society 89
Christianity 21
Churchill, Sir W. 69, 93, 95, 101
Cluness, A. 217
Clyde Valley 156, 159, 204
Coal Board 34
Cobbett, W. 33, 88
Cole, G.D.H. 241
Collingwood, R.G. 15, 16, 32
Cowdenbeath 172, 183
Cross, R.A. 89, 90
Culyer, A.J. 239

Dale, D. 137, 138
Darcy, B. 166
de Tocqueville 22, 208, 209
Disraeli, B. 89, 90
Dogges Troupe, the 192
Dowle, Dr A.K. 155, 174, 181, 184
Dundee 123, 151
Durban 113
Dutch, the 135

East Anglia 113
Eilean Jarmain 185-188
Ensor, R.C.K. 89, 95

Faroe 184, 217
Fetlar 173
Firth, H. 169
Flotta 179
Friedman, M. 57, 222, 224

Gaitskell, H. 103
Gateshead 97
Geddes, Sir P. 142
George, D.Ll. 94-96
George, G.Ll. 69
George, H. 145
German Terrorists 23
Glasgow 156, 195, 198
Grangemouth 82
Greenock 150-169, 181, 227
Gooch, G. 93

Haringey 114, 121
Hayek, F. 57
Henderson, H. 99, 102
Hetherington, A. 169
Hicks, Sir J. 51
Highlands of Scotland 131-149
Hobbes, T. 17
Home, Lord 37, 195
Howard, E. 142-145, 146, 194, 202
Hull 195
Hulton, Sir E. 109
Hume, D. 16, 17, 51, 134, 135
Hungary 66

ILEA 121
Inner Cities Programme 121, 126
IRA 22

Japan 66
Japanese, the 46
Johnson, G. 184
Jones, T. 195, 201

Kent, Duke of 139
Keynes, Lord 47, 49, 57, 62, 91, 99, 102, 107, 109
Khmer Rouge 66
Kirkwall 125
Koreans, the 46

Lakeman, E. 35
Layfield Report 214
Leavis, F.R. 118
Lee, Sir K. 109
Leeds 151
Leningrad 171
Lerwick 170
Lever Family 147
Lithgow Family 156
Liverpool 121, 123, 142, 144, 151, 194, 195, 199, 200, 201, 202, 206, 215
Location of Offices Bureau 128
London 54, 82, 100, 109, 123, 144, 146, 151, 152, 156, 171, 202, 203, 204, 210, 211, 212

MacLean, C. 230, 231
Macrae, N. 82
Malthus, T. 91
Manchester 151, 187, 194
Marshall, A. 57
Marks & Spencer 104-105, 140
Marx, K. 28, 67
Mavis Grind 170, 176
Maynard, A. 15
Meade, Sir J. 47, 221
Merseyside 194
Mill, J.S. 22, 209, 241
Minch, the 135
Minority Rights Group 167

Index

Mondragon 72, 73, 74, 76-79, 115, 138, 196, 215, 224, 228
Moore, G.E. 12, 18, 154
Moray Firth 136
Morris, W. 146
Morrison, H. 110
Moser, Sir C. 150, 152
Moss, L. 215
Mumford, L. 198

NEB 28
Newcastle-upon-Tyne 113
New England 209
New Lanark 137, 138, 139, 146, 227
New York 144, 196, 224
Noble, I. 185, 186, 187
Northern Ireland 113
Northmavine 170-193
Nuffield, Lord 141

Oakeshott, R. 72, 73
Orkney 125, 133, 169, 179, 189, 210
Osborn, F.J. 142, 143
Owen, R. 138, 143, 146, 147, 241

Paisley College of Technology 157, 166
Pareto, V. 239
Peacock, A. 15, 57, 118, 234, 235, 239
Pigou, A.C. 57
Poor Law Amendment Act 1834, 88
Post Office 30, 39
Port Sunlight 139
Prichard, H. 16, 32

Protection of Employment Act 48

Rawls, J. 22, 32
Rhys Williams, Lady 221
Ricardo, D. 241
Robens, Lord 83
Robson, W.A. 52, 53, 54
Ronas Voe 174, 183
Rotterdam 204
Rowntree Family 147
Rowntree, S. 95
Rowntree Social Service Trust 116, 157
Royal College of Physicians 89
Royal Commission on the Poor Laws 1905, 91
Russell, B. 16
Russia 66, 102
Russians, the 22

Sale of Drugs Act 1875, 89
Sampson, J. 174, 175, 176, 179, 182, 188, 189
Scandinavia 117
Scotland 100, 113, 133, 151, 172, 179, 210, 211
Scott Family 156
Scottish Office 64
Seldon, A. 234, 235, 236, 240
Shaftesbury, Lord 70, 142
Shannon 204
Shaw, N. 143
Shetland 135, 152, 169, 170-193
Shore, P. 201
Skerries 172
Skye 185, 187
Smith, A. 57-60
Smith, H. 217
Smith, S. 15

Socrates 15
Somerset 121
South Africa 68, 90
South America 86, 102
South East Asia 67
Southampton 204
Southern Italy 190
Spain 27, 74, 86, 196
Speenhamland System 47
Speer, A. 66
Stalin, J. 29
Steen, A. 202
Storey, R. 184
Stroma 178
Stromness 125, 126
Strone-Maukinhill 158, 162, 163, 165, 168
Sullom 176, 177, 179, 182, 188, 190
Swarbacks Minn 176

Tawney, R.H. 102
Telford, T. 136
Turks 21, 45

Ullapool 136

Urban Programme 120, 123, 126, 132, 137

Wales 100, 113, 151, 219
Warwick University 66
Watson, G. 24
Webb, B. 24, 115
Western Europe 66, 67, 81
Winston R. & C. 66
Wills, J. 169
Winter, R. 157, 166
Woolworths 141
Worcester 152

Young Volunteer Force 160
York 139
Yorkshire 160
Young, R. 155, 156, 159, 166, 167, 168, 215
Youngson, A.J. 132, 134
Yugoslavia 45

Zagreb 164